WORLD POVERTY ISSUES

WORLD POVERTY ISSUES

MARILYN M. WATKINS
EDITOR

Nova Science Publishers, Inc.
New York

Copyright © 2008 by Nova Science Publishers, Inc.

For permission to use material from this book please contact us:
Telephone 631-231-7269; Fax 631-231-8175
Web Site: http://www.novapublishers.com

NOTICE TO THE READER

The Publisher has taken reasonable care in the preparation of this book, but makes no expressed or implied warranty of any kind and assumes no responsibility for any errors or omissions. No liability is assumed for incidental or consequential damages in connection with or arising out of information contained in this book. The Publisher shall not be liable for any special, consequential, or exemplary damages resulting, in whole or in part, from the readers' use of, or reliance upon, this material.

Independent verification should be sought for any data, advice or recommendations contained in this book. In addition, no responsibility is assumed by the publisher for any injury and/or damage to persons or property arising from any methods, products, instructions, ideas or otherwise contained in this publication.

This publication is designed to provide accurate and authoritative information with regard to the subject matter covered herein. It is sold with the clear understanding that the Publisher is not engaged in rendering legal or any other professional services. If legal or any other expert assistance is required, the services of a competent person should be sought. FROM A DECLARATION OF PARTICIPANTS JOINTLY ADOPTED BY A COMMITTEE OF THE AMERICAN BAR ASSOCIATION AND A COMMITTEE OF PUBLISHERS.

LIBRARY OF CONGRESS CATALOGING-IN-PUBLICATION DATA

World poverty issues / Marilyn M. Watkins (editor).
    p. cm.
  ISBN 978-1-60456-057-2 (hardcover)
  1. Poverty. 2. Poverty--Developing countries. 3. Poverty--Psychological aspects. 4. Rural poor.
5. Conservation of natural resources--Developing countries. 6. Agriculture--Economic aspects. I.
Watkins, Marilyn M.
HC79.P6W668 2007
339.4'6091724--dc22
                    2007039058

Published by Nova Science Publishers, Inc. ✦ New York

CONTENTS

PREFACE

Poverty is a social fact of life for billions of people around the world. The developed countries abhor poverty, or seem to, for several reasons. Perhaps it is a blotch on their consciences. Perhaps there is a genuine desire to help those who are not prospering while others around them are. Perhaps they wish to pay lip service to the good cause of eliminating either poverty or the poor, whichever comes first. This new volume concentrates on world poverty issues including alleviation.

Chapter 1 - Poverty exacts an enormous human toll worldwide. Globally, malnutrition and inadequate medical care sap millions of children and adults of their human potential. Even in the affluent West, children and adults still suffer from the negative effects of living without enough. Every day we learn more about the pernicious effects of poverty on cognitive, physical, and psychological development and the mechanisms by which these negative outcomes occur. Understanding such mechanisms provides avenues for intervening in and ultimately helping break the cycle of poverty.

Recent research has highlighted the importance of stress and the body's stress regulation systems in the negative effects of poverty on a variety of physical, psychological, and cognitive outcomes. In this chapter the authors review research documenting the stressors of poverty for children and adults and summarize studies showing how poverty-related stress mediates the association between poverty and various negative outcomes. Next the authors review research showing that stress directly affects our physiological stress regulation systems and that this dysregulation translates directly into several of the negative outcomes under consideration. In addition, the authors summarize research on how children and adults cope with poverty-related stress and the effectiveness of various types of coping. The authors conclude by discussing the incorporation of this corpus of research into interventions for families in poverty—interventions that have the potential to reduce the negative effects of poverty and eradicate some of the barriers to breaking poverty's pernicious cycle. Although focusing mainly on mental health, the authors comment on physical health outcomes where appropriate. In general, many of the processes the authors discuss in the chapter appear to operate quite similarly for both physical and mental health outcomes.

Chapter 2 - Even though many forest villagers have been living on forest department (FD) land and serving the department in northeastern hill forests region of Bangladesh since the early 1950s, their livelihood has not fully explored yet. Taking a sample forest village of the Sylhet forest division, as a case study, this paper deeply examines the livelihoods of villagers and their contribution to forest conservation. Findings of the study indicate that the villagers are well-endowed with all the capitals of sustainable livelihoods framework, though human capital in terms of education is not satisfactory. Existence of several favorable indicators of agricultural sustainability under four broad criteria indicates that the natural capital (i.e., traditional agroforestry system) is quite stable. Strong social capital, stable natural capital, and a productive market-oriented agroforestry system facilitates the generation of financial and physical capitals that make the livelihoods of Khasia people sustainable. At the same time, their reciprocal contributions in terms of forest protection and plantation development support forest conservation. However, some institutional issues such as land tenure and regular agreement renewal problems need to be resolved for the sake of their livelihoods and forest conservation. Lessons learned from the study can be utilized in formulating future participatory forest management schemes in the country.

Chapter 3 - Social scientists are unanimous to acknowledge that urbanization in Africa is fast-growing. Unfortunately, the highest urbanization rate in the world is not accompanied by economic growth. Of greater importance is the fact that most of the researchers in the urban sector predict that by the year 2030 more people will live in cities and towns than in rural areas. A former Congolese Minister in charge of urbanism and habitat recently reiterated this view in his speech during the ceremony of handing-over to the Gizenga government. He declared that in the coming two decades more than a half of Congolese population (presently 60 million) will be living in towns and cities.

As a consequence, satisfying urban dwellers' basic needs in terms of health, food, education, housing, water and other needs could be challenging. Even though cities and towns benefit from most of the local and foreign investments, urban areas experience high rates of unemployment, food insecurity and poverty, which continue to exacerbate.

To alleviate some of these problems, a large number of urban residents in developing countries, particularly in Africa, resort to urban agriculture for food, income generation, and employment. City dwellers convert open spaces (backyards, parks, garbage deposits, power lines and railways, roads, and peri-urban zones) into gardens and farms as a means of reducing urban poverty.

Taking the city of Lubumbashi as a case study, this chapter explores push and pull factors, coupled with the presence of facilitating factors such as availability of land, market proximity, and support from municipal officials and non-governmental organizations (NGOs). This chapter would like to find out who is farming in the city of Lubumbashi, what is produced and for what benefit.

Chapter 4 - Poverty should no longer be understood solely as scarcity of material resources, but reather as the lack of capabilities to gain the social and political empowerment required for a life fully integrated in society. Economic, teological and political views on poverty have been one-sided and uninspiring, suggesting that a fresh approach from the vantage point of ethics is necessary, notwithstanding that ethics has traditionally been devoted to interpersonal relationships and neighbourly assistance.

Poverty is marginal and distant. Does distance elicit ethical concern? The contrary has been the case up till now, for global processes have proved detrimental to the poor, without offering any compensatory policies. According to Pogge, reducing poverty is mandatory because it is a man-made evil that requires a "global resources dividend", to be levied in favour of the destitute.

Since justice is a theoretical principle that has failed to inspire political or social policies, it can hardly be expected that poverty might be reduced by resorting to a just distribution of goods and resources. Instead, it is here proposed to replace the quest for justice with an ethics of protection, where all dealings between individuals, communities and societies would include mandatory clauses demanding the powerfull to benefit the less advantaged in order not only to secure fair dealings and eliminating exploitation and coercion, but also to progressively improve the lot of the destitute.

Chapter 5 - This paper presents a comparative overview of income mobility patterns in Latin America. The authors construct a pseudo-panel for 14 Latin American countries between 1992 and 2003, unprecedented in the Region for its length and breadth. Estimates of time-dependence unconditional income mobility show that this is rather limited, as previously found in the scarce existing literature. However, after introducing personal, socioeconomic, demographic and geographical controls, conditional income mobility rises substantively for the Region. Also, unconditional and conditional income mobility show large variations across countries.

Chapter 6 - Aridity characterizes an expansive area of Southern Africa and almost the whole of Namibia. Although known to be hot and dry, Namibia is characterized by a wide range of microclimates and varying habitats that include some sizable wetlands rich in biodiversity that supports a wide range of plant and animal life. The Namib, the oldest desert in the world, straddles the extremely arid coast of Namibia along its border with the Atlantic Ocean. The Kuiseb River Valley forms one of seven linear oases traversing the Namib Desert. The Kuiseb River Valley and other linear oases traversing the Namib are dotted with numerous small settlements whose inhabitants, depending on the bio-resources, until recently, had successfully adjusted to the conditions created by varying hydrological and climatic elements. Indigenous groups settled here include the Topnaar of the lower Kuiseb valley who had over the last few centuries sustainably exploited the biological resources for food, medicine and fodder for their livestock. Their survival techniques were greatly determined and shaped by the biological resources as determined by climatic variability characterizing their narrow relatively moist habitat along the lower Kuiseb valley. However, recent new developments and interventions in the upper and lower reaches of the valley tipped the scales against the Topnaar. The paper discusses the interactions between biological resources, habitat modifications and society in the lower Kuiseb valley through time and by analyzing recent developments and interventions in the Kuiseb River basin management strategies, highlights undermining of old-age coping mechanisms and increasing vulnerability to risks facing the Topnaar. The strong community spirit and community based activities have been thrown into disarray; the very existence of the Topnaar settlements hangs in balance. Conservation and management of biodiversity based on people centered planning should be adopted where social, economic and environmental consequences of an undertaking are given deserving emphasis. Conservation strategies ought to be multi-disciplinary in nature and consider the entire river basin. Social-economic as well as environmental impacts should be considered alongside the often over-emphasized profit maximization. Stable policies that form part of broader national development strategies need to be formulated and/or revised so as to enhance resilience to dwindling biological resources dictated by recent interventions leading to biodiversity changes affecting the indigenous community inhabiting the lower Kuiseb River Valley. Strong partnerships and indigenous knowledge considerations are necessary to ensure that all aspects of the biological resources on which the inhabitants depend on are included in such studies.

In: World Poverty Issues
Editor: Marilyn M. Watkins, pp. 1-4

ISBN: 978-1-60456-057-2
© 2008 Nova Science Publishers, Inc.

Expert Commentary

SUSTAINABILITY IN TRADITIONAL RURAL LIVELIHOOD SYSTEMS

Josephine Phillip Msangi
University of Namibia, Namibia

Researchers and rural development advocates have defined sustainability severally. Many of those who have endeavored to define sustainability center their definitions around the utilization of the environmental resources while conserving the environment and the resources therein so that they meet the needs of present and future generations. Sustainability has also been distinguished from sustainable development in that sustainability depends on sustainable development just as an economy depends on economic development; therefore sustainable development is a complement of sustainability. In essence sustainability, the core of sustainable development is made up of three attributes: a) stability, b) resilience and c) adaptability. Stability being the ability to resist change; resilience being the ability to recover from change rapidly or bounce back quickly and adaptability being the ability to adjust to change gradually (Edralin and Seong, undated).

Among the much publicized studies and reports on the topic of sustainability, is the report by an advisory panel of the World Commission on Environment and Development (WCED) commonly known as the Bruntland Report released in 1987 that stressed the concept of both equity and sustainability and termed it "sustainable livelihood security". The report defined sustainable development as being "development which meets the needs of the present without compromising the ability of future generations to achieve their needs and aspirations" (WCED, 1987).

Many more studies and definitions followed this historic report leading to the emergence of the concept "sustainable livelihood systems". Livelihood systems are based on income (in cash, in kind or services) obtained from employment and from remuneration through assets and entitlements. In looking at rural traditional livelihood systems, one needs to consider both socio-economic and ecological issues particularly where the livelihood systems are entirely rural in nature and hugely dependent on the exploitation and management of natural resources. Scoones (1998) defined sustainable rural livelihoods as "the capabilities, assets (both material and social resources) and activities required for a means of living. A livelihood is sustainable when it can cope with and recover from stresses and shocks, and maintain or enhance its capabilities and assets, while not undermining the natural resource base". In 2001, Gottret and White commented and elaborated on this definition to include aspects of employment, income as well as poverty reduction. They also included the resilience of livelihoods and natural resource base on which they depend.

Other literature emphasize that sustainable rural livelihoods should focus on people rather than on resources, structures or physical areas and that emphasis should be placed on the indigenous knowledge that has evolved over hundreds of years. There is a distinct call for an appreciation of the survival strategies employed by the rural communities over the years. Among the abundant literature, chapter 26 of Agenda 21 (IDRC, 2005) portrays that in their communities, indigenous people over many generations, have developed a holistic traditional scientific knowledge of their lands, natural resources and environment. It is thus imperative that sustainable development advocates incorporate into their research and analyses, the techniques and strategies employed by rural communities in the utilization, management and conservation of the natural resources at their disposal. Thus the approach to this should be from the grass roots upwards i.e. bottom-up approach, which uses both macro- (policy) and micro- (users, field) levels.

Elaborating on this issue, Chambers (1987) stated that the emphasis placed on physical problems rather than on people hindered research as well as developmental projects that aimed at achieving sustainability. Five years later, together with Conway, they examined how rural households and members within households diversify their activities to increase income, reduce vulnerability and improve the quality of their lives. During this survey, Chambers and Conway came up with the definition stating that a livelihood is sustainable if it "can cope with and recover from stress and shocks, maintain or enhance its capabilities and assets, and provide sustainable livelihood opportunities for the next generations and contribute net benefits to other livelihoods at the local and global levels both in the short and long terms (Chambers and Conway, 1992).

Five years after Chambers and Conway's work was published, Moser and Holland wrote that livelihoods are dynamic and context-specific. Their analysis should include the vulnerability which results from sudden shocks, long-term trends or seasonal cycles and should be studied by examining such assets as labor, social and human capital, productive assets and household relations (Moser and Holland, 1997). Previous to this study, livelihood strategies are said to have remained invisible to both researchers and development specialists due to the fact that different members of a household engage in different types of livelihood activities dictated upon by different factors including time of the year (seasons), age, gender and social standing. In order for this to feature more prominently, the study suggest that these aspects need to be taken into consideration and given emphasis in any study attempting to understand and improve traditional rural livelihoods. What needs to be born in mind is the fact that a change in livelihood strategies will result in changed livelihood outcomes and as the process is dynamic, the outcomes are also not static. As such trends need to be established and reviewed regularly for the dynamism to stand out explicitly.

Traditional rural livelihood systems contain four key components: 1) the state of development (including context), 2) the process of development (livelihood strategies), 3) institutions and organizations and 4) research and development interventions. Livelihood resources (capital) on the other hand dictate possible different production processes. The capital base has five dimensions which include economic/financial capital (assets such as cash, credit/debit and savings); physical capital (household assets and farm infrastructure); natural capital (soils, forests, water, air and genetic resources); human capital (capacities, skills, knowledge, ability to work, good health and physical capability) and social capital networks (social relations, affiliations, associations, norms, trust and disposition to work for the common good). In 1998, Scoones elaborated on livelihood strategies which form part of the sustainable rural livelihoods and stipulated that in order to understand and appreciate restrictions and barriers as well as opportunities available in a given livelihood system, one has to understand institutional processes as well. He argued that due to the fact that formal and informal institutions determine access to livelihood resources, an understanding of institutions and organizations is critical for designing research and development interventions.

Taking traditional rural livelihoods in the drylands as an example, it will be seen that these systems revolve around strategies that enable the inhabitants to meet their needs from the utilization of the range, usually a common property. Meanwhile, it has been stated that the greatest challenges to achieving the United Nations Millennium Development Goals (MDGs) particularly on poverty, hunger and environmental sustainability are found in dry areas (mostly in South Asia and Southern Africa) where extreme poverty and environmental degradation combine and reinforce each other to hold back human development (UNEP, 2006). Therefore, in the drylands, understanding and appreciating the role of indigenous knowledge before incorporating it into development plans, offers an opportunity to come up with viable strategies to sustainably manage the rangelands.

Rangelands, first used by hunter-gatherer societies that depended on the natural environment for most, if not all, of their needs, were exploited and conserved using existing (albeit not written) rules and regulations governing that particular community. Over time, the lifestyles in these lands developed and evolved to include gathering, hunting, subsistence pastoralism and commercial pastoralism or a combination of these livelihood styles such as hunting-gathering, agro-pastoral, subsistence-commercial and many others dictated by the existing conditions such as the available technology and cultural/socio-economic variables. Influence by external forces like the adjacent communities and climatic factors such as droughts may also have a bearing on the emerging traditional livelihood systems.

In the drylands, the livelihood systems maximize usage and utilization as well as management of range resources either for grazing animals or hunting/gathering of wild/natural products. Range management encompasses planning and directing range use so as to meet livelihoods of the entire community. The efficiency obtaining in a given situation is defined by the rules and regulations of a community, which, although not always written, are understood and respected by all members of that community. Indigenous knowledge passed down generations shapes these rules and regulations. Because rangelands do not exist in isolation from non-rangelands ecosystems surrounding them, the livelihood systems often incorporate available resources and the social and economic organization of the adjacent neighborhoods including exchange of goods and services to augment what is extracted from the immediate environment, i.e. the rangelands.

REFERENCES

Chambers R. (1987). Sustainable Livelihoods, Environment and Development: Putting Poor Rural People First. IDS Discussion Paper No. 240. University of Sussex, Institute of Development Studies, Brighton, UK, 37 pp.

Chambers R. and Conway, G. (1992) Sustainable Rural Livelihoods: Practical Concepts for the 21st Century. *IDS Discussion Paper No. 296.* Institute for Development Studies, Brighton, UK.

Edralin, JS and Seong, KT (undated). Sustainable Natural Resource Management and Spatial Planning in Developing Countries. Geo-Information Technology Perspective, United Nations center for Regional Development.

Gottret, MAVN and White, D. (2001). Assessing the impact of integrated natural resource manageent: challenges and experiences. Conservation Ecology 5(2): 17 [online] URL: http://www.consecol.org/vol15/iss2/art 17).

IDRC, (2005) The Local Agenda 21 Planning Guide, Canada: http://web.idrc.ca/ev en.php

Soones, I (1998). *Sustainable Rural Livelihoods: a framework for analysis.* Institute for Development Studies, Brighton, UK.

Moser, C. and Holland, J (1997). Household Responses to Poverty and Vulnerability. Urban Management Program Series No.8, World Bank, Washington, DC.

UNEP (2006). Protecting Natural Capital. From Summit to Sea.

WCED (1987). *Our Common Future. World Commission on Environment and Development.* Oxford University Press, Oxford. UK.

In: World Poverty Issues
Editor: Marilyn M. Watkins, pp. 5-35

ISBN: 978-1-60456-057-2
© 2008 Nova Science Publishers, Inc.

Chapter 1

THE ROLE OF STRESS-AND-COPING PROCESSES IN THE PERNICIOUS EFFECTS OF POVERTY

Martha E. Wadsworth, Catherine DeCarlo Santiago, Brian Wolff, and Christine Reinhard

University of Denver
Denver, Colorado, USA

ABSTRACT

Poverty exacts an enormous human toll worldwide. Globally, malnutrition and inadequate medical care sap millions of children and adults of their human potential. Even in the affluent West, children and adults still suffer from the negative effects of living without enough. Every day we learn more about the pernicious effects of poverty on cognitive, physical, and psychological development and the mechanisms by which these negative outcomes occur. Understanding such mechanisms provides avenues for intervening in and ultimately helping break the cycle of poverty.

Recent research has highlighted the importance of stress and the body's stress regulation systems in the negative effects of poverty on a variety of physical, psychological, and cognitive outcomes. In this chapter we review research documenting the stressors of poverty for children and adults and summarize studies showing how poverty-related stress mediates the association between poverty and various negative outcomes. Next we review research showing that stress directly affects our physiological stress regulation systems and that this dysregulation translates directly into several of the negative outcomes under consideration. In addition, we summarize research on how children and adults cope with poverty-related stress and the effectiveness of various types of coping. We conclude by discussing the incorporation of this corpus of research into interventions for families in poverty—interventions that have the potential to reduce the negative effects of poverty and eradicate some of the barriers to breaking poverty's pernicious cycle. Although focusing mainly on mental health, we comment on physical health outcomes where appropriate. In general, many of the processes we discuss in the chapter appear to operate quite similarly for both physical and mental health outcomes.

POVERTY-RELATED STRESS AS A MEDIATOR OF THE SES – HEALTH LINK

The link between low socioeconomic status (SES) and poor health is very well established. For many health outcomes, there is a steady SES-health gradient, with better health enjoyed at each level up the SES ladder. The types of health problems encompassed by this association include a variety of physical health conditions such as hypertension, heart disease, cancer, and life expectancy, as well as a wide array of mental health problems from depression to schizophrenia. While less research attention has been paid to children than adults, existing research clearly shows that these associations hold for children as well as adults. Research has begun turning attention to the *mechanism* of the SES-health gradient—of *why* the gradient exists. Several models have been proposed to explain *how* poverty or low SES translates into poor health. We explore four models below.

Models of How SES-Health Gradient Operates

The first model is referred to as the "social selection" or "downward drift" hypothesis, which posits that adults with psychological or physical health problems drift down the SES ladder due to their problems and their resulting inability to fulfill expected role obligations. The initial causes of psychopathology or poor health are assumed to be factors unrelated to SES, such as genetic liabilities (e.g., Kendler & Eaves, 1986) or unfortunate circumstances such as an accident. Findings from several studies suggest that SES differences in the rates of a few psychological disorders, including schizophrenia (Dohrenwend et al., 1992), and possibly attention deficit hyperactivity disorder (ADHD; Miech, Caspi, Moffitt, Wright, & Silva, 1999), are consistent with this hypothesis. Thus, schizophrenia, for example, may impair people's ability to secure employment and financial status commensurate with that of their parents. Little research has addressed the possibility of downward drift with regard to physical illnesses, though the few that have looked have not found evidence in support of such selection effects (e.g., Lynch, Kaplan, & Shema, 1997).

The second model arises from observations that people living in poverty are more likely than those not living in poverty to engage in a variety of unhealthy behaviors—behaviors linked to various physical illnesses and diseases (e.g., Wray, Alwin, & McCammon, 2005). Rates of cigarette smoking, for example, are higher among the poor than the non-poor, and the linkages between smoking and diseases such as cancer and heart disease are very strong (Ekberg-Aronsson, Nilsson, Nilsson, Löfdahl, & Löfdahl, 2007). Similarly, higher rates of overweight and obesity are found among the poor, and once again obesity is linked with a variety of poor health outcomes. This is apparently an appealing explanation—poor people smoke, drink, and overeat and that is why they are unhealthy. Unfortunately, the data do not bear out this as a complete explanation of the link between low SES and poor health by any means. In fact, studies have generally found that health risk behaviors such as these at best explain only a quarter of the association between SES and physical health and often explain significantly less than that (e.g., Lantz et al., 2001; Mansson, Rastam, Eriksson, & Israelson, 1998). In addition, as mentioned above, the SES-health gradient exists just as robustly for mental health problems as it does for physical health problems. Yet, there are no compelling reasons to suspect that smoking or overeating leads to ADHD, schizophrenia or anxiety disorders. Thus, while health risk behaviors may add something to the picture of explaining the SES-health gradient, there is much left to be explained by some other mechanism.

The third model explores a related factor that could contribute to the SES-health gradient. In the U.S., millions of poor people do not have adequate access to health insurance. Thus, many poor individuals and families are forced to seek medical care only in emergencies, at which point many health problems are too far advanced to treat easily. While it is intuitively appealing to attribute the gradient to inadequate health insurance, once again this is not borne out in the research that has been conducted. Studies that account for access to healthcare have only found small percentages of the gradient explained by healthcare access and usage (e.g., Sapolsky, 2004). Secondly, the SES-health gradient exists in virtually every country in the world, even in countries with universal healthcare programs such as England and Sweden. Interestingly, the gradient is steepest in countries with the greatest degree of income inequality between the rich and poor such as the U.S. Finally, the SES-health gradient exists even for diseases whose incidence is not related to access to preventative health care such as rheumatoid arthritis and juvenile diabetes (Sapolsky, 2004). Thus, while poor access to healthcare is a problem and certainly does not help the situation created by the gradient, it does not appear to be the primary mechanism of the gradient.

The fourth model, termed "social causation," posits that poor people develop psychological and physical health problems as a result of living with poverty-related adversity. Studies comparing social causation of psychological disorders with alternative models such as social selection generally find strong support for the social causation of multiple disorders such as depression and anxiety (e.g., Wadsworth & Achenbach, 2005). Because of its pervasiveness and chronicity, living with poverty is grueling and demoralizing—it literally wears one down mentally and physically as evidenced by significantly higher mortality rates for those in poverty (e.g., Rehkopf, Haughton, Chen, Waterman, Subramanian, & Krieger, 2006). Research suggests that this wear and tear is not just metaphorical—chronic adversity and stress borne of poverty simultaneously dysregulate the body's physiological stress response system and reduce one's psychological resources for coping with stress. This "allostatic load" eventually weakens resistance to disease-causing agents of both the physical and psychological variety (Kahn & Pearlin, 2006; McEwen, 1998). There is growing support for this fourth model, and especially the importance of stress to the SES-Health gradient (e.g., Almeida, Neupert, Banks, & Serido, 2005). The following section describes the existing research on poverty and the stressors that it creates, exacerbates, and maintains.

Poverty-related Stress - Adults

McLoyd (1990) wrote about the "context of stress" that characterizes life in poverty. The stress of poverty is much more than worries about money—it is also hunger, violence, and illness to name a few. This is especially true for children and adolescents who are not responsible for paying the family's bills, but are nevertheless subjected to food insufficiency, inadequate housing, and frustrated, irritable parents. Building on McLoyd's context construct, we refer to the stressors created, exacerbated, and maintained by poverty collectively as "Poverty-related stress" (PRS; Wadsworth & Berger, 2006).

While the types of stressors captured by PRS vary widely from violence exposure to transportation problems, it is the cumulative nature of PRS that matters more than any particular type of stress (e.g., Evans, 2004; Pearlin, 1989). Cumulative risk studies have consistently failed to identify singularly potent stressors among such candidates as lead exposure and healthcare access, and rather find that it is the sum of stressors that makes the difference—risk for problems increases with each additional stressor in a step-wise fashion (Evans, 2004). In addition, the context of PRS affects how well one is able to mount a response to new threats and challenges; poverty amplifies the negative effects of other stressors (Almeida et al., 2005; DuBois, Felner, Meares, & Krier, 1994). Thus, any stressor that occurs in the context of poverty is affected by that context. In the next sections, we outline the evidence for PRS as a key mechanism of the SES-health gradient for both children and adults. Research has examined PRS from both the psychological and psychobiological perspectives. Both have received strong support in the research literature. Much of this early work focused on the stress of poverty and economic troubles for adults.

Some of the earliest research on the experience and effects of poverty-related stress came from Pearlin and colleagues who wrote of the experience of poverty from a "strain perspective" (e.g., Pearlin, Mehaghan, Lieberman, & Mullan, 1981). According to Pearlin et al., it is the day-to-day events and experiences brought about by major events such as job loss or living in poverty that place strain on the individual as they strive for homeostasis. According to Kahn and Pearlin (2006), "among the array of chronic stressors that people may confront in their daily lives, there is probably none more pivotal than economic hardships and strains" (p.18). For these authors, it is this stress that leads directly to negative outcomes such as depression (Kahn & Pearlin, 2006; Pearlin et al., 1981), anxiety (Pearlin & Radabaugh, 1976), alcohol use (Pearlin & Radabaugh, 1976), and physical health conditions (Kahn & Pearlin, 2006). Our research team has also provided evidence of economic stress' direct link to depression in a sample of rural parents (Wadsworth, Raviv, Compas, and Connor-Smith, 2005). Similarly, Hudson (2005) found that economic stress was a significant route through which SES affected rates of serious mental illness in a data base of over 100,000 Massachusetts psychiatric inpatients.

Expanding this idea, Conger and colleagues have identified economic stress as being a particularly potent catalyst for a variety of problems within a family—problems that partially explain emotional and behavioral problems for children, primarily via the effects on parents and the inter-parental relationship. In a series of studies involving Iowa farm families marked by severe income loss, Conger and colleagues developed the "Family Stress Model" (e.g., Conger & Elder, 1994; Conger et al., 2002). In this model, low family income and negative financial events lead to economic pressure (stress) in the family (Conger, Reuter, & Elder, 1999). This economic stress spawns parental distress and interparental conflict, both of which lead to parenting problems. Ultimately, it is through these parenting problems that childrens's psychological functioning is compromised (e.g., Conger et al., 1992; Conger et al., 1993). In this way, Conger and colleagues have demonstrated a causal pathway through which poverty-related stress (e.g., economic pressure) disrupts interpersonal relationships in a family and contributes to psychological problems for adults as well as children.

Thus, the effects of poverty-related stress on adults are clear. Additionally, the cascade of problems that PRS creates for parents has negative implications for children. A remaining question, however, is whether children themselves experience poverty as being stressful. A major emphasis in our research program has been on uncovering the extent to which children experience PRS and whether PRS affects children the same way that it affects adults.

Poverty-related Stress – Children and Adolescents

A long line of research on cumulative risk has documented various living conditions such as family turmoil and violence exposure that adversely affect children's development (e.g., Evans, Kim, Ting, Tesher, & Shannis, 2007). Despite this excellent research documenting the types of problems that affect children in poverty, understanding of children's own perspectives on what constitutes PRS has been elusive. McLoyd and Wilson (1994) provided some early documentation of adolescents' finance-related concerns. Adolescents' worries about their own financial futures were significantly related to psychological distress. Our work has been among the first to ascertain a fuller representation of the stressful experience of poverty from a child's perspective (e.g., Wadsworth & Compas, 2002).

Focusing primarily on mental health, we have found that children's and adolescents' poverty-related stress mediates the association between SES and health problems. While we originally focused on economic strain as the key type of PRS, our early studies identified other aspects of family stress that play an important role in this process as well. For example, Wadsworth and Compas (2002) found that both economic strain and family conflict served as mediators of the association between SES and children's mental health problems. We then expanded our poverty-related stress definition to include a variety of problems that coincide with life in poverty, such as family changes and transitions, and family and neighborhood violence (Wadsworth & Berger, 2006). We found that this expanded poverty-related stress construct had direct linkages with a variety of children's psychological disorders and syndromes, as well as physical health indicators and academic functioning (Wadsworth et al., 2007).

WHAT ARE THE STRESSORS OF POVERTY?

Based on the above review, we know that PRS is detrimental to the health and well-being of people of all ages and that PRS may be an important mechanism of the SES-health gradient. What exactly is stressful about poverty for children, adolescents and adults? In our various studies, we have asked parents and children living in poverty about the stress in their lives.

Adults' Poverty-related Stress

For adults, many of the situations and circumstances included under poverty-related stress are those directly linked to not being able to provide for their family. In our urban sample, parents reported having experienced financial hardship for an average of 10 years. Parents reported frequent attempts to cut back on expenses to make ends meet in the last six months, including cutting back on recreation/social activities (74%), postponing household purchases (64%), selling possessions (21%), postponing medical care (29%), and applying for federal assistance (30%). Forty-eight percent of this sample reported that they were having major or severe financial problems currently. These current financial problems were strong predictors of a variety of mental health syndromes and disorders, including substance use disorder, depression, and generalized anxiety disorder.

Other studies have examined fairly similar indices of poverty-related stress. Conger and colleagues' studies have generally included three indices of economic pressure or strain: (1) the extent to which parents in their study felt they could make ends meet; (2) the extent to which they had the money needed to provide the necessary material needs for their family; and (3) the number of changes they have made in response to financial difficulties in the past year. A latent variable analysis containing these three indicators robustly predicts parental depression and inter-parental conflict (e.g., Conger et al., 1994). Other studies have been less specific and included a series of retrospective questions about individuals' levels of financial hardship during particular periods in their lives (i.e., during childhood, early adulthood, and middle age; Kahn & Pearlin, 2006) or non-specific interviews regarding conflicts, frustrations, and threats in their economic lives (e.g., Pearlin & Radabaugh, 1976). All methods have yielded highly consistent results, with economic stress strongly predicting negative health outcomes such as depression and alcohol use.

School-age Children's Poverty-related Stress

Since children are not responsible for the family's finances, we could not assume that the same aspects of economic pressure were stressful for them as for their parents. Therefore, we started from the bottom up, and asked children aged 6-10 about the money troubles that their family has and whether or not they are of concern to them. From children, we heard about a very wide array of problems that cause them stress. While many children reported that not getting a particular toy or game was their money trouble, a large percentage of children this age reported that things such as not being able to pay the rent, not having heat in the winter, and not having food were their money troubles. Some children even reported highly specific, parentified concerns such as hoping that their mother got that job she just interviewed for because it pays $16 per hour or that they hope their mother will find the money to pay rent that month so they do not have to go stay in a shelter. These types of parentified concerns were significantly related to children's anxiety symptoms. In addition, many of these young children reported that they worried about finances and money troubles more than their parents do. Fifty-four percent of these children reported worrying about finances often or very often, and 25% believed that they worry about finances more than their parents do.

We also asked parents to tell us what poverty-related stressors bother their children. Many parents were optimistic that their children did not have many finance-related concerns and that they were generally unaware of the family's financial problems. The remaining parents seemed to believe that the only finance-related concerns their children had were child-appropriate, and included such concerns as being upset about not getting a new toy.

Adolescents' Poverty-related Stressors

We have obtained adolescents' reports of economic strain and poverty-related stress in several studies now. Overall, adolescents appear to provide reliable and meaningful reports of poverty-related stress. Rural teens enrolled in their school's free/reduced price lunch program (a poverty indicator) in Wadsworth and Compas' (2002) study reported more economic strain than non-enrolled teens, such as not having enough money for school clothes, their parents not having enough money to pay the bills, not having enough money to go places they wanted to go, and the family not having money left over to do something fun as a family. These economic strains predicted symptoms of anxiety, depression, and aggression over the course of one year (Wadsworth & Berger, 2006) and significantly mediated the link between SES and these symptoms (Wadsworth & Compas, 2002). Thus, a portion of the relation between SES and adolescent psychological symptoms was explained by economic strain.

Similarly, adolescents in our urban sample (e.g., Wadsworth et al., 2007) reported that a variety of poverty-related events and circumstances are stressful for them, including their parents' inability to pay bills, the inability to obtain needed school supplies, and the inability to get dental or orthodontic care when needed. A surprisingly large proportion of teens also reported on not having enough to eat, mentioning having to skip meals because there was no money for food, having to beg for food at the supermarket, and running out of food at the end of the month. Several teens commented on feeling guilty about asking their parents for things they needed and feeling stressed by seeing their mother so depressed about money all the time. Many adolescents reported that the family's financial troubles were highly stressful (57%) and many indicated that they worry about having to go on Welfare as an adult (49%). Girls reported significantly more embarrassment and sadness resulting from poverty-related stress than boys, and they indicated that they worry more about losing their job as an adult and having to depend financially on a spouse as an adult. These adolescent-reported poverty-related stressors predicted significant increases in internalizing and externalizing symptoms over the course of a year.

Thus, it is clear that stress plays a critical role in placing adults and children alike at risk for a variety of mental health problems. How do these findings regarding poverty-related stress align with research examining the physiological effects of PRS and links between dysregulated physiological systems and key mental health outcomes? The next section explores these crucial linkages.

POVERTY AND PHYSIOLOGICAL STRESS REACTIVITY

These exceptionally high levels of stress place parents and children at risk both for patterns of high physiological reactivity and impaired mental health. Some of the influence of chronic stress on mental health comes *indirectly* from the physiological impact stress has on the human body. Repeated stress actually *sensitizes* multiple components of the nervous system, heightening physiological reactions to even mildly stressful or threatening events in the environment (e.g., perceived mean "looks" from other people, or having a supervisor/teacher demand something from you) (Repetti, Taylor, & Seeman, 2002). People become hyper-vigilant to relatively small and/or irrelevant social and environmental stimuli

(Sanchez, Ladd, & Plotsky, 2001), perceiving more threats and sources of harm than actually exist. Physiological responses not only occur more frequently, but also tend to increase in magnitude and duration, taking longer to regulate back to baseline levels (Heim & Nemeroff, 2001). Unfortunately, these repeated and exaggerated stress responses become entrenched, placing individuals at risk for developing stable patterns of high-reactivity (Cohen & Hamrick, 2003; Matthews, Salomon, Kenyon, & Allen, 2002) and abnormal brain development (e.g., Gianaros et al., 2007). Finally, in stressful environments, from childhood through adulthood, patterns of high-reactivity are associated with mental health impairment (Pine, Cohen, Gurley, Brook, & Ma, 1998; Weems et al., 2005).

In this section, we examine empirical evidence illustrating the ways in which stress-induced changes in physiology link poverty-related stress to impaired mental health.

The Effects of Poverty-related Stress on Physiological Reactivity

Physiological activation in response to an acute stressor is designed to prepare humans for real environmental threats while providing a system to regulate such responses and maintain physiological homeostasis. Humans have two primary neurobiological systems to accomplish this task – the autonomic nervous system, which includes both sympathetic and parasympathetic branches, as well as the hypothalamic-pituitary-adrenal (HPA) axis. With its electrical impulses emanating from the brain to the cardiovascular system, the autonomic nervous system acts quickly as the body's first response to perceived threat, a response also known as "fight or flight." Autonomic nervous system sympathetic activation rapidly provides physiological resources to deal with threat, primarily by increasing heart rate and respiration. In contrast, autonomic nervous system parasympathetic activation serves to regulate the body, allowing humans to return to a more normative baseline state. A typical healthy response to an acute stressor involves temporary sympathetic activation along with parasympathetic withdrawal, followed by a steady increase in parasympathetic activation to return to physiological homeostasis. In contrast to the quick-acting mechanisms of the autonomic nervous system, the HPA axis secretes relatively slow-acting steroid hormones (i.e., glucocorticoids) in response to stress. The primary stress response steroid hormone in humans is cortisol, which is released between ten and thirty minutes following an acute stressor. Although the exact function of the HPA-axis as a stress response mechanism is not entirely known, heightened levels of cortisol responding are associated with the experiences of uncontrollability and feelings of defeat (Bauer, Quas, & Boyce, 2002).

Poverty-related stress elevates risk for repeated, intense, and prolonged physiological stress responses, in both the autonomic nervous system and HPA-axis (Chen, Matthews, & Boyce, 2002; Evans & English, 2002). Much evidence for this link between poverty and dysregulated physiological reactivity in humans comes from animal analogue models. Such models examine the direct experimental effects of early deprivation or high exposure to stress on rodent and nonhuman primate physiological reactivity. Early deprivation and stress exposure manipulations are thought to be a partial proxy for the experience of human poverty, although naturalistic studies of human experiences are important to help confirm animal-based research. Stress exposure studies of rodents (Caldji, Francis, Sharma, Plotsky, & Meaney, 2000) and nonhuman primates (Sanchez et al., 2001) suggest that early exposure to stress can alter both autonomic nervous system and HPA stress response systems. Early stress exposure in rats produces marked changes in HPA functioning, resulting in hyper-reactivity to mildly stressful events throughout the rats' lifespan (Sanchez et al., 2001). Caldji et al. (2000) found that when rat pups were repeatedly separated from their mothers, they developed increased HPA activation. This HPA activation was associated with increased fearfulness to novel situations among deprived pups compared to those pups exposed to higher levels of maternal licking and grooming.

Nonhuman primate studies have found similar results to rodent studies. One common method of inducing high levels of stress among nonhuman primates is to artificially create a variable foraging demand, meaning that the young primates and their mothers experience unpredictable alternating periods of food scarcity and abundance. Primates can adapt well to either scarcity or abundance, however, fluctuating these environments in unpredictable and uncontrollable ways elicits high levels of physical and behavioral distress (Sanchez et al., 2001). This type of unpredictability and uncontrollability created in primates' environments is quite similar to the real human experience of living in poverty. Poverty-related stress, such as high residential mobility, economic strain, and unforeseen expenses such as car repairs, usually involves unpredictability. Creating a variable foraging demand leads to long-lasting physiological and behavioral hyper-reactivity to stress among the stressed primates, providing further evidence for the link between adversity and long-term physiological dysregulation. These findings are supported by other manipulations of early primate environments, such as forced maternal separation, which has been linked to increased cortisol levels and more pronounced frontal lobe electroencephalogram (EEG) asymmetries favoring the right hemisphere (Kalin, Larson, Shelton, & Davidson, 1998). This pattern of EEG responding has also been linked to increased distress in human infants in response to maternal separation (Davidson & Fox, 1989), an early sign of anxiety.

Similar to the early deprivation and high stress levels created in these animal models, poverty-related stress (Wadsworth et al., 2007) is a form of early adversity experienced by humans that has lasting effects on physiological reactivity patterns over time. In a direct examination of the effect of poverty-related stress on physiological reactivity, Evans and English (2002) assessed the level of stress exposure experienced by low-income and middle-class families, as well as their physiological response profiles and socioemotional adjustment. Families living in poverty were compared to matched middle-income families. The authors found that children living in poverty had higher resting blood pressure and greater levels of overnight urinary epinephrine (an indicator of HPA activity). Additionally, the authors found that much of the linkage between poverty status and alterations in physiological responding could be accounted for (i.e., mediated) by exposure to multiple poverty-related stressors. Poor children were exposed to greater cumulative levels of stress than their middle-income counterparts, which in turn increased cardiovascular and hormonal indices of physiological reactivity (Evans & English, 2002). A similar effect was found among adults; lower socioeconomic status (SES) was associated with higher cortisol responses, an indicator of heightened HPA activity (Cohen, Doyle, & Baum, 2006). Interestingly, Cohen and colleagues (2006) found that this association between low SES and cortisol elevations was partially mediated in their sample by differences in health practices and social factors, such as increased rates of smoking, not eating breakfast, and less diverse social networks. This research highlights the complexity of the poverty-reactivity association, and the importance of testing for a multitude of mediating influences.

Unfortunately, such direct tests of mediators of the association between poverty and heightened reactivity are rare in the literature. However, considerable evidence exists linking overall chronic stress to reactivity (McEwen, 1998). Higher stress exposure and its consequent repeated physiological stress responses takes a toll on the body, a process termed "allostatic load" (McEwen, 1998). Allostatic load is associated with dysregulation throughout the autonomic nervous system and HPA stress response systems, as well as impaired physical and mental health outcomes. Adults with higher levels of chronic life stress, including economic strain, show exacerbated autonomic nervous system and HPA responses to acute stressors in the laboratory (Pike, Smith, Hauger, & Nicassio, 1997). Children's and adolescents' physiological responses to laboratory stress also appear to be affected by individual differences in their background chronic stress levels. Children and adolescents with higher self-reported levels of chronic life stress had higher blood pressure levels as well as elevations in other cardiovascular indices of stress reactivity (Matthews, Gump, Block, & Allen, 1997). This study also found higher levels of interpersonal stress among lower-income families, providing further support for the links between poverty, poverty-related stress, and heightened physiological responding.

Children raised in families with more inter-adult anger and general turmoil, two poverty-related stressors, show heightened physiological stress reactivity (El-Sheikh, Cummings, & Goetsch, 1989; Matthews et al., 1997). Young children's blood pressure levels increase when listening to angry interactions between adults (El-Sheikh et al., 1989). Furthermore, young children identified as being "concerned/distress" type responders to stress showed heart rate increases in response to angry adult interactions, suggesting an association between high reactivity and internalizing symptoms. Interestingly, children identified as being "angry/ambivalent" showed significant *decreases* in heart rate responding to the angry interaction, providing possible evidence for an association between low-reactivity and externalizing symptoms such as aggression and oppositionality (El-Sheikh et al., 1989).

In sum, a growing compendium of animal and human studies point to the harmful impact of adversity and poverty-related stress on individuals' physiological reactivity. More specifically, stress and adversity appear to sensitize autonomic nervous system and HPA stress reactivity systems, heightening physiological arousal and increasing hyper-vigilance to mild, acute stressors in the environment. As these maladaptive physiological alterations become more entrenched, individuals of all ages are placed at increasingly heightened risk for mental health outcomes.

Stability of Physiological Reactivity Patterns

Unfortunately, heightened vigilance and sensitized physiological reactivity appear to become trait-like over time, especially when individuals continue to be exposed to high levels of stress. In a recent review of the stability of autonomic and endocrine measures of stress reactivity, Cohen and Hamrick (2003) concluded that there is considerable continuity of physiological reactivity across tasks and over time for individuals across the entire lifespan, strongly suggesting a dispositional component to reactivity. Evidence of such stability exists longitudinally and across multiple cohorts of children for indices of parasympathetic reactivity from four months to four years of age, measured over multiple time points and across multiple types of challenge (Bar-Haim, Sutton, Fox, & Marvin, 2000; Calkins &

Keane, 2004). The stability of heart rate and physiological reactivity among preschool-age children also shows moderate continuity extending into later childhood (Alkon et al., 2003; Marshall and Stevenson-Hinde, 1998), adolescence (Matthews et al., 2002) young adulthood (Cohen & Hamrick, 2003; Kamarck, Jennings, Pogue-Geile, & Manuck, 1994; Sherwood et al., 1997), and later adulthood (Kamarck et al, 1994).

This dispositional, stable component to reactivity, however, is not a fixed genetic characteristic. Social and contextual factors, especially early in development, have considerable influence over reactivity patterns (Alkon et al., 2003; Boyce & Ellis, 2005). Continuity in reactivity patterns over time likely reflects continuity in one's environment over time. That is, high levels of poverty-related stress over a given time period may result in stable patterns of high physiological reactivity. Fortunately, environmental changes can alter physiological reactivity levels. Providing social support, for example, during stressful situations reduces sympathetic reactivity and enhances the body's regulatory processes following stressors (Uchino, Cacioppo, & Kiekolt-Glaser, 1996). Such changes in physiological activation in response to social support provision have even been found in experimental laboratory settings by varying the levels of adult supportiveness provided to participants during stressor tasks (e.g., Hilmert, Kulik, & Christenfeld, 2002). Also, familiarity and comfort level may play a role in modulating reactivity levels. For children, simply changing the venue of physiological assessments appears to influence reactivity levels, with the lowest levels found in home assessments compared to those conducted in laboratories or child care settings (Alkon et al., 2003). Positive environmental changes can result in commensurate reductions in reactivity, which over time could help highly reactive individuals adopt patterns of lower reactivity.

Unfortunately, living in poverty carries a dual risk for low-income families: risk for developing patterns of high physiological reactivity and risk for developing stability of such patterns over time. Remaining in poverty for long periods of time likely leads to steady, if not worsening, physiological reactivity patterns over time for individuals of all ages. However, as noted above, reducing stress exposure and increasing environmental protective factors (e.g., social support) holds promise for improving children's and adults' reactivity patterns over time, which can help ameliorate risk for psychopathology.

Effects of High Physiological Reactivity on Psychopathology

High physiological reactivity constitutes a considerable risk for developing psychopathology. More specifically, autonomic nervous system and HPA hyperarousal strongly predicts the development of internalizing disorders in children and adolescents (Beidel, 1991; Friedman, 2007; Granger, Weisz, & Kauneckis, 1994; Gunnar, 2001; Scheeringa, Zeanah, Myers, & Putnam, 2004; Wadsworth et al., 2005; Weems et al., 2005) as well as among young adults (Hoehn, Braune, Schiebe, & Albus, 1997; Hughes, Watkins, Blumenthal, Kuhn, & Sherwood, 2004). While physiological activation is an adaptive response to acute stress; chronic over-activation of the stress response damages healthy development and impairs mental health. The accumulated effect of repeated and prolonged physiological responding increases allostatic load, depleting the body's overall physiological resources (Johnston-Brooks, Lewis, Evans, & Whalen, 1998; McEwen, 1998).

Examining the link between stress and anxiety in children, a number of studies have found higher heart rate, blood pressure, and sympathetic activation levels in both community and clinical samples of children with anxiety symptoms and disorders (Beidel, 1991; Scheeringa et al., 2004; Weems et al., 2005). For example, children with PTSD show inhibited parasympathetic activation (i.e., less regulation) in response to the presentation of traumatic situations and memories (Scheeringa et al., 2004). Among adults, individuals with anxiety disorders also show elevations in physiological reactivity compared with healthy control patients. In response to mental arithmetic and improvised speech tasks in a laboratory, patients with panic disorder showed greater autonomic nervous system and HPA activation than non-anxious participants (Hoehn et al., 1997). Increased sympathetic activation in response to stress has been found in depressed and anxious women in their forties and fifties (Hughes et al., 2004). Clearly, heightened stress reactivity places individuals of all ages at risk for psychopathology, including anxiety and other internalizing disorders.

Higher stress reactivity also appears to exacerbate key risk factors and inhibit protective factors that impact the development of psychopathology over time. High stress reactivity limits the ability of primary control coping to mitigate the impact of poverty-related stress on aggressive behavior (Wadsworth & Berger, 2006). Additionally, higher reactivity has been found to exacerbate the impact of poverty-related stress on children's, adolescents', and adults' anxiety symptoms over the course of one year (Wolff, DeCarlo, & Wadsworth, 2007). Finding this in a relatively homogenous sample of low-income families living in an urban area suggests the powerful impact even incremental differences in reactivity and poverty-related stress has on the development of anxiety symptoms among individuals of all ages.

In sum, high physiological reactivity, especially when combined with current poverty-related stress, is strongly predictive of impairment in psychological and social-emotional functioning. It should be noted that exceptionally *low* reactivity is also predictive of psychopathology, particularly externalizing disorders such as oppositional-defiant disorder and conduct disorder (Boyce et al., 2001; Raine, Venables, & Mednick, 1997). However, despite some evidence for the relationship between low reactivity and aggression among individuals from low socioeconomic status levels (Kindlon, Tremblay, Mezzacappa, & Earls, 1995), this relationship actually appears to be strongest among individuals from higher SES levels (Raine, Reynolds, Venables, & Mednick, 1997; Raine & Venables, 1984). Higher levels of aggression among children and adults living in poverty likely results from other variables prevalent in impoverished families and neighborhoods, such as greater exposure to, and modeling, of harsh discipline and violence, poor parental supervision, and the effects of alcohol and substance use on behavior, among others (e.g., Farrington & Loeber, 2000; Friedman, 1998).

COPING WITH POVERTY-RELATED STRESS

One very promising avenue to explore in terms of preventing dysregulated stress response systems is coping. Given the host of negative outcomes that results from chronic PRS, it is crucial to understand the processes that mitigate or alternatively enhance the relationship between PRS and negative outcomes. This portion of the chapter focuses on how adults and children cope with PRS, what is helpful and what is not, and the effects of coping on adjustment.

Current definitions of coping conceptualize it as a conscious and voluntary process that includes attempts to manage emotions and cognitions, regulate behavior and arousal, and act on the environment to alter or decrease a source of stress (Compas, Connor-Smith, Saltzman, Thomsen, & Wadsworth, 2001). In other words, coping includes voluntary attempts to handle stress by focusing on emotions, thoughts, or actions that one can take. Most conceptualizations of coping distinguish between taking action to confront a problem versus taking action to avoid a problem (e.g. Compas, Malcarne, & Fondacaro, 1988; Ebata & Moos, 1991). In addition, coping can focus on the problem, for example, problem solving; or coping can focus on resulting emotions, such as trying to regulate emotional reactions (Ayers, Sandler, & Twohey, 1998).

Connor-Smith, Compas, Wadsworth, Thomsen, and Saltzman (2000) proposed the Responses to Stress Model, which distinguishes between coping (voluntary) responses to stress, and involuntary (automatic) stress responses. Among voluntary or coping responses, we can distinguish between responses that demonstrate engagement with or disengagement from the stressor or reactions to the stressor. Voluntary engagement responses include primary control coping strategies and secondary control coping strategies. Primary control strategies are used to directly alter the stressor or one's emotional reactions to it. For example, problem-solving, emotional expression, and emotion regulation all fall under primary control coping. Secondary control coping includes strategies that aim to adapt oneself to the stressor—cognitive coping strategies fall under this category (Connor-Smith et al., 2000). Voluntary disengagement strategies are used to avoid the stressor both behaviorally and cognitively. In addition to coping responses defined by the Responses to Stress model, researchers have identified social support, religious coping, and substance use as other ways of coping with stress.

How children and adults cope with PRS can buffer or exacerbate the effects of this stress on a number of outcomes. Examining the effectiveness of different forms of coping in the context of PRS informs understanding of what is helpful in the face of this kind of stress and what is likely to make matters worse.

Adult Coping

Adults engage in a variety of strategies to cope with stress, including social support, primary control, secondary control, disengagement coping, religious coping and substance use. Although stress can undermine engagement in some strategies, research has confirmed that certain types of coping are helpful and are superior to other types in the context of PRS.

Social Support

Social support may buffer against PRS by serving several functions. Often social support provides tangible help and resources such as family members helping with child-care or lending money in a time of extra need. In addition, social support provides the opportunity for venting and expressing your emotions, and for discussion about how to solve a particular problem (two strategies encompassed by primary control coping). Talking with someone about financial stress can also allow for validation that times are hard and that one is doing the best he or she can. In these ways, social support serves as a buffer against the negative impact of poverty (Leadbeater & Linares, 1992). However, poverty in itself often decreases the availability of social support because of fewer available resources, dangerous neighborhoods, and increased stress (McLoyd & Wilson, 1994).

Despite the decreased availability of social support for adults coping with poverty, those who believe they have adequate social support often show buffering effects against a range of stressors common to poverty. Those adults who perceive high levels of social support report lower levels of economic strain, suggesting that social support buffers adults from economic stress (Henly, Danziger, & Offer, 2005) and protects low-income parents from depressed mood (Ennis, Hobfall, & Schröeder, 2000). Social support is also helpful when coping with discrimination, an element of PRS. Those who perceive social resources and support feel more empowered to confront racial bias, which in turn, contributes to a sense of efficacy and well-being (Noh & Kaspar, 2003). Similarly, marital support also promotes resilience. By demonstrating care, concern, and affection, marital support has a "soothing" effect on the negative effects of financial stress (Conger et al., 1999). However, some studies indicate that social support does not buffer against all types of stress, such as parenting stress for low-income mothers (Raikes & Thompson, 2005). Thus social support is a positive resource for low-income families, though not a panacea or the only useful option available.

Social support and primary control strategies inherently overlap as seeking social support often involves expressing or trying to get help regulating how one is feeling. Social support fosters direct coping strategies and vice versa (Lever, Piñol, & Uralde, 2005; Rayburn et al., 2005). Thus engagement in primary control coping strategies and perceiving and utilizing a social support network are intertwined and likely promote each other.

Primary Control or Active Coping

Primary control coping strategies include problem solving, emotional expression, and emotional regulation. Although primary control strategies are generally related to better psychological functioning, poverty often undermines their use. Despite low-income mothers' reports that active problem solving and thinking about the future are helpful ways of coping (Cosgrove & Flynn, 2005), poverty predicts less use of both (Klebanov, Brooks-Gunn, & Duncan, 1994). Likewise, when utilized, problem solving can benefit low-income adults at high risk for depression (Vinokur, Price, & Schul, 2002). In addition, active coping can reduce the impact of perceived discrimination on depression by fostering a sense of taking control and confronting discrimination (Noh & Kaspar, 2003).

Wadsworth and colleagues (2005) examined primary control as a moderator, an influence that strengthens or weakens the relationship between two other factors. For adults, primary control weakened the impact of economic stress on depression. Parallel results were found for parents coping with family PRS. Primary control coping was related to less symptoms for a range difficulties from anxiety and depression to aggression, attention problems and social difficulties (Wadsworth & DeCarlo, 2007). Thus primary control coping is helpful in the face of PRS and protects against a range of problems. However, because poverty undermines the use of primary control strategies, intervention and prevention programs should target teaching these skills.

Secondary Control Coping

Secondary control coping strategies include acceptance—acknowledgement that circumstances are unlikely to change; distraction—engaging in other activities to get one's mind off stressful circumstances; positive thinking—trying to see the positive in stressful times; and cognitive restructuring—thinking about a situation in a way that allows one to see what he or she is gaining or learning from the problem (Conner-Smith et al., 2000). Secondary control strategies may be particularly helpful for problems for which there is little control. Thinking about a problem differently in order to adapt to stressors that are difficult to change is especially relevant for coping with poverty. For example, when there are few jobs available to apply for or when there is no better housing available within an affordable range, accepting the situation or thinking differently about it may be the best one can do. In addition, distraction allows low-income adults to "take a break" from stress by engaging in something else that is more positive, thus promoting psychological health.

Secondary control coping strategies, such as reappraising the situation in a more positive way, are particularly helpful for middle-aged and older adults (Wrosch, Heckhausen, & Lachman, 2000). Additionally, secondary control coping mediates the association between life stress and parental hostility (Wadsworth et al., 2005), suggesting that life stress undermines the ability to engage in secondary control coping strategies, though these strategies predict less hostility. Secondary control strategies such as cognitive restructuring are also helpful when coping with discrimination (Yoo & Lee, 2005), as these strategies allow for people to think differently about the discrimination, for example attributing the discrimination to the ignorance of others. In addition, for parents coping with family PRS, secondary control coping strategies are associated with fewer problems across a range of domains including anxiety and depression, withdrawal, somatic problems, thought problems, aggression, attention problems and social difficulties (Wadsworth & DeCarlo, 2007). Because poverty is often associated with structural barriers, feelings of powerlessness and lack of control are not uncommon (Belle & Doucet, 2003). Thus secondary control strategies that involve adapting oneself to a stressor may be especially potent for coping with PRS.

Disengagement Coping

Disengagement coping consists of strategies that attempt to orient the individual away from a stressful event or away from their emotional reactions and includes avoidance, denial, and wishful thinking. Avoiding and denying stress provides temporary and welcome escape from stress, but is unlikely to promote psychological health in the long-term because such strategies do not address or solve problems. Effortful attempts to suppress unwanted thoughts, for example, eventually lead to increased frequency of unwanted thoughts (Wegner, 1994) and sometimes a sense of failure and self-blame (Kelly & Kahn, 1994). Thus, cognitive avoidance is likely to lead to negative long-term psychological effects. Behavioral avoidance also may provide temporary relief from stress, but is likely to have long-term negative consequences (Compas et al., 2001). Thus for a person avoiding or denying financial trouble, he or she is likely unable to suppress thoughts for extended amounts of time. Eventually a person will be reminded of the trouble and may feel even worse about it because they have not addressed the situation, creating a sense of incompetence.

In the context of PRS, avoidance coping is related to depression for poor mothers (Banyard & Graham-Bermann, 1998; Rayburn et al., 2005). Thus, trying to forget about problems, ignoring or denying them, often prevents one from seeking validation and support, leaving one feeling isolated with a problem that does not get fixed. Disengagement coping exacerbates the effects of economic strain on depressive symptoms for low-income parents (Wadsworth et al., 2005). Thus, disengagement coping may provide short-term relief from stress, but it is likely to promote negative psychological consequences when unaccompanied by engagement in more positive activities (distraction) or problem-solving.

Substance Use

Stress and poverty are related to drinking more often and larger quantities of alcohol (Khan, Murray, & Barnes, 2002; Pierce, Frone, Russell, & Cooper, 1996) and alcohol is commonly used to cope with stressful circumstances (Pearlin & Radabaugh, 1976). There is evidence to suggest that alcohol use can buffer adults from negative effects of acute stress (Levenson, 1980) particularly for men (Neff, 1993). Other research suggests that alcohol consumption coupled with positive distraction activities induces positive mood (Steele, Southwick, & Pagano, 1986), suggesting that drinking while socializing or engaging in other positive activities may be beneficial and act similarly to distraction coping strategies.

However, a substantial literature suggests that alcohol consumption is an ineffective coping strategy and may compound symptoms in the end (Abrams & Wilson, 1979; Keane & Lisman, 1982). High levels of alcohol consumption are related to negative health and social outcomes for older adults though lower levels of consumption are unrelated to negative outcomes (Hunter & Gillen, 2006). Drinking to relieve stress may be appealing as a way to escape temporarily. However, for those under high levels of stress, it may take larger amounts of alcohol to "escape," leading to negative consequences. Thus it appears that adults coping with PRS may turn to alcohol, especially men, which may provide temporary relief from stress. However, drinking large quantities of alcohol is problematic and ineffective for coping with stress. It is likely that long-term effects of alcohol when it is used to avoid problems is similar to the exacerbating effects of disengagement coping, in that drinking to escape temporarily does very little to actually change problems.

Religious Coping

Although religious coping is sometimes helpful when coping with acute loss such as that incurred through natural disasters and other traumas (Pargament, Cole, Vandecreek, Belavich, Brant, & Perez, 1999), few studies have examined religious coping in the context of chronic PRS. However, there is evidence to suggest that religiosity can buffer against the negative effects of stress. Overall well-being is associated with religion that is internalized, intrinsic, and based on a secure relationship with God (Bergin, Masters, & Richards, 1987; Pargament, Kennell, Hathaway, & Grovengoed, 1988). Religiosity may be especially helpful for socially marginalized groups who embed religion more fully into their lives and because religion offers accessible resources, such as a social network provided by one's church (Pargament, 1997). Indeed, we find higher levels of religiosity among a number of groups including African Americans (Pargament, 1997), older populations (Gurin, Veroff, & Feld, 1960), and less educated people (Gallup, 1994), suggesting that for these groups religion is a central and important aspect of their lives.

Religiosity and religious coping likely serve several functions to buffer against stress. For those highly involved in religious communities, religiosity provides a social support network, a place for people to get validation and be accepted. In addition, certain forms of religious coping promote cognitive strategies, such as acceptance, hope or positive thinking, as well as making meaning out of stressful times, which is similar to cognitive restructuring. Although research is needed to examine religiosity and religious coping in the context of PRS, research suggests that religiosity can also buffer in times of stress and that religious coping may be particularly relevant to the lives of marginalized and ethnic minority adults (Pargament, 2002; Pargament, 1997).

Child Coping

Research on children's coping has mirrored conceptualizations of adult coping (Compas et al., 2001). The Responses to Stress model is a useful framework for understanding child coping along the dimensions of primary control coping, secondary control coping, and disengagement coping. In addition, children engage in social support strategies. Some teens also begin to use alcohol or other substances to cope and begin to engage in religious coping. Thus, this section reviews how each of these forms of coping relates to child adjustment in the face of PRS.

Social Support

Social support for young children often comes in the form of support-seeking from parents, caregivers, or other family members. Poor children often receive less social support and have parents that are less responsive and more authoritarian (Evans, 2004). A strong social support network does promote resiliency in the face of adversity for children (Masten, Best, & Garmezy, 1990), suggesting that when poor children do have a network of support they often fare better. Social support is related to higher self-esteem for children, though it does not always buffer the impact of stress on child adjustment (e.g., Guest & Biasini, 2001). Seeking support as a coping strategy may be helpful in some contexts and not others. This is because sometimes seeking support for children reflects distress or anxiety and not simply a positive attempt to cope with stress. For example, seeking social support when coping with discrimination is related to lower levels of distress (Scott & House, 2005), but seeking support when coping with family conflict is often associated with distress or depression (e.g. Sandler, Tein, & West, 1994). Thus, in some contexts, seeking social support can help to buffer the impact of stress, especially for a stressor external to the family, like an incident of discrimination, and in other contexts, seeking social support likely reflects distress. In addition, when a source of stress is within the family such as family conflict, seeking support from caregivers to cope with the conflict may be impossible or ineffective. However, primary control strategies that overlap with social support, such as emotional expression, are often associated with fewer mental health problems across contexts (Wadsworth & Compas, 2002).

Primary Control Coping

As discussed above, primary control strategies include emotional expression, emotion regulation, and problem solving. These strategies predict less anxious/depressed symptoms and aggressive problems for teens coping with PRS (Wadsworth & Berger, 2006; Wadsworth & Compas, 2002). Directly approaching the problem tends to predict fewer symptoms for young people coping with general stress (Compas et al., 2001). Thus attempting to directly alter the stressful situation or to alter one's emotional reactions to the stressor is effective in coping with economic stress. In addition, primary control coping strategies are related to less problems across multiple psychological domains ranging from anxiety and depression to aggression and attention problems (Wadsworth & DeCarlo, 2007). However, when coping with specific types of stress such as family conflict, primary control coping may be less helpful (O'Brian, Margolin, & John, 1995) or differentially helpful for one gender. Recent data in this area suggests that primary control coping strategies are associated with fewer internalizing symptoms for low-income girls when faced with family conflict, but have no impact for low-income boys (DeCarlo & Wadsworth, 2007).

In addition, primary control coping strategies are helpful in the face of PRS, but PRS undermines the use of these strategies (Wadsworth & Berger, 2006; Wadsworth & Compas, 2002). Perhaps poor children and teens are using less primary control strategies under high conditions of stress due to the uncontrollable nature of PRS for children and teens who have little power over their family's financial situation. Thus, secondary control strategies may be particularly relevant for poor children coping with a burden of uncontrollable stress.

Secondary Control Coping

Secondary control coping strategies, such as positive thinking, acceptance, cognitive restructuring and distraction, appear to be particularly helpful for children coping with PRS. Boys and girls who use high levels of secondary control coping tend to have fewer aggressive behaviors and suffer from less anxiety and depression (Wadsworth & Berger, 2005; Wadsworth & Compas, 2002; Wadsworth et al., 2005). Still, children who live in poverty are less able to make use of secondary control coping, suggesting that PRS and coping affect each other (Wadsworth et al., 2005), pointing to the need for intervention and prevention programs to target these skills. Secondary control coping protects children and teens across many domains of psychological functioning including anxiety and depression, withdrawal, somatic complaints, thought problems, aggression, attention problems and social difficulties (Wadsworth & DeCarlo, 2007). Children coping with PRS are in a position of little control—their actual ability to problem solve or create change is very small. Thus, intervention and prevention programs should target secondary control coping strategies that focus on adapting to a stressor that is not likely to change or dissipate. Primary control strategies should be targeted to daily stressors that arise in the context of PRS for which children might have more actual ability to affect such as difficulties with peers.

Disengagement Coping

Disengagement strategies such as avoidance, denial, and wishful thinking are generally not beneficial for children coping with poverty. Disengagement strategies either have no effect or actually worsen symptoms for poor children (Wadsworth & Berger, 2005; Wadsworth & Compas, 2002; Wadsworth et al., 2005). In addition, under high levels of stress, many poor youths respond by trying to disengage themselves from the stressor, both behaviorally and cognitively, in an effort to escape an overwhelming burden of stress. A natural response for such large burdens of stress would be to try to "get away" or escape. However, these strategies do little to actually change the situation or adapt to the stress.

However, research has suggested that disengagement coping may actually be helpful in some circumstances such as family conflict (O'Brian et al., 1995). In some cases, disengaging or avoiding potentially dangerous conflict situations is helpful for children and teens. Recent findings suggest that disengagement coping is not related to worse outcomes for low-income teens coping with family conflict in the short-term, but is detrimental for teens in the long-term. Because disengagement coping does little to fix or change the problem, the negative effects of the stress are likely to catch up to teens later on. In addition, unlike secondary control strategies, disengagement coping does not allow teens to adapt themselves to the stressor in any positive way. Essentially, disengagement coping allows teens to ignore stress temporarily, but eventually teens recognize that the problem has not dissipated and may feel worse or more powerless. Disengagement coping was unrelated to internalizing symptoms for low-income teens coping with family conflict within a single time point, but moderated the effect of family coping across time, such that more use of disengagement coping predicts more internalizing symptoms a year later (DeCarlo & Wadsworth, 2007). Thus, although disengagement may be functional in the short-term, the long-term effects of using disengagement strategies, uncoupled with any more positive strategies such as distraction or problem-solving, is harmful for low-income teens.

Substance Use

Stress and poverty are associated with greater use of alcohol and other substances among poor teens (Chassin, Pillow, Curran, Molina, & Barrera, 1993; Windle & Weisner, 2004). Teens may be engaging in substance use as a way to cope with stress, though it does not appear to work very well. In fact, using substances to cope is often associated with negative mood (e.g., Chassin et al., 1993; Newcomb and Harlow, 1986; Wills, 1986). In addition, teens motivated to use alcohol to cope with stress quickly develop more serious alcohol problems (Rafnsson, Jonsson, & Windle, 2006). Thus, teens may be motivated to use alcohol or other substances to cope, but have difficulty regulating this strategy, making substance use a problem for teens and a developmentally inappropriate strategy.

Religious Coping

Little research has examined religious coping among poor teens. Collaborative religious coping is related to less suicidal risk compared to self-directed religious coping for African American teens (Molock, Puri, & Matlin, 2006), suggesting that some forms of religious coping supply a support network, which is beneficial for teens. In addition, religious coping appears to benefit both psychological health and physical health for some low-income teens. For Mexican American teens, religious coping was associated with both physical health and less depression, and for Asian American teens, religious coping was associated with less depression (Vaughn & Roesch, 2003). Thus, religious coping may buffer low-income teens from PRS, though this may depend on ethnic and cultural socialization.

IMPLICATIONS FOR INTERVENTION AND AMELIORATION

How can we use the above information to provide information about amelioration of the harmful effects of poverty? Effective coping is probably not going to alter a family's economic situation. However, we propose that having the ability to cope effectively with PRS could prevent the development of depression and other psychological problems that interfere with success in occupational, academic, and interpersonal realms. Thus, prevention and early intervention are promising avenues through which psychologists may be able to have a long-term positive impact on the lives of children and adults in poverty.

Several large scale programs have been designed and implemented with the intention of preventing academic and social difficulties in children living in poverty. Head Start (e.g., Ripple & Zigler, 2003) and the Perry Preschool Program (Weikart & Schmeinhart, 1992) are successful prevention programs targeting poor families with preschool children to prevent the emergence of behavioral difficulties and promote positive social skills, emotional competence, and academic achievement. Both of these programs focus on providing families with access to basic human necessities such as food, housing, education and health care, as well as high quality childcare. As target children are so young, coping is not a central theme in the curricula of Head Start and Perry Preschool, though both of these programs likely foster positive emotional control skills, the building blocks of later efficacious coping.

A relatively new program aimed at preventing the emergence of conduct problems in school-age children, the Fast-Track program, has shown some success with low-income children. As with the above programs, Fast-Track provides a wide array of basic services to families. In addition, however, Fast-Track incorporates the teaching of basic emotion regulation and coping skills into units developed for both parents and children. Children participating in Fast-Track receive a classroom program, called PATHS (Promoting Alternative Thinking Strategies). PATHS helps children work on self-control skills by teaching emotional awareness and understanding. It also helps children enhance peer-related social skills and social problem solving to increase social competence (Bierman et al., 2002). The program began with a sample of 1st graders and plans to follow them to their 10th grade year. So far results of the program have been reported through the 3rd grade, and they are promising but modest. According to Bierman et al. (2002) the high-risk intervention group has shown a significant decrease in aggressive, disruptive and disobedient behavior in school and at home.

As we have seen above, the stressors of poverty may play a key role in creating the pervasive and potentially permanent negative effects on children. As such, it is possible that intervention programs may see enhanced efficacy by more directly targeting PRS and directly teaching skills for how to cope with it. A number of intervention programs directly target the very coping skills research shows to be effective for coping with poverty-related stress. Two such evidence-based programs, Coping Cat (Kendall, 2000) and Primary and Secondary Control Enhancement Training (PASCET; Weisz, Thurber, Sweeney, Proffitt, & LeGagnoux, 1997), provide evidence that more sophisticated coping skills are teachable and that learning coping skills translates into measurable reductions in psychological disorders and symptoms. Both of these curricula have been effective in treating and preventing psychological disorders such as depression and anxiety in at-risk children and adolescents.

Coping Cat, developed by Kendall (2000) is a cognitive behavioral treatment that assists school age children (8-17 year-olds) in recognizing anxious feelings and physical reactions to anxiety. This program helps children and adolescents clarify that they are thinking and feeling (physically and emotionally) in anxiety-provoking situations, and teaches them how to develop and evaluate a plan to cope with the situation. The intervention effectively uses behavioral training strategies such as modeling real-life situations, role-playing, relaxation training, and contingent reinforcement. Social reinforcement is also used throughout the sessions to encourage and reward the children's coping efforts, and the children are encouraged to verbally reinforce their own successful coping. Acquisition of coping skills as a result of this program has been linked to improvements in children's anxiety. This provides strong evidence for the relevance of coping for at-risk children, and demonstrates that coping can be taught to young children.

The second example, the Primary and Secondary Control Enhancement Training (PASCET) program developed by Weisz et al (1997) is a manual-based intervention addressing the needs of depressed children. This program targets depression by using a "two-process model of control," which is closely aligned with the primary/secondary control coping described earlier in the chapter (Weisz et al., 1997). The first process, the *primary control process*, addresses what a child can actively do to alter (either through the use of activity selection and/or setting attainable goals) a situation to fit their own wishes. The second process, called *secondary control process*, refers to what a child can alter within themselves in order to buffer against the impact of the situation/environment (e.g., replacing negative thoughts with positive thoughts, etc.). Through engaging activities such as role-playing, games, videos, and weekly homework assignments, PASCET teaches children to apply primary control coping skills when faced with distressing conditions they can alter (i.e., situations which they have some direct control over), and to apply secondary control coping skills when confronted by situations beyond their direct control. In a study examining PASCETs' impact on children with mild to moderate depression, findings suggest that children enrolled in PASCET (i.e., the treatment group) showed significantly greater reductions in depressive symptoms than depressed children in the control condition (Weisz et. al., 1997). This provides evidence for the usefulness of matching coping skills with aspects of the stressful context. Addressing the controllability of a situation, or the lack of direct control that an individual might have over a certain context such as poverty, can be helpful for children in determining how to best solve a particular problem.

The aforementioned programs are both effective in alleviating symptoms of anxiety and depression in children (Kendall, 2000; Weisz et al, 1997). They are prime illustrations of how enhancement of coping skills can be helpful in addressing a psychological problem once present. At present though, both of these programs are designed as a treatment program for preexisting psychological problems, rather than a program to prevent the onset of the problems. The public health approach of preventing the development of problems before they begin is the only way to lower incidence rates of psychological disorders in the population. This is one avenue through which efforts at breaking the cycle of poverty can begin.

Intervention Focused on Coping with Poverty: FACES

While numerous prevention programs target low-income children, and one program includes enhancement of some emotion regulation skills in at-risk youth, no programs to date have been aimed specifically at assisting children and their parents in developing skills to cope with the stresses of economic hardship. In addition, few prevention or intervention programs have targeted multiple coping strategies or systematically demonstrated that changes in coping skills resulting from the intervention are associated with changes in symptoms. The Families Coping with Economic Strain (FaCES) intervention developed by Raviv and Wadsworth (2006) was designed to address these limitations of prior research.

The FaCES program was adapted from the manual-based Primary and Secondary Control Enhancement Training (PASCET) treatment program for child depression (Weisz et al.,

1997) with several important modifications. First, additional components were designed to help children and parents constructively discuss and cope with issues specific to familial financial stress. Second, the PASCET program was designed primarily for use with children; therefore, material regarding parenting and parental coping was developed.

The goal of FaCES was to teach children and their parents primary and secondary control coping strategies shown to be effective for individuals dealing with poverty-related stress. Children and parents were taught these skills in separate groups. Both groups engaged in various activities such as role-playing, watching video-clips, and playing games to facilitate learning of new skills. The sessions 1) introduced various ways of coping 2) taught emotion regulation skills (i.e., relaxation) and 3) educated parents and children about the effects of poverty on the family and the benefits of having strategies to utilize when stressors came their way.

Raviv & Wadsworth (2006) conducted a pilot study and utilized a multiple baseline design to implement and evaluate the feasibility and efficacy of the FaCES program. Participants were children (8-12 years-old) and their parents. FaCES showed promising results. Children demonstrated significant improvements in the proximal coping variables targeted by the intervention for their potential to reduce risk for psychopathological symptoms. Findings also revealed a decrease in internalizing and externalizing symptoms and deviations from pre-intervention symptom trajectories. Finally, FaCES was very accessible to participating families and that is important to note since program accessibility is very much interlinked with participation rates and overall program effectiveness. FaCES results indicated attrition rates were low and parent-reported levels of satisfaction with the program were high.

In conclusion, prevention and intervention programs focused on increasing an individual's repertoire of strategies for coping with PRS appear to be beneficial to low-income children and families. Coping may well be one to add to the list of protective factors that are both teachable and effective for children and adults alike.

IMPLICATIONS FOR FUTURE RESEARCH

Individuals from families in poverty are exposed to toxic levels of stress with pervasive and long-lasting effects. While additional research simply reiterating this link is not needed, there remain several important avenues for further research. For example, the relative strength of the effects of a child's personal PRS versus the effects through parental processes has yet to be evaluated. This information will assist in fine-tuning interventions so that they provide adequate emphasis on skills relevant for both adults and children. Similarly, determining whether children's age-appropriate PRS has different psychological implications than more parentified PRS concerns will assist in determining how parents can best provide support and assistance to their children as they struggle to understand and cope with PRS.

The research on poverty-related physiological reactivity problems provides strong evidence for significantly increased risk for developing various forms of psychopathology across the lifespan. Although there is substantial empirical evidence supporting the individual components of this model, little research has attempted to examine the model in its entirety. Naturalistic studies examining the effects of human poverty, as well as animal models exploring the impact of early deprivation, on *both* physiological reactivity and psychosocial outcomes, can provide even greater clarity on how these multiple factors interact. Finding ways to easily assess reactivity and intervene to reduce chronic stress can help prevent the development of stable patterns of heightened reactivity among individual and families living in poverty, ultimately reducing risk for anxiety and other internalizing disorders.

There are a number of areas for future study with regard to coping as well. Primary and secondary control coping appear to be effective coping strategies for both the short- and long-term, though other coping strategies may have differing effects depending on the time-course. Understanding the time-course for primary and secondary control strategies, but also and especially for disengagement coping and substance use could enhance our understanding of coping's effectiveness. Also, disengagement coping appears to be related to symptoms differently depending on the type of stress and gender. Substance use as a coping strategy is generally considered problematic but additional research could focus on disentangling the circumstances where substance use may ameliorate the effects of stress, albeit temporarily and in moderation. In addition, further research is needed to fully understand the role of religious coping in the context of chronic PRS. Religious coping has not been fully explored in the context of PRS or with children and teens. A rich area of future research involves examining the effectiveness of religious coping as well as the contexts in which it is appropriate, including the cultural, ethnic, gender, and age contexts and influences. Likewise, what is most effective and for whom is an enduring question that cuts across coping strategies—thus gender, ethnic, and age differences should be more fully explored.

Although certain forms of coping have obvious protective benefits, a theme for both children and adults, is that PRS actually reduces coping resources, making it more difficult to engage in the sorts of behaviors that help. For example, poverty decreases social support networks for adults because of reduced resources and dangerous neighborhoods. For children, stressed adults are less able to provide the nurturing and supportive environment that may buffer them from stress. Both children and adults also have a more difficult time engaging in primary and secondary control strategies that benefit their mental health. High levels of stress make it more difficult to find the cognitive and emotional resources necessary to think more positively about a problem or to effectively regulate emotions, for example. Rather, adults and children are more inclined to disengage from high levels of stress providing only temporary relief. Thus, intervention and prevention efforts can focus on increasing primary and secondary control strategies and combining these with certain disengagement strategies when appropriate and necessary.

Primary and secondary control strategies stand out as effective ways of coping with PRS and they are related to less mental health problems and difficulties. In addition, secondary control coping is especially relevant for coping with uncontrollable stressors making it an especially effective set of strategies for poor children. Adults coping with PRS are faced with a number of relatively uncontrollable stressors, or stressors that are unlikely to change quickly, such as inadequate housing or debt. Children coping with PRS have even less control over their family's financial situation or the stress that accompanies living with less than they need. Thus, prevention and intervention programs targeting low-income families should emphasize secondary control strategies. These strategies are associated with fewer symptoms of anxiety and depression, and fewer aggressive problems and appear to aid in preventing a range of difficulties for low-income children and families. Additional research is needed to test the effectiveness of intervention efforts that incorporate primary and secondary control coping strategies for both children and adults.

In this way, research-based intervention programs can apply decades of research to attacking the problem of poverty. While promoting effective coping and parental support will not directly eradicate poverty, eradicating the psychological problems that result from poverty is a move in the right direction. From there, children and families can make better use of other programs and opportunities to get ahead unhampered by psychological problems.

REFERENCES

Abrams, D. B. & Wilson, T. G. (1979). Effects of alcohol on social versus physiological processes. *Journal of Abnormal Psychology, 88,* 162-173.

Alkon, A., Goldstein, L.H., Smider, N., Essex, M.J., Kupfer, D.J. & Boyce, W.T. (2003). Developmental and contextual influences on autonomic reactivity in young children. *Developmental Psychobiology, 42(1),* 64-78.

Almeida, D., Neupert, S., Banks, S., & Serido, J. (2005). Do daily stress processes account for socioeconomic health disparities? *Journals of Gerontology: Series B: Psychological Sciences and Social Sciences, 60,* 34-39.

Ayers, T.S., Sandler, I.N. & Twohey, J.L. (1998). Conceptualization and measurement of coping in children and adolescents. *Advances in Clinical Child Psychology, 20,* 243-301.

Banyard, V.L. & Graham-Bermann, S.A. (1998). Surviving poverty: Stress and coping in the lives of housed and homeless mothers. *American Journal of Orthopsychiatry, 68(3),* 479-489.

Bar-Haim, Y., Sutton, D.B., Fox, N.A. & Marvin, R.S. (2000). Stability and change of attachment at 14, 24, and 58 months of age: Behavior, representation, and life events. *Journal of Child Psychology and Psychiatry, 41(3),* 381-388.

Bauer, A.M., Quas, J.A. & Boyce, W.T. (2002). Associations between physiological reactivity and children's behavior: Advantages of a multisystem approach. *Journal of Developmental & Behavioral Pediatrics, 23(2),* 102-113.

Beidel, D.C. (1991). Determining the reliability of psychophysiological assessment in childhood anxiety. *Journal of Anxiety Disorders, 5(2),* 139-150.

Belle, D. & Doucet, J. (2003). Poverty, inequality, and discrimination as sources of depression among U.S. women. *Psychology of Women Quarterly, 27(2),* 101-113.

Bergin, A.E., Masters, K.S., & Richards, P.S. (1987). Religiousness and mental health reconsidered: A study of an intrinsically religious sample. *Journal of Counseling Psychology, 34(2),* 197-204.

Bierman, K., Coie, J., Dodge, K., Greenberg, M., Lochman, J., McMahon, R., et al. (2002). Using the Fast Track randomized prevention trial to test the early-starter model of the development of serious conduct problems. *Development and Psychopathology, 14,* 925-943.

Boyce, W., & Ellis, B. (2005). Biological sensitivity to context: I. An evolutionary-developmental theory of the origins and functions of stress reactivity. *Development and Psychopathology, 17,* 271-301.

Boyce, W., Quas, J., Alkon, A., Smider, N., Essex, M., Kupfer, D., et al. (2001, August). Autonomic reactivity and psychopathology in middle childhood. *British Journal of Psychiatry, 179,* 144-150.

Caldji, C., Fancis, D., Sharma, S., Plotsky, P.M. & Meaney, M.J. (2000). The effects of early rearing environment on the development of GABA-sub(A) and central benzodiazepine receptor levels and novelty-induced fearfulness in the rat. *Neuropsychopharmacology, 22(3),* 219-229.

Chassin, L., Pillow, D.R., Curran, P.J., Molina, B.S.G., Barrera, M. Jr. (1993). Relation of parental alcoholism to early adolescent substance use: A test of three mediating mechanisms. *Journal of Abnormal Psychology, 102(1),* 3-19.

Chen, E., Matthews, K.A. & Boyce, W.T. (2002). Socioeconomic differences in children's health: How and why do these relationships change with age? *Psychological Bulletin, 128(2),* 295-329.

Cohen, S., Doyle, W.J. & Baum, A. (2006). Socioeconomic status is associated with stress hormones. *Psychosomatic Medicine, 68(3),* 414-420.

Cohen, S. & Hamrick, N. (2003). Stable individual differences in physiological response to stressors: Implications for stress-elicited changes in immune related health. *Brain, Behavior and Immunity, 17(6)* 407-414.

Compas, B.E., Connor-Smith, J.K., Saltzman, H., Thomsen, A.H. & Wadsworth, M.E. (2001). Coping with stress during childhood and adolescence: Problems, progress, and potential in theory and research. *Psychological Bulletin, 127(1),* 87-127.

Compas, B.E., Malcarne, V.L. & Fondacaro, K.M. (1988). Coping with stressful events in older children and young adolescents. *Journal of Consulting and Clinical Psychology, 56(3),* 405-411.

Conger, R.D., Conger, K.J, Elder, G.H., Lorenz, F.O., Simons, R.L. & Whitbeck, L.B. (1992). A family process model of economic hardship and adjustment of early adolescent boys. *Child Development, 63(3),* 526-541.

Conger, R.D., Conger, K.J, Elder, G.H., Lorenz, F.O., Simons, R.L. & Whitbeck, L.B. (1993). Family economic stress and adjustment of early adolescent girls. *Developmental Psychology, 29(2),* 206-219.

Conger, R.D. & Elder, G.H. Jr. (1994). *Families in troubled times: Adapting to change in rural America.* Hawthorne, NY: Aldine de Gruyter.

Conger, R.D., Ge, X., Elder, G.H. Jr., Lorenz, F.O. & Simons, R.L. (1994). Economic stress, coercive family process, and developmental problems of adolescents. *Child Development, 65(2),* 541-561.

Conger, R.D., Rueter, M.A. & Elder, G.H. Jr. (1999). Couple resilience to economic pressure. *Journal of Personality and Social Psychology, 76(1),* 54-71.

Conger, R.D, Wallace, L.E., Sun, Y., Simons, R.L., McLoyd, V.C. & Brody, G.H. (2002). Economic pressure in African American families: A replication and extension of the family stress model. *Developmental Psychology, 38(2),* 179-193.

Connor-Smith, J.K., Compas, B.E., Wadsworth, M.E., Thomsen, A.H. & Saltzman, H. (2000). Responses to stress in adolescence: Measurement of coping and involuntary stress responses. *Journal of Consulting and Clinical Psychology, 68(6),* 976-992.

Cosgrove, L. & Flynn, C. (2005). Marginalized mothers: Parenting without a home. *Analysis of Social Issues and Public Policy, 5,* 127-143.

Davidson, R.J. & Fox, N.A. (1989). Frontal brain asymmetry predicts infants' response to maternal separation. *Journal of Abnormal Psychology, 98(2)*, 127-131.

DeCarlo, C. & Wadsworth, M.E. (2007). Coping with family conflict: What's helpful and what's not for low-income teens. Manuscript in preparation.

Dohrenwend, B.P., Levav, I., Shrout, P.E., Schwartz, S., Naveh, G., Link, B.G., Skodol, A.E. & Stueve, A. (1992). Socioeconomic status and psychiatric disorders: The causation-selection issue. *Science, 255(5047)*, 946-952.

DuBois, D., Felner, R., Meares, H. & Krier, M. (1994). Prospective investigation of the effects of socioeconomic disadvantage, life stress, and social support on early adolescent adjustment. *Journal of Abnormal Psychology, 103(3)*, 511-522.

Ebata, A.T. & Moos, R.H. (1991). Coping and adjustment in distressed and healthy adolescents. *Journal of Applied Developmental Psychology, 12(1)*, 33-54.

Ekberg-Aronsson, M., Nilsson, P.M., Nilsson, J.A., Löfdahl, C.G. & Löfdahl, K. (2007). Mortality risks among heavy-smokers with special reference to women: A long-term follow-up of an urban population. *European Journal of Epidemiology, 22(5)*, 301-309.

Ennis, N.E., Hobfoll, S.E. & Schröder, K.E.E. (2000). Money doesn't talk, it swears: How economic stress and resistance resources impact inner-city women's depressive mood. *American Journal of Community Psychology, 28(2)*, 149-173.

El-Sheikh, M., Cummings, E.M. & Goetsch, V.L. (1989). Coping with adults' angry behavior: Behavioral, physiological, and verbal responses in preschoolers. *Developmental Psychology, 25(4)*, 490-498.

Evans, G.W. (2004). The environment of child poverty. *American Psychologist, 59*, 77-92.

Evans, G.W. & English, K. (2002). The environment of poverty: Multiple stressor exposure, psychophysiological stress, and socioemotional adjustment. *Child Development, 73(4)*, 1238-1248.

Evans, G.W., Kim, P., Ting, A.H., Tesher, H.B. & Shannis, D. (2007). Cumulative risk, maternal responsiveness, and allostatic load among young adolescents. *Developmental Psychology, 43(2)*, 341-351.

Farrington, D., & Loeber, R. (2000). Epidemiology of juvenile violence. *Child and Adolescent Psychiatric Clinics of North America, 9*, 733-748.

Friedman, B.H. (2007). An autonomic flexibility-neurovisceral integration model of anxiety and cardiac vagal tone. *Biological Psychology, 74(2)*, 185-199.

Gallup, G., Jr. (1994). *The Gallop poll: Public opinion 1993*. Wilmingtong, DE: Scholarly Resources.

Gianaros, P.J., Horenstein, J.A., Cohen, S., Matthews, K.A., Brown, S.M., Flory, J.D., Critchley, H.D., Manuck, S.B. & Hariri, A.R. (2007). Perigenual anterior cingulated morphology covaries with perceived social standing. *Social Cognitive and Affective Neuroscience.*

Granger, D.A., Weisz, J.R. & Kauneckis, D. (1994). Neuroendocrine reactivity, internalizing behavior problems, and control-related cognitions in clinic-referred children and adolescents. *Journal of Abnormal Psychology, 103(2)*, 267-276.

Guest, K.C. & Biasini, F.J. (2001). Middle childhood, poverty, and adjustment: Does social support have an impact? *Psychology in the Schools, 38(6)*, 549-560.

Gunnar, M.R. (2001). *The role of glucocorticoids in anxiety disorders: A critical analysis.* New York, NY: Oxford University Press.

Gurin, G., Veroff, J. & Feld, S. (1960). *Americans view their mental health: A nationwide interview survey*. Oxford, England: Basic Books.

Heim, C. & Nemeroff, C.B. (2001). The role of childhood trauma in the neurobiology of mood and anxiety disorders: Preclinical and clinical studies. *Biological Psychiatry, 49(12),* 1023-1039.

Henly, J.R., Danziger, S.K. & Offer, S. (2005). The contribution of social support to the material well-being of low-income families. *Journal of Marriage and Family, 67(1),* 122-140.

Hilmert, C.J., Kulik, J.A. & Christenfeld, N. (2002). The varied impact of social support on cardiovascular reactivity. *Basic and Applied Social Psychology, 24(3),* 229-240.

Hoehn, T., Braune, S., Schiebe, G. & Albus, M. (1997). Physiological, biochemical and subjective parameters in anxiety patients with panic disorder during stress exposure as compared with healthy controls. *European Archives of Psychiatry and Clinical Neuroscience, 247(5),* 264-274.

Hudson, C.G. (2005). Socioeconomic status and mental illness: Tests of the social causation and selection hypotheses. *American Journal of Orthopsychiatry, 75(1),* 3-18.

Hughes, J.W., Watkins, L., Blumenthal, J.A., Kuhn, C. & Sherwood, A. (2004). Depression and anxiety symptoms are related to increased 24-hour urinary norepinephrine excretion among healthy middle-aged women. *Journal of Psychosomatic Research, 57(4),* 353-358.

Hunter, I. R. & Gillen, M. C. (2006). Alcohol as a response to stress in older adults: A counseling perspective. *ADULTSPAN Journal, 5,* 114-126.

Johnston-Brooks, C.H., Lewis, M.A., Evans, G.W. & Whalen, C.K. (1998). Chronic stress and illness in children: The role of allostatic load. *Psychosomatic Medicine, 60(5),* 597-603.

Kalin, N.H., Larson, C., Shelton, S.E. & Davidson, R.J. (1998). Asymmetric frontal brain activity, cortisol, and behavior associated with fearful temperament in rhesus monkeys. *Behavioral Neuroscience, 112(2),* 286-292.

Kamarck, T.W., Jennings, J.R., Pogue-Geile, M. & Manuck, S.B. (1994). A multidimensional measurement model for cardiovascular reactivity: Stability and cross-validation in two adult samples. *Health Psychology, 13(6),* 471-478.

Kahn, J.R. & Pearlin, L.I. (2006). Financial strain over the life course and health among older adults. *Journal of Health and Social Behavior, 47(1),* 17-31.

Keane, T. M. & Lisman, S. A. (1982). Alcohol and social anxiety in males: Behavioral, cognitive, and psychological effects. *International Journal of Rehabilitation Research, 5,* 82-83.

Kelly, A.E. & Kahn, J.H. (1994). Effects of suppression of personal intrusive thoughts. *Journal of Personality and Social Psychology, 66(6),* 998-1006.

Kendall, P. C. (2000). *Coping cat workbook*. Ardmore, PA: Workbook Publishing.

Kendler, K.S. & Eaves, L.J. (1986). Models for the joint effect of genotype and environment on liability to psychiatric illness. *American Journal of Psychiatry, 143(3),* 279-289.

Khan, S., Murray, R.P. & Barnes, G.E. (2002). A structural equation model of the effect of poverty and unemployment on alcohol abuse. *Addictive Behaviors, 27(3),* 405-423.

Kindlon, D., Tremblay, R., Mezzacappa, E., & Earls, F. (1995). Longitudinal patterns of heart rate and fighting behavior in 9- through 12-year-old boys. *Journal of the American Academy of Child & Adolescent Psychiatry, 34,* 371-377.

Klebanov, P.K., Brooks-Gunn, J. & Duncan, G.J. (1994). Does neighborhood and family poverty affect mothers' parenting, mental health, and social support? *Journal of Marriage & the Family, 56(2),* 441-455.

Lantz, P., Lynch, J., House, J., Lepkowski, J., Mero, R., Musick, M., et al. (2001). Socioeconomic disparities in health change in a longitudinal study of US adults: The role of health-risk behaviors. *Social Science & Medicine, 53,* 29-40.

Leadbeater, B.J. & Linares, O. (1992). Depressive symptoms in Black and Puerto Rican adolescent mothers in the first 3 years postpartum. *Development and Psychopathology, 4(3),* 451-468.

Levenson, R.W. (1980). Alcohol and stress response dampening: Pharmacological effects, expectancy, and tension reduction. *Journal of Abnormal Psychology, 89(4),* 528-538.

Lever, J.P., Piñol, N.L. & Uralde, J.H. (2005). Poverty, psychological resources and subjective well-being. *Social Indicators Research, 73(3),* 375-408.

Lynch, J.W., Kaplan, G.A. & Shema, S.J. (1997). Cumulative impact of sustained economic hardship on physical, cognitive, psychological, and social functioning. *New England Journal of Medicine, 337(26),* 1889-1895.

Mansson, N.O., Rastam, L., Eriksson, F.K., & Israelsson, B. (1998). Socioeconmic inequalities and disability persion in middle aged men. *International Journal of Epidemiology, 27,* 1019-1025.

Marshall, P.J. & Stevenson-Hinde, J. (1998). Behavioral inhibition, heart period, and respiratory sinus arrhythmia in young children. *Developmental Psychobiology, 33(3),* 283-292.

Masten, A.S., Best, K. M., & Garmezy, N. (1990). Resilience and development: Contributions from the study of children who overcome adversity. *Development and Psychopathology, 24,* 425-444.

Matthews, K.A., Gump, B.B., Block, D.R. & Allen, M.T. (1997). Does background stress heighten or dampen children's cardiovascular responses to acute stress? *Psychosomatic Medicine, 59(5),* 488-496.

Matthews, K.A., Salomon, K., Kenyon, K. & Allen, M.T. (2002). Stability of children's and adolescents' hemodynamic responses to psychological challenge: A three-year longitudinal study of a multiethnic cohort of boys and girls. *Psychophysiology, 39(6),* 826-834.

McEwen, B.S. (1998). *Stress, adaptation, and disease: Allostasis and allostatic load.* New York, NY: New York Academy of Sciences.

McLoyd, V.C. (1990). The impact of economic hardship on Black families and children: Psychological distress, parenting, and socioemotional development. *Child Development, 61(2),* 311-346.

McLoyd, V.C. & Wilson, L. (1994). The strain of living poor: Parenting, social support, and child mental health. In A.C. Huston (Ed.) *Children in poverty: Child development and public policy.* Cambridge, UK: Cambridge University Press.

Miech, R.A., Caspi, A., Moffitt, T.E., Wright, B.R.E. & Silva, P.A. (1999). Low socioeconomic status and mental disorders: A longitudinal study of selection and causation during young adulthood. *American Journal of Sociology, 104(4),* 1096-1131.

Molock, S. D., Puri, R., & Matlin, S. (2006). Relationship between religious coping and suicidal behaviors among African America adolescents. *Journal of Black Psychology, 32,* 366-389.

Neff, J.A. (1993). Life stressors, drinking patterns, and depressive symptomatology: Ethnicity and stress-buffer effects of alcohol. *Addictive Behaviors, 18(4)*, 373-387.

Newcomb, M.D. & Harlow, L.L. (1986). Life events and substance use among adolescents: Mediating effects of perceived loss of control and meaninglessness in life. *Journal of Personality and Social Psychology, 51(3)*, 564-577.

Noh, S. & Kaspar, V. (2003). Perceived discrimination and depression: Moderating effects of coping, acculturation, and ethnic support. *American Journal of Public Health, 93(2)*, 232-238.

O'Brian, M., Margolin, G. & John, R.S. (1995). Relation among marital conflict, child coping, and child adjustment. *Journal of Clinical Child Psychology, 24(3)*, 346-361.

Pargament, K.I. (1997). *The psychology of religion and coping: Theory, research, practice.* New York, NY: Guilford Press.

Pargament, K.I. (2002). The bitter and the sweet: An evaluation of the costs and benefits of religiousness. *Psychological Inquiry, 13(3)*, 168-181.

Pargament, K.I., Cole, B., Vandecreek, L., Belavich, T., Brant, C. & Perez, L. (1999). The vigil: Religion and the search for control in the hospital waiting room. *Journal of Health Psychology, 4(3)*, 327-341.

Pargament, K.I., Kennell, J., Hathaway, W. & Grevengoed, N. (1988). Religion and the problem-solving process: Three styles of coping. *Journal for the Scientific Study of Religion, 27(1)*, 90-104.

Pearlin, L.I. (1989). The sociological study of stress. *Journal of Health and Social Behavior, 30(3)*, 241-256.

Pearlin, L.I., Menaghan, E.G., Lieberman, M.A. & Mullan, J.T. (1981). The stress process. *Journal of Health and Social Behavior, 22(4)*, 337-356.

Pearlin, L. I. & Radabaugh, C. W. (1976). Economic strains and the coping functions of alcohol. *American Journal of Sociology, 82*, 652-663.

Pierce, R. S., Frone, M. R., Russell, M. & Cooper, M. L. (1996). Financial stress, social support, and alcohol involvement: A longitudinal test of the buffering hypothesis in a general population survey. *Health Psychology, 15*, 38-47.

Pike, J., Smith, T., Hauger, R. & Nicassio, P. (1997). Chronic life stress alters sympathetic, neuroendocrine, and immune responsivity to an acute psychological stressor in humans. *Psychosomatic Medicine, 59(4)*, 447-459.

Pine, D.S., Cohen, P., Gurley, D., Brook, J. & Ma, Y. (1998). The risk for early-adulthood anxiety and depressive disorders in adolescents with anxiety and depressive disorders. *Archives of General Psychiatry, 55(1)*, 56-64.

Rafnsson, F.D., Jonsson, F.H. & Windle, M. (2006). Coping strategies, stressful life events, problem behaviors, and depressed affect. *Anxiety, Stress & Coping: An International Journal, 19(3)*, 241-257.

Raikes, H.A. & Thompson, R.A. (2005). Efficacy and social support as predictors of parenting stress among families in poverty. *Infant Mental Health Journal, 26(3)*, 177-190.

Raine, A., & Venables, P. (1984). Tonic heart rate level, social class and antisocial behaviour in adolescents. *Biological Psychology, 18*, 123-132.

Raine, A., Venables, P., & Mednick, S. (1997). Low resting heart rate at age 3 years predisposes to aggression at age 11 years: Evidence from the Mauritius Child Health

Project. *Journal of the American Academy of Child & Adolescent Psychiatry, 36*, 1457-1464.

Raviv, T., & Wadsworth, E. (2006). An evaluation of the FaCES prevention program for children in poverty. Poster presented at the annual meeting of the Society for Prevention Research, San Antonio, Texas.

Rayburn, N.R., Wenzel, S.L., Elliott, M.N., Hambarsoomians, K., Marshall, G.N. & Tucker, J.S. (2005). Trauma, depression, coping, and mental health service seeking among impoverished women. Journal of Consulting and Clinical Psychology, 73(4), 667-677.

Rehkopf, D.H., Haughton, L.T., Chen, J.T., Waterman, P.D., Subramanian, S.V. & Krieger, N. (2006). Monitoring socioeconomic disparities in death: Comparing individual-level education and area-based socioeconomic measures. *American Journal of Public Health, 96(12),* 2135-2138.

Repetti, R.L., Taylor, S.E. & Seeman, T.E. (2002). Risky families: Family social environments and the mental and physical health of offspring. *Psychological Bulletin, 128(2),* 330-366.

Ripple, C.H. & Zigler, E. (2003) Research, policy, and the federal role in prevention initiatives for children. *Special issue: Prevention that works for children and youth,* 482-490.

Sanchez, M.M., Ladd, C.O. & Plotsky, P.M. (2001). Early adverse experience as a developmental risk factor for later psychopathology: Evidence from rodent and primate models. *Development and Psychopathology, 13(3),* 419-449.

Sandler, I.N., Tein, J-Y. & West, S.G. (1994) Coping, stress, and the psychological symptoms of children of divorce: A cross-sectional and longitudinal study. *Child Development, 65(6),* 1744-1763.

Sapolsky, R.M. (2004). Social Status and Health in Humans and Other Animals. *Annual Review of Anthropology, 33,* 393-418.

Scheeringa, M.S., Zeanah, C.H., Myers, L. & Putnam, F. (2004). Heart period and variability findings in preschool children with posttraumatic stress symptoms. *Biological Psychiatry, 55(7),* 685-691.

Scott, L. D., Jr., & House, L. E. (2005). Relationship of distress and perceived control to coping with perceived racial discrimination among Black youth. *Journal of Black Psychology, 31,* 254-272.

Sherwood, A., Girdler, S.S., Bragdon, E.E., West, S.G., Brownley, K.A., Hinderliter, A.L. & Light, K.C. (1997). Ten-year stability of cardiovascular responses to laboratory stressors. *Psychophysiology, 34(2),* 185-191.

Steele, C.M., Southwick, L. & Pagano, R. (1986). Drinking your troubles away: The role of activity in mediating alcohol's reduction of psychological stress. *Journal of Abnormal Psychology, 95(2),* 173-180.

Uchino, B.N., Cacioppo, J.T. & Kiecolt-Glaser, J.K. (1996). The relationship between social support and physiological processes: A review with emphasis on underlying mechanisms and implications for health. *Psychological Bulletin, 119(3),* 488-531.

Vaughn, A.A. & Roesch, S.C. (2003). Psychological and physical health correlates of coping in minority adolescents. *Journal of Health Psychology, 8(6),* 671-683.

Vinokur, A.D., Price, R.H. & Schul, Y. (2002). Impact of the JOBS intervention on unemployed workers varying in risk for depression. In T.A Revenson, A.R. D'Augelli, S.E. French, D.L. Hughes, & D. Livert (Eds.), *A quarter century of community psychology: Readings from the American Journal of Community Psychology (pp. 477-511). New York: Kluwer Academic/Plenum Publishers.*

Wadsworth, M.E. & Achenbach, T.M. (2005). Explaining the link between low socioeconomic strata and psychopathology: Testing two mechanisms of the social causation hypothesis. *Journal of Consulting and Clinical Psychology, 73,* 1146-1153.

Wadsworth, M.E. & Berger, L.E. (2006). Adolescents coping with poverty-related family stress: Prospective predictors of coping and psychological symptoms. *Journal of Youth and Adolescence, 35(1),* 57-70.

Wadsworth, M.E. & Compas, B.E. (2002). Coping with economic strain and family conflict: The adolescent perspective. *Journal of Research on Adolescence, 12,* 243-274.

Wadsworth, M.E. & DeCarlo, C. (2007). When life hands you lemons: Families coping with poverty-related stress. Manuscript submitted for publication.

Wadsworth, M.E., Raviv, T., Compas, B.E., & Connor-Smith, J.K. (2005). Parent and adolescent responses to poverty-related stress: Tests of mediated and moderated coping models. *Journal of Child and Family Studies, 14(2),* 283-298.

Wadsworth, M.E., Raviv, T., Reinhard, C., Wolff, B.C., DeCarlo, C. & Schachter, L. (2007). An indirect effects model of the association between poverty and child functioning: The role of children's poverty-related stress. *Stress, Trauma and Crisis: An International Journal.* Special issue: *Poverty and Mental Health, 10 (3/4).*

Weems, C.F., Zakem, A.H., Costa, N.M., Cannon, M.F. & Watts, S.E. (2005). Physiological response and childhood anxiety: Association with symptoms of anxiety disorders and cognitive bias. *Journal of Clinical Child and Adolescent Psychology, 34(4),* 712-723.

Wegner, D.M. (1994). Ironic processes of mental control. *Psychological Review, 101(1),* 34-52.

Weikart, D.P. & Schweinhart, L.J. (1992). *High/Scope Preschool Program outcomes.* New York, NY: Guilford Press.

Weisz, J.R., Thurber, C.A., Sweeney, L., Proffit, V.D., LeGagnoux, G.L., (1997). Brief treatment of mild-to-moderate child depression using primary and secondary control enhancement training. *Journal of Counseling and Child Psychology, 65 (4),* 703-707.

Wills, T.A. (1986). Stress and coping in early adolescence: Relationships to substance use in urban school samples. *Health Psychology, 5(6),* 503-529.

Windle, M. & Wiesner, M. (2004). Trajectories of marijuana use from adolescence to young adulthood: Predictors and outcomes. *Development and Psychopathology, 16(4),* 1007-1027.

Wolff, B.C., DeCarlo, C. & Wadsworth, M.E. (2007). Poverty-related stress and involuntary engagement stress responses: Examining the link to anxiety symptoms within low-income families. Manuscript submitted for publication.

Wray, L., Alwin, D., & McCammon, R. (2005). Social status and risky health behaviors: Results from the health and retirement study. *Journals of Gerontology: Series B: Psychological Sciences and Social Sciences, 60,* 85-92.

Wrosch, C., Heckhausen, J. & Lachman, M.E. (2000). Primary and secondary control strategies for managing health and financial stress across adulthood. *Psychology and Aging, 15(3),* 387-399.

Yoo, H.C. & Lee, R.M. (2005). Ethnic Identity and Approach-Type Coping as Moderators of the Racial Discrimination/Well-Being Relation in Asian Americans. *Journal of Counseling Psychology, 52(4),* 497-506.

In: World Poverty Issues   ISBN: 978-1-60456-057-2
Editor: Marilyn M. Watkins, pp. 37-67   © 2008 Nova Science Publishers, Inc.

Chapter 2

Forest Villagers in Northeastern Hill Forests of Bangladesh: Linkages Between Villager's Livelihood and Forest Conservation

Tapan Kumar Nath[*]

Institute of Forestry and Environmental Sciences, The University of Chittagong,
Chittagong 4331, Bangladesh

Inoue Makoto

Department of Global Agricultural Sciences, Graduate School of Agricultural and Life
Sciences, The University of Tokyo, 113-8657, Japan

Abstract

Even though many forest villagers have been living on forest department (FD) land and serving the department in northeastern hill forests region of Bangladesh since the early 1950s, their livelihood has not fully explored yet. Taking a sample forest village of the Sylhet forest division, as a case study, this paper deeply examines the livelihoods of villagers and their contribution to forest conservation. Findings of the study indicate that the villagers are well-endowed with all the capitals of sustainable livelihoods framework, though human capital in terms of education is not satisfactory. Existence of several favorable indicators of agricultural sustainability under four broad criteria indicates that the natural capital (i.e., traditional agroforestry system) is quite stable. Strong social capital, stable natural capital, and a productive market-oriented agroforestry system facilitates the generation of financial and physical capitals that make the livelihoods of Khasia people sustainable. At the same time, their reciprocal contributions in terms of forest protection and plantation development support forest conservation. However, some institutional issues such as land tenure and regular agreement renewal problems need to

---

[*] E-mail: tknath@fr.a.u-tokyo.ac.jp, tapankumarn@yahoo.com

be resolved for the sake of their livelihoods and forest conservation. Lessons learned from the study can be utilized in formulating future participatory forest management schemes in the country.

Keywords: Forest villagers, agroforestry, sustainability, livelihood, forest conservation

INTRODUCTION

In most of the developing countries, forests are inhabited by the poor, which means that millions and billions of rural poor live in remote forested areas and obtain their food, fuel, medicine, and other essentials from forest resources. Forests are not only considered a socioeconomic buffer for the poor, but also to provide important basics for the livelihood development of the rural communities (Kijtewachakul et al., 2004: 634). Scholars (for example, Mcsweeney, 2004: 39-40) believe that forest resources serve as 'natural insurance' for the livelihoods of rural poor and that the earnings from forests, although small, help bridge income gaps and, therefore, play a critical role in livelihood security. Confronted with poverty due to small landholdings and scarce non-farming employment opportunities, villagers have benefited considerably from forest resources (Pandit and Thapa, 2004: 1). Forest resources are often the most important available resource for poverty alleviation in these areas (Belcher, 2005: 83). However, achieving poverty reduction with forest products requires the creation of wealth by means of forest product production, processing, and marketing, and having mechanisms, which ensure that the intended beneficiaries get some of that wealth (Belcher, 2005: 84). Investment in the building of institutions and capacity within forest communities, and facilitating the devolution of rights and responsibilities for local resource management that increases local access to forest rents, can be a direct pathway to poverty alleviation (Belcher, 2005: 88; Sunderlin et al., 2005: 1393). If economic development and community participation are not promoted in conjunction with environmental conservation, then local populations will have no interest in protecting resources (Virtanen, 2005: 1). Improving local people's access to resources in their vicinity and their capacity to transform them is critical for enabling them to attain better health, education, and other well-being improvements (Dewi et al., 2005: 1431).

As in other South Asian countries, the hill forests of Bangladesh, which constitute more than 40 percent of the total forests area, are dominated by different ethnic communities. The Khasia ethnic community is predominant in the northeastern hill forests of Bangladesh. Some of them have been serving the FD as forest villagers since the early 1950s[1]. Even though these forest villagers have been living on FD land and utilizing forest resources for their survival for more than half a century, their livelihood is not fully explored yet. It is necessary to know how they maintain their livelihood and what roles they play in forest conservation. This study examines the livelihood of the forest villagers using the Department for International Development's (DFID's) sustainable livelihood framework.

---

[1] Even though forest villagers were settled in the 1950s, there are no remarkable published articles and/or evaluation reports, in between 1950s and 2006, related to their activities, livelihood, and their contribution to forest conservation.

More specifically, the study will examine:

a) the situation of livelihood assets, or human, physical, natural, financial, and social capitals, which are forest villagers' livelihood building blocks;
b) the livelihood strategies, which Khasia people adopted to support themselves;
c) the institutions and level of local governance that facilitate resource utilization and management; and
d) what roles Khasia people play in forest conservation

The next section of this chapter begins with background information on forest villages in Bangladesh, and then elaborates the methods used in conducting the study. This paper's core comprises a number of sub-sections, which analyze situations of different capitals, sustainability of natural capital (i.e., agroforestry), local governance issues, livelihood diversification strategies, problems of the villagers, and forest conservation. It concludes with a brief analysis of important findings and their implications for development policy initiatives.

BACKGROUND

Bangladesh has a century of plantation history starting with the introduction of teak (*Tectona grandis*) from Burma in 1871. The first plantation was established with teak in the Chittagong Hill Tracts on a very small scale, and plantation activities were subsequently expanded to other parts of the country by converting low-density heterogeneous forests into commercial mono-plantations, mainly of teak. As plantation programs gained momentum, the FD faced problems with labor because population density was lower in the forested hilly areas during that period. To supplement the labor force, the FD introduced the forest village concept. This concept was first applied in the Chittagong and Chittagong Hill Tracts forest divisions in 1872 and 1909, respectively (Saha, 1998 cited in Saha and Azam, 2004). In the forest villages, local people (20-50 families) living near the forest were settled in villages where they were supposed to supply their labor to the FD whenever and wherever necessary, and in return they could practice agroforestry practices on the allotted land.

As in other places, scientific management of Bangladesh's northeastern hill forests, which are under Sylhet forest division jurisdiction, started in the 1900s. In order to meet the demand of labor for forestry operations, the FD introduced the forest village concept here in the 1950s and invited Khasia people to be forest villagers by granting forest land for their house construction and agroforestry development. They practice the agri-silvicultural type of agroforestry system where the main agricultural component is betel leaf (*Piper betel*).

METHODOLOGY

Selection of the Study Village

This study intended to investigate the livelihoods of forest villagers registered with the Sylhet forest division. As such, we asked forest officers holding different positions how many villages were registered with their divisions. Unfortunately, they could not tell us the exact number. Then we searched the literature and found one article saying 10 villages are registered with the Sylhet forest division (Saha and Azam, 2005), but not all village names were given. Finally, we asked two headmen (*mantri*) of two registered Khasia forest villages (*punji*). They gave the names of six Khasia *punji* (Amchari, Doublechara, Kalenji, Kuroma, Lawachara, and Magurchara) that are officially recognized as Sylhet forest division's forest villages. Their information was quite authentic because they have a Khasia welfare society that comprised all Khasia *punji* including those not registered as forest villages. From their records, they could thus tell the exact names and number of registered forest villages.

We then asked the forest officers whether there are differences among forest villages in fulfilling FD objectives. They replied that the Khasia are very simple and are obliged to perform assigned duties. All villagers are helpful in forest management activities. As such, we decided to select one representative village randomly from six for the study. Yin (2003) also suggests selecting one representative case study site if there are no remarkable differences among sites. We selected Lawachara Khasia *punji* located within Lawachara National Park.

Lawachara National Park

The study site was Lawachara National Park, previously known as West Bhanugach Reserved Forest. Part of the reserve was declared as park in mid-1996, covers an area of 1,531 ha (FSP, 2000), and is under the administration of Sylhet forest division. The park's coordinates are 24°30′ to 24°32′N and 91°37′ to 91°39′E. Topographically the park consists of many hillocks (*tila*) having an elevation of not more than 50 m with fairly moderate slopes.

Park forests consist of mixed semi-evergreen old secondary re-growth. Almost 100-year-old plantations created multistoried dense forest looking like virgin natural forest. The most commonly visible plant species include *Tectona grandis*, *Artocarpus* spp., *Quercus* spp., and *Amorphophallus* spp. Commonly found wildlife includes *Hoolock hoolock*, *Macaca* spp., *Trachypithecus* spp., and many species of birds.

Agro-ecologically the site belongs to the northern and eastern hills of Bangladesh and the general soil types are brown hill soils (Banglapedia, 2001). Soil organic matter and fertility level are generally low and texture is generally sandy loam or silty loam. The area has a maritime climate characterized by a period of high rainfall from April to September, and relatively dry from November to March. Humidity remains high at 70 to 85 percent throughout the year, and daytime temperatures remain above 30 degrees Celsius from April to October, and normally below 20 degrees Celsius from November to March (Saha and Azam, 2005).

Livelihood Analysis

The methodology that we followed for livelihood analysis of forest villagers is similar to that we used for planters of Upland Settlement Project in chapter one.

Criteria and Indicators for Evaluating Sustainability of Agroforestry System

In order to identify the criteria and indicators of sustainability, here we, first, describe the issues of sustainable development and agricultural sustainability, and then shed light on the sustainability of agroforestry and on identifying the sustainability indicators that were used to assess the sustainability of the agroforestry system studied.

Sustainable development and sustainable resource use are terms used constantly by development agencies, but scholars and agencies, in some cases, do not agree on the concept of sustainable development. For example, neoclassical economic theories of sustainability prioritize profit maximization, economic growth, and wealth accumulation (Lamberton, 2005). Naturalists, on the other hand, claim that sustainability implies an ongoing dynamic development, driven by human expectations about future opportunities, and it is based on present economical, ecological, and societal issues and information (Bossel, 1999, cited in Peterseil et al., 2004). Peterseil and others also added that ecological sustainability plays an important role in fully understanding and supporting sustainable development at the regional level (Peterseil et al., 2004). Sustainability requires that economic objectives be achieved while preserving the ecological and social systems that support humankind (Lamberton, 2005). The concept of sustainable development, however, is the result of growing awareness of the global links between mounting environmental problems, socio-economic issues to do with poverty and inequality, and concerns about a healthy future for humanity (Hopwood et al., 2005).

The livelihoods of rural people depend on their village's natural capital (land, water, trees, forests, etc.), which provides all natural resources required by villagers (Komatsu et al., 2005), and hence sustainability has foremost importance to sustaining their livelihoods. Like sustainable development, agricultural sustainability also has considerable appeal. Despite variation in the concept of sustainable agriculture, there is a consensus on three basic features (Rasul and Thapa, 2004; Zhen et al., 2005): (a) maintaining environmental quality (reasonable use of external inputs to prevent resource degradation and reduce risks of human health hazards), (b) economic viability (ensuring stable and profitable production activities), and (c) socio-institutional acceptance (food sufficiency, technology adoption, and effective institutional services such as markets, policy, etc.). Dumanski et al. (1998) mention five pillars of sustainable land management: maintenance or enhancement of productivity/services, reduction of production risk, protection of the natural capital base, economic viability, and social acceptability.

The sustainability attributes of agroforestry are based mainly on soil productivity and other biophysical advantages such as erosion control, addition of organic matter, improvement of physical properties, N_2-fixation, improved nutrient cycling, and reclamation of degraded lands (Nair, 1993). At present, there is no quantitative measure of sustainability and until such criteria and indices for assessment are fully developed and widely accepted, we will have to do with qualitative statements about the sustainability of agroforestry, as is the case with other land-use systems (Nair, 1993). Very recently, the International Tropical Timber Organization (ITTO), after repeated revision, developed seven criteria with several indicators of sustainable forest management (ITTO, 2005). These criteria can be grouped into three major categories: enabling conditions (ITTO criteria 1), ecological criteria (ITTO criteria 1-6), and socioeconomic criteria (ITTO criteria 7).

Though there are no criteria or indicators for measuring the sustainability of agroforestry systems, we summarize four broad criteria for evaluating the sustainability of Khasia's agroforestry system by considering the above-mentioned issues of sustainability:

i.   Ecological sustainability: In assessing the system's ecological sustainability, we used cropping patterns, species composition, pest and disease management, soil erosion, and soil fertility management as indicators.

ii. Economic sustainability: Trends of productivity, profitability, food security and savings are used as indicators of economic sustainability.

iii. Social and cultural sustainability: People's beliefs, self-sufficiency of inputs, and equity are used as indicators of this criterion. Input self-sufficiency means availability of local inputs, while equity means the ability of the agroforestry system to generate employment (Rasul and Thapa, 2004).

iv. Institutional sustainability: Policy, land tenure, and markets are used as indicators of institutional sustainability.

It is assumed that presence of these four criteria would represent some favorable indicators of the sustainability of the agroforestry system, which underpins the sustainable livelihood of the Khasia people.

Data and Data Collection Methods

We collected both quantitative data and qualitative information to ensure methodology pluralism and to minimize the weaknesses of the methods. We conducted household interviews for quantitative data at 21 of 23 households from Lawachara Khasia *punji*. The remaining two household members were not at home during the study. They had gone to another non-registered *punji*, where they have a betel leaf garden, to perform agroforestry chores. We conducted a participatory wealth-ranking exercise to stratify the households. Four key informants including *mantri* took part in the exercise. Initially they identified variables such as income, household labor, and the number of agroforestry plots (each of which is equivalent to 1.01 ha of forest land) in each household. After a long discussion, the informants concluded that the main factor affecting household wealth in this forest village area is the number of agroforestry plots. Their argument was that households having more *jhums* could harvest products sustainably and thus have a regular income flow. Based on their opinion, we placed all 21 households into one of two categories:

- Category A: more than one agroforestry plots (six households)
- Category B: only one agroforestry plot (15 households)

We found an average of 3.92 agroforestry plots for category A, and it was significantly (*P*<0.000) different from category B households with only one plot in this *punji*. However, for agroforestry sustainability, the analysis was done by considering the 21 household as a whole population; we did not divide them into above-mentioned categories. The reason is that sample size in each category is small and as a whole population, it would give a comprehensive picture of agroforestry system.

After a series of discussions with colleagues and testing at the research site, and with necessary revision and modification, we prepared a questionnaire containing some structured questions and a checklist for a semi-structured interview. The questions were designed to help collect data on all five capitals of the livelihood framework, and on variables pertaining to governance. We used one questionnaire for each household and carried out interviews over a period of several weeks in May and June 2005. One Khasia boy always accompanied me during household interviews.

To estimate the monetary values of physical capitals (e.g., televisions, cassette players, and motorcycles except livestock) we asked what physical capitals they have, and their estimated monetary values. Then we calculated the mean equivalent value of physical capitals. Ordered scales were used to measure different variables of governance and social capital.

We collected most of the quantitative data to assess the agroforestry system's profitability, food security, and savings, which indicate economic sustainability. Profitability was measured according to gross annual income and cost-benefit ratio. We estimated household expenditures to get a general picture of savings. To assess households' income and expenditures, we asked people's weekly incomes and their expenditures for certain items. We found that people could recall their weekly income and expenditures more accurately than monthly or yearly. For example, they recalled how much they spend for food in a week and how much they earn from agroforestry products per week. Those figures were converted to an annual basis. Villagers said that even though expenditures may vary from week to week, this estimate gives a general picture of household expenditures. The principal input cost in agroforestry is labor, and therefore we asked them how many men and women they employ for how many days in season and off season, and also annually, and the cost for wages in addition to their own labor. We did not include households' own labor costs in calculating total costs.

To gather qualitative information, we conducted a group discussion with villagers, informal talks with Khasia people of different ages, forest officials, and NGO staff members, along with informal personal observations. Group discussion involved six men and two women, and highlighted issues such as their views on agroforestry systems, management of soil fertility, pest and diseases control, markets for products, and problems related to agroforestry systems and to livelihood, local institutions, their FD activities, and daily activities. A separate semi-structured questionnaire facilitated the discussion. Talks with forest officials dealt with Khasia participation in forest management activities, what the FD is doing for the forest villagers' welfare, their perceptions on the role of villagers in forest conservation, problems with villagers, policy, land tenure issues and other matters. We talked with Khasia people of different ages about social issues such as social relations, conflicts, *mantri*'s activities, their education, and daily activities. NGO staffs told about their activities in the *punji*.

Statistical Analysis

We summarized all quantitative data into averages and percentages find out standard deviation and conducted analysis of variance (one-way ANOVA) to find statistically significant differences among the means of different variables of two categories of Khasia people. The Pearson correlation (two-tailed) was also used to find the correlation between different variables. All statistical analysis used the SPSS (Statistical Package for the Social Sciences) version 12.

Respondents' Profiles

Household interviews involved whomever was available, both men and women. Eight of the 21 interviewees were female. The respondents' mean age was 38. Eight interviewees had no formal education; 12 had primary (five years) schooling, and secondary (10 years) schooling. Only one person had graduated (14 years of schooling).

FINDINGS AND INTERPRETATION

In this section, we first explain the state of five different capitals of the livelihood framework, followed by issues of local-level governance, and other relevant issues of livelihood. Then we discuss the Khasia role in conservation and management of forests.

State of Livelihood Capitals

In the rural livelihoods framework, the ability of households to pursue livelihood strategies depends on their available livelihood assets or capitals (Cramb et al., 2004: 264). We investigated all five capitals of the sustainable livelihoods framework. The variables of the capitals we assessed were mostly of individual household capitals. Village-level capital was present in the form of social capital only. Below we describe the five capitals:

Human Capital

We evaluated human capital in terms of household size, age gradations, literacy, current school enrollment, and household members that contribute remarkably to households cash income (Table 1). In 21 sampled households, the total number of household members was 118, and the average was 5.62. Mean household sizes of categories A and B were 7.33 and 4.9, respectively. Even though gross literacy and male and female literacy percentages were higher in category A than in B, the present female education rate was higher in B than in A. This is due to parental awareness raised mainly by NGOs. Male education, however, was considerably higher in category A. The reason cited was distant schools and involvement in agroforestry activities. Public schools are about 7 to 10 km from their village and communication is very bad, especially in the monsoon season. Better-off families send their children (sons only) to Christian missionary schools where they have to bear the costs of tuition, lodging, and other living costs. Years of schooling were higher in category A than in

B. The higher schooling of category A indicates that some of their children gained the secondary school certificate (SSC) and entered colleges, which is absent in category B. In category A, we found one person (*mantri*) who had graduated and obtained an SSC from missionary school. However, most of the children dropped out after seven or eight years of schooling, then engage in agroforestry activities and contribute to household income. All people more than 12 years old are involved in agroforestry activities. When we considered the mean number of active members contributing very much to household income, we found a highly significant ($P<0.003$) difference between the two categories. The mean number of income-earning members in category A was more than twice that of B.

Physical Capital

Physical capital that we considered comprised various household assets such as the condition of houses, appliances (e.g., televisions, radios, cassette players, CD players, and batteries), vehicles, irrigation equipment (e.g., deep tube-wells), agricultural implements, and livestock. We estimated equivalent monetary values of household appliances based on the opinions of households. The findings indicate that only one category B household has a bamboo mat-walled house thatched with sun grass (*Imperata cylindrica*). All other households of both categories have mud-walled houses with corrugated iron sheet roof (Table 1). On my first visit to the village, we thought that all houses were brick-walled. Everybody thought so until they asked the villagers. The reason is that they put a thin layer of cement on the wall and then colored it. All houses have cement floors, and around the base of wall there is earth (*dela*) that is also coated with cement. The two reasons for cement coating are to improve appearance and, more importantly, to keep the wall from absorbing water. Due to the remote location and lack of recreation facilities, almost all households of the *punji* have either a television, or cassette player or CD player, or even a radio. Those without TVs watch their neighbors' TVs. Antenna on long bamboo poles bring in programs from around India. Because they are off the grid, they use nine-volt batteries to run their televisions and other appliances. It costs Tk. 200 a week to charge a battery. Among other physical capital, one household (*mantri*) had a motorcycle and a deep tube-well. He can irrigate his agroforestry plots in the dry season with the deep tube-well (installed at the base of the hillock) by using long plastic pipe. He also uses the well for household water. Some households obtain drinking water from the *mantri*'s house, but all other households of the *punji* use ring-wells. Though one is abandoned, they have two other ring-wells for drinking water. Being open-top wells, the water becomes contaminated and villagers suffer from stomach diseases. Considering estimates by households, the mean equivalent monetary values of the physical capital were Tk. 7,310 for category B and Tk. 20,583 for category A. The difference between them was statistically significant ($P<0.052$), and the difference was obviously due to the greater capital endowment of category A.

The state of livestock husbandry in Khasia *punji* is not good. Only three households out of 21 have livestock. *Mantri* has three cows and four goats. Two category-B households have cows and chickens. The villagers told that they are interested in raising cattle, but the problem is the shortage of land at their homesteads. If they allow open livestock grazing, livestock might damage the betel leaf plants. *Mantri* employs a boy to look after his livestock while they graze in the adjacent forest.

Table 1. Different Variables of Livelihood Capitals at Household Level of the Lawachara Khasia *punji*, Bangladesh (Source: Field survey May-June, 2005)

Capitals	Category		
	A (n=6)	B (n=15)	Sig. level
Human capital			
Mean household size (no.)	7.33(1.20)	4.9(1.79)	
Male: female	1:1	1.1.1	
Members ≤ 11 years (no.)	7	19	
Members 11-59 years (no.)	36	55	
Literacy (%)	89	57	
Male/female literacy (%)	100/77	52/48	
Average schooling years	9.50	8.25	
Current school enrollment (%)			
Primary (male/female)	12/6	8/9	
Secondary (male/female)	27/-	5/7	
Mean members contributing cash income (no.)	5.33	2.53	0.003
Physical capital			
Mud wall house with tin roof (%)	100	87	
Bamboo mat wall house with Sun grass thatch (%)	-	13	
Television (% of households)	83	53	
Cassette player (% of households)	67	20	
CD player (% of households)	33	20	
Radio (% of households)	33	33	
Battery (% of households)	100	53	
Motorcycle (% of households)	16	-	
Deep tube-well (% of households)	16	-	
Agricultural tools (% of households)	100	100	
Mean equivalent money (Tk.)	20583	7310	0.052
Livestock (no.)			
Cows	3	1	
Goats	4	-	
Chickens	-	3	
Natural capital			
Mean landholding (ha)	4.42	1.21	0.000
Forest conditions			
Good (% of households)	100	100	
Financial capital			
Households having loan (no.)	2	3	
No. of loans	1	1	
Sources and amount (Tk.)			
NGOs	9000	7667	

Note: Figures in parenthesis indicate standard error of mean.

Natural Capital

We assessed natural capital in terms of landholdings, and forest conditions of the agroforestry plots (Table 1). From FD-granted land (2.1 ha), every household allocates 1.01 ha for an agroforestry plot and the remaining 0.2 ha for a house. All households built their houses in a compound at the top of hillock that is surrounded by their agroforestry plots. Even though all households supposedly have equal quantities of land in this *punji*, we found that households of category A possessed more land than category B. As head of the *punji*, the *mantri* said that their families got 2.42 ha of land, but forest officers said that all villagers were granted equal amounts of land. Another person of that category said he bought some land from others. Other households got the land of their kin (*gousti*-extended male-lineage family members) after death. Of these two categories, the variations in landholdings were highly significant ($P<0.000$).

Landholding status indicates that some households hold more land than granted. We tried bringing this to the attention of forest officers, who described the overall situation as follows:

'Over the years, the Khasia people encroach upon forest land. Being very rich, they persuade [with money] local influential people, politicians, forest officers, and other concerned parties, and then illegally occupy the forest land to raise plantations, grow betel leaf, and invite relatives to settle down on encroached land. They occupy other areas using the same strategy. When the FD goes to recover the land and to evict the unauthorized villagers, they [Khasia people] first try to persuade [by money] the concerned officer, and if that fails, the case is filed in court. By this time, their welfare society makes contact with influential donor agencies, humanitarian organizations, and others to get a judicial verdict in favor of them. In addition, in almost all cases, the verdict goes in favor of villagers, for many reasons. The Khasia *punji* now become the burden of the FD' (pers. comm. 2005).

Though there is no record of how many hectares of forest land have been encroached by the Khasia, one study indicates that around 29 ha of Lawachara National Park have been taken by two Khasia *punji* (NACOM, 2003). However, it also reports that non-Khasia people, Bengalis who have migrated here, illegally occupy much more land.

In addition to landholding, we used a four-level scale (4=very good, 3=good, 2=fairly good, and 1=not good) to ask villagers about the conditions of their agroforestry plots and whole forest area. All households of both categories replied that agroforestry conditions are good in terms of their subsistence value. They also said that forest conditions of the national park are good enough to conserve the biodiversity of the region, even though there is some illicit felling. We also asked similar questions to forest officers. They replied that though agroforestry plots do not support wildlife, overall biodiversity conditions of the forest are reasonably good.

Rural livelihood depends, to a larger extent, on the sustainability of natural capital. As such, here, we evaluate the sustainability of agroforestry system that Khasia people practice since their settlement in this *punji*.

Plate 1. An agroforestry plot beside the Lawachara Khasia *punji*, Bangladesh. Photo shows trees of different ages are being used as support trees for betel vines.

Sustainability of the Agroforestry System

Ecological Aspects of Sustainability

Khasia people practice an agroforestry system (agri-silvicultural type) that has the two components of trees and betel leaf, in which perennial betel leaf is grown along with trees. Trees support the betel vines. To maintain the ecological sustainability of the system, villagers practice agroforestry in mixed patterns. Though they prefer fluid-rich trees (e.g., *Artocarpus heterophyllus* and *Artocarpus chaplasha,* whose bark produces much latex), all trees at agroforestry plots are used as supporting trees (Plate 1). Trees of different ages are present. We identified 36 tree species on agroforestry plots, which supports the observation of Alam and Mohiuddin (1995). If not affected by disease or damaged by cattle, every betel vine is satisfactorily productive for 10 to 15 years. However, within this period they replant new cuttings at the base of the support trees. To replace the old vines, at two-year intervals they cut rooted leafy cuttings from the very productive vines during June and July. Cuttings grow vigorously after planting. This practice makes it possible to maintain different age groups of betel vines to ensure continuous production.

Two diseases that are common in agroforestry plots, *uttram* and *uklam*, mostly occur during the rainy season (June through August). *Uttram* damages leave from the outside to the inside, and can spread through the whole agroforestry plot within a week if precautions are not taken. Villagers generally cut off the affected branches, bury them far from the agroforestry plots, wash all cloths and tools with hot water, and then take a bath so that the disease can't spread anymore. *Uklam* causes root-rot and villagers reported that it is very dangerous. Whole vines become yellowish and if preventative measures are not taken at the first sign of infection, the whole agroforestry plot may be damaged within two or three days. They uproot the affected vine, bury it far away, wash all materials, and take a bath. There were no incidences of spreading of diseases to other plants due to burying of the uprooted disease infected betel plants. They said that heavy damage due to diseases occurs sometimes in some agroforestry plots, but not frequently. During the study, I observed two agroforestry plots of two households with serious damage. In very severe cases, villagers clear all vines, keep the agroforestry plot vacant for 2-3 years, and then replant with cuttings. However, their long experience plus regular and intensive care prevents the outbreak of severe diseases. The Khasia people told that many Bengalis (the main ethnic group of Bangladesh) tried betel leaf, but they could not keep their agroforestry plots productive for long because after six or seven years diseases damaged the agroforestry plots. Bengalis could not identify the diseases at the beginning even though they worked long hours in Khasia agroforestry plots. They proudly feel that "the *paan* (betel leaf) is given to us by God and only we can take care of it."

Maintaining productivity at an increasing or constant level makes it essential to improve soil fertility. The Khasia traditionally manage soil fertility by using available plant materials. Every year, just before the monsoon season, they prune all the branches from support trees and topped someone, and allow them to dry out at agroforestry plots. When all the leaves have been shed, big branches are collected for fuelwood and the decayed leaves are spread evenly at the bases of betel vines. Agroforestry plots are weeded twice in a year and the weeds are used as mulching. If mulching is insufficient, villagers collect weeds from the forest. They believe that this humus is enough to maintain soil fertility and they have followed this traditional method in practicing agroforestry for more than 50 years on the same agroforestry plots. During my visits to some agroforestry plots, we observed that the ground was covered with half-decomposed weeds, leaves, and small branches. Topsoil was black and full of organic matter. However, some people told that because the forest had been declared a national park, collection of weeds was prohibited. For that reason, some of them want to use chemical fertilizer in future. Though two households applied inorganic fertilizer this year, they warn that it may increase the possibility of *uklam* as being experienced in other *punji*. Moreover, villagers dig a very small pit when planting betel cuttings, which does not create any soil erosion. Mulching at the bases of vines helps to hold moisture during the dry season.

Economic Features of Sustainability

To assess economic sustainability we first describe the trend of productivity and then the profitability of the system. We used a three-level scale (increasing, constant, or decreasing) to examine yield trend. The findings are as follows: two households (10 percent) who applied chemical fertilizer reported increasing yield trends, 17 households (80 percent) reported a constant level, and two households, whose agroforestry plots were affected by diseases, reported a decreasing rate. This means that without using any chemical fertilizer and if there is no disease, it is possible to get a constant level of production under present traditional management.

In general, if benefit is greater than the costs, then we assume the business is profitable. To measure profitability, we assessed all costs involved over the last year and gross income from the sale of agroforestry products (Table 2). The main cost involved with agroforestry is labor (*kamla*). Besides households' labor, they employ wage labor of which the major portion is women. Women do weeding, cleaning the ground, and mulching. Men do the hard and specialized jobs such as pruning and plucking. We found a male-female wage disparity. Women's wages varied from Tk. 25 to Tk. 50, whereas men's wages ranged between Tk. 50 and Tk. 80. Number of days worked and labor costs of men and women vary both in and off season (Table 2). Villagers divide the year into the in season (May through August) and off season (September through January) based on rainfall. From late May to August, the region receives monsoon rain, and from September to January, there is occasional rainfall. February to April is the dry season.

Category A households employs more number of men labor than that of category B though it was not significantly different (Table 2). They reason is that male of members of category B families do plucking along with other agroforestry chores by themselves and recruit male labors during pruning only. Category A members, on the other hand, employs more men labor and they only supervise labor's work. Similar trend of labor employment was also observed while recruiting women labor, but it was significantly different between two categories. We observed that some villagers of category A employ female labor for whole year not only for agroforestry purposes but also for household tasks. Category B villagers employ female labor when they needed. Recruitment of more labors by category A villagers imposed higher costs, which was significantly higher than that of category B (Table 2).

Table 2. Mean annual costs and income from the agroforestry system at Lawachara Khasia *punji*, Bangladesh (Source: Field data collection, May-June 2005).

Variables	Category		
	A (n=6)	B (n=15)	Sig. level
Mean costs			
Labor costs			
Men working days	178	93	0.189
In season	82	40	
Off season	96	53	
Women working days	548	111	0.005
In season	211	47	
Off season	337	64	
Costs for men(Tk.)	10879	4883	0.203
In season	5012	2027	
Off season	5867	2856	
Costs for women (Tk.)	3662	4368	0.026
In season	5260	1855	
Off season	8402	2513	
Mean costs/year/household (Tk.)	24541	9251	0.013
Mean income			
Betel leaf production (*kuri*)	380	198	0.004
In season	195	107	0.005
Off season	185	91	0.007
Sale value (Tk)			
In season	59467	31770	0.004
Off season	134800	64143	0.013
Mean annual income (Tk.) from betel leaf	194267	95913	0.010

Regarding profitability, the main benefits (gross mean annual income per household) come from the sale of betel leaf. The unit of productivity and selling of leaves is the *kuri* (1 *kuri*= 2880 individual leaves). Leaf productivity and prices vary in and off season. In season, leaf production per week per agroforestry plot is between 2.5 and 4 *kuri* and the price is between Tk. 250 and Tk. 300 per *kuri*, while off-season productivity varies from one to three *kuri* per week, with price between Tk. 650 and 700, and even more than Tk. 1000 February through March. Because category A households have more number of agroforestry plots, leaf productivity was also significantly higher than that of category B. Higher yield fetches greater sale values resulting significantly higher mean annual agroforestry income of category A than that of category B villagers (Table 2).

Table 2 shows only the costs and income of the agroforestry production system. It does not say anything about the interactions of different factors of the system. To have an idea about interactions of some important factors as well as their impacts on agroforestry income, we conducted multiple regression analysis considering 21 sampled households as a whole population. However, possibly due to small number of sample size it did not produce meaningful results and showed some contradictory findings such as negative effects of agroforestry plot number on agroforestry income. Then we performed a correlation test, which shows imperative results (Table 3).

The correlation tests (Table 3) revealed that total input costs have no significant contribution to agroforestry income. It indicates that agroforestry income depends more on other factors than that of labor which entail more costs. Therefore, in order to make the agroforestry system more profitable, it is important to employ less labor. Household members who are skilled enough to perform plucking and pruning should be encouraged to do these tasks instead of employing paid labor. Discussions with villagers and forest workers found that household members, mostly of category A, nowadays do little work at their agroforestry plots because they have become affluent and have regular and steady incomes from agroforestry. They only check the agroforestry plots for signs of disease.

Agroforestry plot numbers are significantly related with agroforestry income (Table 3 & Figure 1). The reasons are that villagers could pluck more leaves sustainably from more number of agroforestry plots. If diseases outbreak in an agroforestry plot, villagers have alternative to pluck leaves from other unaffected agroforestry plots. Similarly, agroforestry plot numbers have significant relationships with in season and off season production as well as in season sale values and off season sale values (Table 3 & Figure 1). However, off season leaf production and off season sale values are strongly correlated with agroforestry income than in season production and sale values. The reasons are that even though off season production is relatively low, but due to higher market demand and lower supply, these fetch higher prices resulting better contribution to the agroforestry income.

Higher off season sale values indicate that if villagers could irrigate their agroforestry plots during the dry seasons, they could expand plucking period and earn more income. In this regard, they could arrange collective irrigation programs. During the study, we observed that there is a perennial stream just beside their *punji* from which they could irrigate their agroforestry plots. They could collectively make a temporary (for the dry season, November through March) dam to create a reservoir for irrigating their agroforestry plots with a shallow water pump connected with a long pipe. The costs for a shallow pump would be not more than Tk. 5000, and could be used for many years. We observed that the *mantri* [leader of the *punji*] has a deep tube well by which he irrigates his agroforestry plots February through

March and fetches higher prices (even Tk. 1300 per *kuri*). After March, all leaves become yellow and shed.

We asked farmers about their food security status using a three-level scale: surplus, sufficiency, and shortage. All households said that the income they get from agroforestry is sufficient to cover the costs of food and other necessities. A look at household income-expenditures (Table 6) shows that after covering all expenditures including input costs, they can still save a handsome amount of money. However, they could not tell how much money they save annually and what they do with their savings. However, forest officers and some villagers told that almost all households invest their savings in acquiring more agroforestry plots in other non-registered Khasia villages. These additional agroforestry plots ensure them steady incomes in case of disease infestation in agroforestry plots in the *punji*. Extended family members or relatives look after these agroforestry plots, which they visit occasionally for maintenance.

Social and Cultural Sustainability

In explaining the social and cultural sustainability or acceptability of this agroforestry system, the villagers claim that "*paan* (popularly known as Khasia *paan*, the local name of betel leaf) is our blood, our life. All of our culture and festivals are based on *paan*. We are the only people who can grow *paan*." This statement expresses how deeply the agroforestry system is rooted in their lives. They believe the agroforestry plot is a sacred place. Every morning they bathe before entering the agroforestry plot and wear clothes used exclusively for agroforestry plot activities. They feel hurt if outsiders enter an agroforestry plot without bathing because they believe that outsiders may bring hazardous germs. Their beliefs and culture are strongly connected with agroforestry plots. Walker (2004) also mentions that upland agriculture is intrinsically linked by locally specific belief systems and cultural practices. Traditional culture, which is embedded in human knowledge and experience within religious faith and which is deeply rooted in the minds and hearts of small-scale farmers, makes agriculture meaningful and sustainable (Alhamidi *et al.*, 2003).

If we consider input self-sufficiency and equity in order to justify the socio-cultural sustainability of the system, the earlier discussion (ecological and economic sustainability) indicates that this agroforestry system depends, to a greater extent, on the local labor force and locally available plant materials for soil fertility management. The system creates employment opportunities for the surrounding local people. Both Bengalis and ethnic people work in agroforestry plots. We found that over one year 271 men days and 659 women days were employed in the study *punji* (Table 2). Moreover, some people get employment during marketing of products. The *paikar* (middlemen; five *paikar* come each day) buy betel leaves from the *punji* (3 days a week) and employ labor (six to eight men each day) to transport the produce to the main road. Therefore, it seems that the agroforestry system is quite input self-sufficient and has an equity effect in generating local employment.

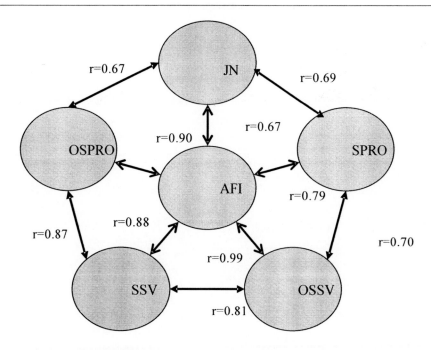

Figure 1. Correlations among some important variables of agroforestry production systems practiced by the Khasia forest villagers, Sylhet forest division, Bangladesh. Meaning of different variables are shown in Table 3.

Institutional Aspects of Sustainability

Explaining institutional sustainability involves first discussing government policy and the land tenure status of the Khasia people, then the market issue. Regarding policy, the FD initially granted land to the villagers on a renewal basis for 99 years with the agreement that they provide their labor in developing and managing forest plantations. The conditions for renewal are that the villagers supply their own labor in developing and managing the plantation in addition to the protection of forest from pilferage. Villagers as well as forest officers reported that the villagers cooperate in forest management activities very cordially. Renewal is done for the same area of land allotted to each household. In accordance with policy, the agreement between the FD and the forest villagers is to be renewed every two years. The *mantri* informed that the agreement was last renewed in 1982, since which there has been no renewal. We asked the local forest officer about the renewal status of the agreement, and he replied that he sent all the papers for renewal to the divisional office last year (2004). However, another senior officer said that since 1982 there has been no activity to renew the agreement. The *punji* people wonder what might happen if the FD does not renew their agreement. It is significant that though they have been living in the *punji* since the early 1950s, they still do not have legal land tenure status. Even though the FD says there is no problem, villagers are appealing for permanent tenure. However, FD officers suspect that if they provide permanent land tenure, the villager would not abide by the agreement. We suggest that the FD should at least renew the agreement regularly so that villagers know they have land security. Considering market issue of institutional sustainability, it can be claimed that this product (betel leaf) has huge local and foreign markets (Rashid, 1991; Nath et al., 2003).

Table 3. Correlation matrix showing relationships among different variables in agroforestry production system of the studied forest village of Sylhet forest division, Bangladesh (Source: Field survey May-June, 2005)

Variables	AFI	JN	HHM	MWD	WMD	MW	WW	SSV	OSSV	SPRO	OSPRO
JN	0.67**										
HHM	0.21	0.57**									
MWD	-0.03	0.18	0.27								
WMD	0.56**	0.95**	0.56**	0.33							
MW	0.01	0.26	0.35	0.96**	0.38						
WW	0.49*	0.88**	0.51*	0.40	0.97**	0.43					
SSV	0.88**	0.68**	0.35	0.11	0.59**	0.17	0.52*				
OSSV	0.99**	0.63**	0.18	-0.07	0.49* -0.04	0.43	0.81**				
SPRO	0.79**	0.69**	0.45*	0.18	0.64**	0.24	0.57**	0.97**	0.70**		
OSPRO	0.90**	0.67**	0.28	0.04	0.60**	0.06	0.53*	0.87**	0.87**	0.85**	
TINPUT	0.38	0.72**	0.67**	0.77**	0.80**	0.84**	0.80**	0.48*	0.31	0.54*	0.41

AFI= Mean annual income from agroforestry; JN= Agroforestry plot number; HHM= Household member; MWD= Men working days; WMD= Women working days.

MW = Men wage; WW= Women wage; SSV= In season sale value; OSSV= Off season sale value; SPRO= In season production; OSPRO= Off season production; TINPUT= Total input costs, ** indicates significant difference at $P<0.00$ level and * at $P<0.05$ level.

Financial Capital

We used three indicators for measuring households' financial capital: loans, credit, and credit amount (Table 1). As all the households are fairly well off, they generally do not need loans. However, if agroforestry production declines or households need money for emergency purposes (e.g., purchasing land in other areas), they get loans. During the study, we found five households that have loans: two in category A and three in category B. Every household has one credit, and national NGO Caritas provides credit to them with an interest rate of 12 percent. Repayment is in 22 installments, one per month.

Social Capital

Indigenous people in the uplands are accustomed to solving problems by relying mainly on their own resources (Danchev, 2005: 30). These resources are social ties and networks, which are collectively expressed as social capital. Societies with high-quality social capital attained high achievements in their development despite restricted access to resources and technologies (Danchev, 2005: 25). In measuring household-level social capital, we used four indicators (see Table 4). For groups and networks, I used three variables. By household communication network (HCN), we mean the number of households (whether kin, relatives, or friends in their own or nearby villages) with whom a member of a household (mainly a household's head) can share problems, ask for help, and also request loans. As such, we found a significant difference ($P<0.004$) among households of the two categories having different HCNs. The value of HCNs was almost two times higher in category A than in B. A similar trend was observed when I consider the number of people willing to help by giving money, and the number of people currently able to provide that money. The variations of these two variables are also significantly ($P<0.004$ and $P<0.000$, respectively) higher in category A than in B. Household's networks have developed not for making visits to relatives, but for getting monetary help during economic hardship too. Although many households do not get loans, they do believe that they would get them on request. The extent of their beliefs can be understood when we analyze trust and solidarity. According to the scale we utilized (see note of Table 4), it is evident that people of the *punji* have strong confidence in their fellow people and strong faith in their leader (*mantri*). Scholars (for example, Danchev, 2005: 27) believe that no form of capital can be sustained unless there is confidence among the members of the community (tribe, village, town, region, etc.). Though one category-A interviewee (who felt that young men (*mantri*) cannot serve as *mantri* and he should be fairly old) is not satisfied, other villagers are satisfied with the *mantri*'s activities, responsiveness, and honesty. They share their personal problems with the *mantri*. Sometimes they could get loans from the *mantri* for emergencies such as sickness or school fees for their children. Villagers also help each other by loaning money, but for purchasing land in other areas, they do not provide loans. In that case, villagers ask close relatives or their kin groups.

Though villagers (except *mantri*) do not have direct contact with forest officers, they believe that FD personnel are responsive, mostly honest, and would not do anything that might hamper their livelihoods. Their mutual trust helps them to live very closely inside the forest. While there is income disparity, it does not create remarkable social stratification. Most villagers opined that the wealth differential has created a small extent of social stratification, which does not induce conflicts. *Mantri* told us that it is very rare for major conflicts to arise in a Khasia *punji*. They have similar relations with their relatives and kin groups living in other *punji*. They visit them occasionally and also causally. All households of the *punji* visit relatives every year. The reasons for such visits are apparently to learn and help in farming activities, to visit and stay for leisure, to share their problems, and perhaps to get loans. More than 90 percent of households of two categories said that they learn agroforestry techniques such as crop improvement, disease prevention, and soil management from relatives. For example, two households of this *punji* applied inorganic fertilizer this year for the first time under inspiration by relatives (fathers-in-law) who live in nearby *punji*, and have better betel leaf production (greener and bigger leaves which fetch better prices). Wu and Pretty (2004: 87) also mention that social connectedness in uplands helps to spread and adopt ideas and technologies. Visits to relatives are also associated with household loans; last year two category-B households received loans from their relatives and pay back that money within six months. Besides household-level social capital, we also investigated village-level social capital in the form of collective action and cooperation. Almost all households of the *punji* take part in social development activities such as repairing access roads, and maintaining wells and prayer halls. Last year they donated four or five days of social work. People are not criticized for inability to participate for good reason (e.g., sickness or emergency work). Households donate equal amounts to cover needed costs for maintaining wells, roads, and prayer halls. In addition to social work, we also observed collective action in farming activities. If any household needs weeding on its agroforestry plots, it sometimes invites some villagers to help, and for this, the household arranges a feast for the villagers who help.

Table 4. Some selected variables of social capital of Lawachara Khasia *punji*, Bangladesh (Data source: Field survey, May-June 2005)

Variables	Category		
	A (n=6)	B (n=15)	Sig. level
Groups and Networks			
Household communication network	13.42	9.30	0.004
No. of people willing to help by giving money in emergency	8.25	5.57	0.004
No. of people currently able to provide this money	6.50	3.87	0.000
Trust and Solidarity			
Opinion on the statements[a]			
Most people living here can be trusted	1.50	1.53	0.897
One has to be alert or someone is likely to take advantage of you	4.67	4.8	0.541
Most people are willing to help if needed	1.83	1.87	0.853
People generally do not trust each other in lending or borrowing money	4.50	4.6	0.694
Trust the following people[b]			
People of same ethnic group	4.60	4.93	0.505
Village leader	4.60	4.75	0.900
Leader responsiveness	4.60	4.80	0.398
Forest Department (FD) personnel	3	-	
FD personnel responsiveness	3	-	
Village group members	4.17	4.07	0.505
Social Cohesion and Inclusion			
Feeling of togetherness or closeness			
Somewhat close	33	20	
Very close	67	80	
Social stratification			
Neither great nor small extent	17	-	
Small extent	83	80	
Very small extent	-	20	
Information and Communication			
Sources of information related to farming systems			
Relatives	100	100	
Neighbors	17	-	
Kin group	50	20	
Times traveled to relatives last year	8.08	5.77	0.008

[a] values were derived using five-level scale [1= agree strongly, 2= agree somewhat, 3= neither agree nor disagree, 4= disagree somewhat, 5= disagree strongly]; b= Figures were derived using five-level scale [1= to a very small extent, 2= to a small scale, 3= neither small nor great extent, 4= to a great extent, 5= to a very great extent]; c= Figures indicate percentage of households

Finally, we tried to examine some issues of empowerment, such as feelings of happiness as a forest villager, self-control and power in making decisions that affect their livelihoods, and the overall impact of the forest on sustaining livelihoods. On a five-level scale (1=very happy to 5=very unhappy), all households felt that they are moderately happy being forest villagers. The forest as the venue for the agroforestry system has a very big impact on their livelihoods. With the present economic situation (not described in this paper) and social connectedness, all villagers are mostly able to make the decisions, which change their livelihoods. They are strongly connected with other *punji*. All Khasia *punji* form a Khasia welfare society that has a strong liaison with different national and international NGOs and several donor agencies. It deals with all problems and interests of the Khasia people and organizes a 36-hour seminar twice a year in different *punji*. People from all *punji* join at the seminar and share information on their situations. All people of the *punji* where a seminar is held help defray seminar costs.

This society has a very strong lobbying capacity to elicit decisions, which favor themselves, which is evident from the following statement:

> 'This society is so powerful that if anything happened, at any *punji*, against members' interests they could bring the matter quickly to the influential agencies (e.g., foreign embassies or donor agencies) to take immediate and necessary action, even before our national government or the concerned agency knows about it' (senior forest officer, pers. comm. 2005).

SELECTED ISSUES OF GOVERNANCE AT LOCAL LEVEL

FD considers forest villagers to be resident labor that engages in plantation and other scheduled tasks in forests. Villager participation in forest management is only as labor. In accordance with need, local personnel (Beat officers) call the *mantri* to discuss the schedules of activities (e.g., nursery work, planting, and patrolling), and decide how many people they need for labor. Usually the *mantri* ask the FD to restrict the number of villagers so it does not exceed one-third of the *punji*'s households in a day. Villagers said that agroforestry management would be hampered if more than one-third of the households were called out in a day. In most cases, the FD agrees, but more labor is needed for large works. If villagers cannot supply adequate labor from their *punji*, they hire outside laborers. The *mantri* decides these matters. The FD also invites him to attend meetings. Though he does not play a very active role in decisions made at meetings, the *mantri* feels fairly satisfied with their deliberative quality, decisions, and convenience.

Forest villagers are not paid for their labor. We asked the *mantri* and local forest officers repeatedly whether villagers are paid. After a series of talks, the *mantri* said that the FD gave him money last year for their labor. However, local FD personnel said that they pay no money to forest villagers. To be further confirm this we put the same question to higher-level forest officers, who replied that forest villagers are no longer unpaid labor because they now receive wages under government rules. Finally, we asked villagers whether they receive money from the FD. They replied that they still are not paid for their labor in forest management.

Table 5. Some Selected Issues of Local-Level Governance at Lawachara Khasia *Punji*, Bangladesh (Source: Field survey, May-June, 2005)

Variables	Category		
	A (n=6)	B (n=15)	Sig. level
Participation in local institution meetings			
How many times	4.17	3.43	0.005
Had a say[a]	100	100	
Role in decision making[a]			
Leader	17	-	
Very active	-	-	
Active	17	-	
Somewhat active	67	73	
Does not participate	-	27	
Meeting indices[†]			
Satisfaction with meetings	3.83	3.93	0.505
Comfort and convenience	4.00	3.93	0.541
Deliberative quality	3.83	3.93	0.505
Leader's responsiveness[a]			
Very responsive	83	93	
Fairly	17	7	
Satisfaction with leader activities[a]			
Very satisfied	17	-	
Satisfied	83	100	
Equity[a]			
Access to benefits			
Land allocation	100	100	
Access to information			
Policy change	17	-	
Market information	100	100	
Women's participation			
Local meetings	100	80	
Meeting decisions	83	7	
Know activities such as			
Fund for common work 100	100		
Programs available	100	100	

[a] Values indicate percentage of households.

[†] Values indicate means of scales [1= disagree strongly, 2= disagree somewhat, 3= neither agree nor disagree, 4= agree somewhat, 5= agree strongly].

Even though not all villagers can attend FD meetings, they have access to their local institution meetings. At *punji*, they have a *darbar*[2] committee. All household heads are members of this committee, which is chaired by the *mantri*. The *mantri* is selected

---

[2] *Darbar* committee means a village committee in a Khasia community which looks after day-to-day affairs. All decisions related to social development, festivals, resolution of social conflicts, duties in forests, and other matters are made by the *darbar* committee.

hereditarily, but he/she should be literate, acceptable to the majority, be of sound health, and be able to liaison with the FD and other agencies. When he feels, for example, a need for road construction, or the FD wants plantation labor, then the *mantri* convenes a *darbar* meeting at his house. Every year four or five general meetings are called, and in most cases, all members attend, though category-B members attended less (Table 5). They do not generally criticize if some members cannot participate occasionally, but warn if it happens repeatedly. Every member can participate in making decisions. First, the *mantri* states the agenda, and then all attendees participate in the discussion, reach a consensus, and finally make decisions based on majority support. We found that though some members do not participate, most members take part somewhat actively in decision-making processes (Table 5). Using a five-level scale (see note of Table 5), we measured three indices of *darbar* meetings. Values of indices reveal that all households are quite satisfied with the meetings; they feel comfort and convenience, and express their satisfaction with deliberative quality at the meetings. As a measure of governance, we also assessed several variables of equity. Findings show that all households have equal access to granted forest land, and are aware of how their own funds are used for common social work and common development programs in their *punji*. However, except for the *mantri*, they do not know about policy changes in FD activities. Women too can participate in local meetings. Villagers said that women attend at *darbar* meetings with their husbands, and play a role in decision-making processes.

In addition to *darbar* committees, there is a savings committee. Household members (men and women over 12 years old) can be a member. At present, there are 40 members. Every member deposits Tk. 20 per month. They can get loans from this committee at a very nominal interest rate. However, the committee convenes meetings to decide the amounts and number of loans that can be given to members.

LIVELIHOOD DIVERSIFICATION STRATEGIES

Discussions with villagers and forest officers, and personal observations disclose that there is very limited diversification of livelihood means in Khasia *punji*. Rural households may choose not to diversify, preferring instead to specialize in a product to have greater returns (Perz, 2005, p.1195). This study reveals that all their efforts are concentrated on betel leaf production, which can use low-capital inputs (local labor, organic fertilizer) and generates better returns. Some households cultivate pineapples, lemons, and other crops in agroforestry plots, but these are for household consumption, not to sell. A very few households have livestock, one girl works for Caritas (an NGO), and two women, after finishing their own work, work part-time in other households of the *punji*. The *mantri* receives tax from *paikar* who come to *punji* to buy betel leaves. As a rule, the *paikar* must pay Tk. 2 (a kind of tax) for one *kuri* of betel leaves and must get a receipt from the *mantri*. The receipt shows how many *kuri* of betel leaves the *paikar* bought from the *punji*, and it must be shown to the *aratdar* (market wholesaler) when selling the goods. Without a receipt, the *aratdar* would not buy the products, which would be regarded as smuggled.

However, in order to maintain steady production from the agroforestry system, all households invest their savings in getting more agroforestry plots. Even though they avoided answering our questions, forest officers said that every household has agroforestry plots in other areas. Extended family members or relatives look after these agroforestry plots, which they visit occasionally to care for. We talked with boys of the *punji*, who also said that all households have more agroforestry plots in other non-registered *punji*.

HOUSEHOLD INCOME - EXPENDITURE SITUATION

In both categories of villagers, the principal source of income is betel leaf. We found significant differences in income from betel leaf ($P<0.004$) and mean household income ($P<0.007$) between two groups. It's always not easy to clearly portray accurate household expenses. Villagers usually do not keep any record. We tried to have at least a fairly estimate of household expenditures. The major expenditure involves food that includes rice, ingredients of curry (e.g., vegetables, fish, meat, spices, etc.), snacks, confectionary, tea, etc. Other spending includes health care, education, social work, rearing of livestock, etc. Regarding health care, they could tell costs that involved in major treatment. In cases of ordinary treatment such as fever, cough, etc. they could not say how much it cost. The costs for education is generally fixed (e.g., price of book, tuition fee, daily costs, etc.) and as such they could give almost accurate figure. Considering all the costs, the study finds that more than 85 percent of total expenditure is used for food (Table 6).

Table 6. Mean annual income - expenditure (Tk.) situation of the sampled households of the Lawachara Khasia *punji*, Bangladesh (Source: Field survey, May-June 2005)

Variables	Category		
	A (n=6)	B (n=15)	Sig. level
Income			
Betel leaf	194267	95913	0.004
Livestock			
Cow	2720	-	
Part-time wage labor	-	768	
Service (in NGO)	4080	-	
Tax	532		
Gross mean annual income per household	201599	96681	0.007
Expenditure			
Input costs	24541	9251	0.013
Food	65167	39360	0.005
Health care	825	-	
Education	2417	275	
Livestock	850	-	
Social work	567	283	
Guard	2490	600	
Mean total expenditure/household	96857	49769	0.003
Mean expenditure/person	12850	9955	0.202

Note: Figures in parenthesis indicate percentage of households.

Within food item, they purchase rice, fish, meat, spices, oil, etc. from market. They collect most of the vegetables from forests. They informed that more than 80 percent of their vegetables are collected from forest and their maximum dietary requirements are fulfilled from forest resources. Occasionally they buy fish and meat from markets. However, there are substantial differences among households of two categories in food costs as well as total households' expenditures. Households having more income expense more than others. For social works (e.g., Christmas day, New Years day, etc.) they contribute as per their capacity. Those who could not patrol forests must give Tk. 250/month to *mantri* and with this money, *mantri* employ temporary forest guards.

This expenditure situation roughly expresses how much they expense annually. There are many other items such as clothing, daily expenses, etc. that we did not assess. However, from this expenditure, and gross annual income, it can be confirmed that there remain some savings.

NGOs AND OTHER DEVELOPMENT PROGRAMS

NGO-driven activities are operationally flexible, responsive, and capable of promoting human capital development (Bingen et al., 2003: 412). For the last three years Caritas, a national Christian NGO, has been operating in Lawachara Khasia *punji*. Its activities include a credit program, savings program, education, legal awareness, and a leadership development program. To get loans, every member (women only) must be a member of the savings program and deposit Tk. 20 per month. After depositing this monthly fee for six months, a member can get a loan. Caritas established a primary school in the *punji*. Each student must pay Tk. 10 tuition monthly. In order to increase legal awareness, and for capacity building, Caritas arranges a monthly meeting in the *punji*. All elderly women participate at the meetings. They encourage women to enroll their children not only in primary schools, but also in higher education.

In addition to Caritas there is Nishorgo, a joint project of the FD and USAid, also operating in the *punji* as a broader part of protected area management. As Lawachara national park is a protected area, for its effective management Nishorgo is developing a co-management plan for the area where forest villagers will be involved as a key stakeholder. Under the project, social forestry programs, ecotourism, and other income-generating activities will be initiated (Philip J. DeCosse, e-mail com., 2005). It also provides training for alternative livelihood sources. The *mantri* said that he attended aquaculture training last year.

PROBLEMS OF THE VILLAGERS

In group discussion, the villagers pointed out some problems that require attention for betterment of their livelihoods. The principal problem is lack of safe drinking water. Hilly topography prevents installation of shallow tube wells. They are planning to establish another ring well with closed top. For this, they received some rings from a former NGO, the Integrated Rural Program for Khasia (IRPK). Every *punji* household contributes Tk. 150 for installing the well. The second problem is the distance to schools, which induces many children to give up further schooling after completing primary education in the *punji*. Poor roads (dirt forest roads) prevent students from going to schools, especially during the monsoon season. The other minor problem is the lack of a common fund. The *darbar* committee does not have a fund. A fund must be raised for any program. The *mantri* said that they would discuss the matter to create a common fund for social development.

ROLE OF FOREST VILLAGERS IN FOREST CONSERVATION

Present forest villagers play a two-fold role in forest conservation: protection and plantation expansion. Forest protection involves patrolling the forests with FD guards. Nine people in three shifts (three persons in one shift, each shift for eight hours), working with FD guards, provide round-the-clock duty along forest boundaries everyday. Although this is inadequate, it still goes a long way toward protecting forests from theft. Thanks to patrols, the forests still look like deep natural forest. In addition to these nine people, the FD calls more people if it needs an emergency force to tackle organized gangs. The villagers cooperate actively, even in the dead of night.

The FD carried out plantation activities almost every year. Villagers participate in all phases of plantation work from nursery preparation, to site preparation, planting, weeding, and other tasks. Due to readily available labor, the FD can run plantation programs smoothly. Moreover, villagers plant seedlings on their agroforestry plots. They take care of trees on agroforestry plots along with betel leaf, but they cannot harvest the trees. They claim that 'As long as there are trees (forests), we can practice agroforestry.' It means that forests are inevitable for their agroforestry plots and conversely on their livelihoods. With this in mind, they cordially participate in forest conservation activities, and have been living in forests peacefully for more than 50 years. Scholars (for example, Walker, 2004: 321) believe that the coexistence of people and forests is possible only due to the intimate relationship between rural livelihoods and forest ecosystems.

LINKAGES BETWEEN LIVELIHOOD AND FOREST CONSERVATION

The linkages between livelihood and forest conservation can be illustrated by Figure 2. It shows that forests provide the asset base to Khasia people on which they practice agroforestry and considered it as natural capital for their livelihood. Life-long experience, skilled household labor, and deep-rooted cultural beliefs, which are regarded as human capital, support the sustainability of the agroforestry system. Existence of strong social capital among villagers as well as with outsiders helps to learn farming technologies, and even to take loan for investment in agroforestry. Having both internal as well as foreign markets of the agroforestry products, the agroforestry generates financial capital and with this financial capital villagers purchase household's equipments, agricultural tools, repair village infrastructure (e.g., road, prayer hall, etc.) that are known as physical capital. On the other hand, they invest these financial and physical capitals for smooth production of the agroforestry system, development of human capital (e.g., education), helps peers in emergencies by giving loan, and above all maintain all household expenditure to sustain their living. Reciprocally, villagers provide labor (human capital) for the conservation and development of forest resources.

CONCLUSION

The study found that the Khasia are well-endowed with all the capitals of the sustainable livelihood framework, but some issues need more attention for better livelihood outcomes and forest conservation. For example, in terms of human capital, the current school enrollment rate is very discouraging. Except for the *mantri*, nobody had a secondary school certificate. Our observation is that to be the *mantri*, he was sent to missionary school because he has to maintain liaison with many agencies. Even though Khasia people seem quite rich (their average annual income is about three times higher than average per capita income of Bangladeshi people, Nath et al., 2003), they are not interested in education. For the improvement of human capital, there is a need for a human capacity building program. The investment in human capacity requires a long-term and focused commitment, and willingness to develop human skills (Bingen et al., 2003: 417). Although Caritas has an education program, more facilities (e.g., infrastructure) should be developed so that children can continue their education after primary school.

The Khasia have very limited diversity of income-generation activities. Small-scale livestock husbandry programs can be promoted. The homestead area, as we observed, is sufficiently large enough to rear some livestock such as chickens and goats, at least for household consumption, to reduce the hunting of wild animals. I also observed that they built some small buildings for their work, which could be used instead to house livestock. The natural capital (forests) and the agroforestry system appear good enough to sustain their livelihoods. However, land encroachment disputes need a reasonable solution. Due to lack of monitoring by forest personnel, and by observing encroachment by Bengalis who have migrated here, they have gradually extended their boundaries. Experience shows that forced eviction could not affect a satisfactory solution to illegal land occupation. The solution should involve villagers in the co-management of national parks, as Nishorgo is trying to do. It is increasingly argued that conservation areas and buffer zone management today have come to rely on user groups based in settlements located close to or within protected area boundaries (Agrawal and Gupta, 2005: 1103).

Though Lawachara National Park was created 10 years ago, it neither involves villagers in its management, nor has a buffer zone from which they could collect wood for household use. The encroached land could be buffer zones in which they could grow fuel wood and grass for agroforestry plots. This would reduce pressure on park resources. Even though villagers claim that they meet fuelwood demand from their agroforestry plots, my observations show that the branches from pruning are not enough to provide fuel to cook three meals a day. Moreover, they provide lunch to paid labor. However, the question may arise whether recovery of encroached land would hamper their livelihoods. My observation is that all of them have agroforestry plots in other areas. Furthermore, regression results indicate that having more number of agroforestry plots in this *punji* do not have significant effect on agroforestry income. Hence, it does not hinder their livelihood. The important point is that they need to be motivated and convinced, and be given a good understanding of their participation in co-management. Policy regarding benefit sharing and the level of participation should be clearly formulated based on negotiations with villagers and the FD. Qualitative information and social capital results indicate that the villagers have strong confidence and faith in the *mantri*, who is beneficial to the *punji*, but is somewhat exploitive. Although villagers are paid labor of the FD, they do not receive their wages. Even they do not know that they are now paid labor. Local forest officers and the *mantri* might share this wage money. Therefore, to implement co-management, the FD should involve other villagers along with the *mantri* in decision-making meetings. This will increase the level of transparency and accountability. Otherwise, influential people will receive most of the benefits.

The interesting and remarkable finding of this study is that the forest villagers, by conserving and utilizing forest resources, have been able to maintain their livelihoods in a sustainable way. We have forest villagers in other parts of the country, but they are wage labor and sometimes involved in illegal logging (Nath et al., 2003). They do not have productive farming or agroforestry systems that support their livelihoods. A similar scenario can also be observed in social forestry projects in upland areas, which can be brought under productive farming systems by tailoring their comparative advantages. Effective strategies for developing upland areas depend, however, upon identifying and implementing socially profitable investments in different environments and opportunities (Pender, 2004: 363). Particular development pathways that are appropriate for uplands offer location-specific opportunities for poverty alleviation and sustainable resource management (Ruben and Pender, 2004: 313). In areas with better agroecological conditions and access to markets and infrastructure, land use intensification and/or diversification into high-value crops (e.g., horticulture) are of major importance, also generating employment opportunities (ibid.: 313). If farmers can realize sustainable benefits, they would find it in their own interests to maintain the production system whether it is forestry, agricultural, or any other kind of development intervention. This study indicates that because villagers realize continuous benefits from the agroforestry system, they expend many resources on conserving their agroforestry plot as well as the government's forests.

Finally, it can be said that strong social capital helps villagers to get moral, technological, and financial support from fellows, and competent manpower for the management of agroforestry plots that stable natural capital, facilitates the generation of financial and physical capitals, and the re-investment and utilization of financial and physical capitals,, therefore making the livelihoods of the Khasia people sustainable, gaining in return their support for the conservation of forests in Lawachara National Park. However, to better assure the villagers' livelihoods and to avoid possible conflicts between the FD and forest villagers, land tenure issues should be resolved and regular renewal of the agreement should be confirmed. The lessons that learned from this study can be utilized in formulating future participatory forest management schemes in the country.

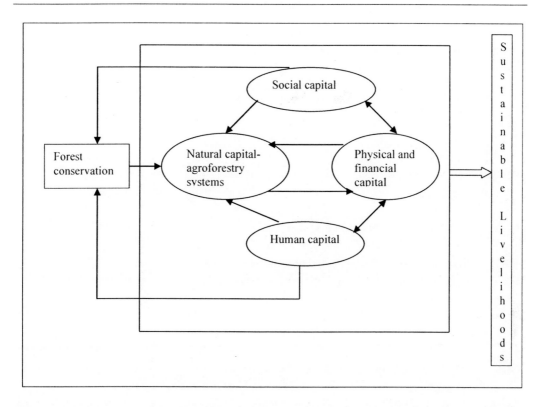

Figure 2. The reciprocal relationship between forest conservation and livelihoods of the Khasia people.

REFERENCES

Agrawal, A. & Gupta, K. (2005). Decentralization and participation: The governance of common pool resources in Nepal's Terai. *World Development, 33*, 1101-1114.

Alam, M. K. & Mohiuddin, M. (1995). Conservation of Tree Diversity through betel-leaf (*Piper betel*) based Agroforestry in Sylhet. *Bangladesh Journal of Forest Science, 24*, 49-53.

Alhamidi, S. K., Gustafsson, M., Larsson, H. & Hillbur, P. (2003). The cultural background of the sustainability in the Ghouta, the oasis of Damascus, Syria. *Agriculture and Human Values, 20*, 231-240.

Banglapedia (Encyclopedia of Bangladesh). (2001). BANGLAPEDIA: Khasia, *The.* [http:// banglapedia.search.com.bd/HT/K_0215.htm, accessed on October 2005].

Belcher, B. M. (2005). Forest product markets, forests and poverty reduction. *International Forestry Review, 7*, 82-89.

Bingen, J., Serrano, A. & Howard, J. (2003). Linking farmers to markets: different approaches to human capital development. *Food Policy, 28*, 405-419.

Bossel, H. (1999). Indicators for sustainable development: Theory, Method, Applications. Winnipeg: International Institute for Sustainable Development.

Cramb, R. A., T. Purcell, & Ho, T. C. S. (2004). Participatory assessment of rural livelihoods in the central highlands of Vietnam. *Agricultural Systems, 81*, 255-272.

Danchev, A. (2005). Social capital influence on sustainability of development (case study of Bulgaria). *Sustainable Development,* 13, 25-37.

Dewi, S., Belcher, B. & Puntodewo, A. (2005). Village economic opportunity, forest dependence, and rural livelihoods in East Kalimantan, Indonesia. *World Development,* 33, 1419-1434.

Dumanski, J., Terry, E., Byerlee, D. & Pieri, C. (1998). Performance indicators for sustainable agriculture. Discussion Note. *Rural Development Sector,* Washington, D.C.: The World Bank.

FSP (Forestry Sector Project). (2000). *First Five Year Management Plan for Lawachara National Park, Volume 1: Management Plan.* Ministry of Environment and Forests: Dhaka, Bangladesh.

Hopwood, B., Mellor M. & O'Brien, G. (2005). Sustainable development: mapping different approaches. *Sustainable Development,* 13, 38-52.

ITTO. (2005). Revised ITTO criteria and indicators for the sustainable management of tropical forests including reporting format. *ITTO Policy Development Series No. 15.* Yokohama, Japan: ITTO.

Kijtewachakul, N., G. P. Shivakoti, & Webb, E. L. (2004). Forest health, collective behaviors, and management. *Environmental Management,* 33, 620-636.

Komatsu, Y., Tsunekawa, A. & Ju, H. (2005). Evaluation of agricultural sustainability based on human carrying capacity in dry lands – a case study in rural villages in Inner Mongolia, China. *Agriculture, Ecosystem and Environment,* 108, 29-43.

Lamberton, G. (2005). Sustainable sufficiency – an internally consistent version of sustainability. *Sustainable Development,* 13, 53-68.

Mcsweeney, K. (2004). Forest product sale as natural insurance: The effects of household characteristics and the nature of shock in eastern Honduras. *Society and Natural Resources,* 17, 39-56.

NACOM (Nature Conservation Management). (2003). Secondary data collection for pilot protected areas: Lawachara National Park. In: Co-management of Tropical Forest Resources of Bangladesh, [online available: www.nishorgo.org/files_pdf/Secondary Data on Lawachara NP.pdf, accessed on October 2005].

Nair P. K. R. (1993). *An introduction to agroforestry.* The Netherlands: Kluwer Academic Publishers.

Nath, T. K., M. Inoue, M. J. Islam, & Kabir, M. A. (2003). The Khasia tribe of northeastern Bangladesh: their socio-economic status, hill farming practices and impacts on forest conservation. *Forests, Trees and Livelihoods,* 13, 297-311.

Pandit, B. H. & Thapa, G. B. (2004). Poverty and resource degradation under different common forest resource management systems in the mountains of Nepal. *Society and Natural Resources,* 17, 1-16.

Pender, J. (2004). Development pathways for hillsides and highlands: some lessons from Central America and east Africa. *Food Policy,* 29, 339-367.

Perz, S. G. L. (2005). The importance of household asset diversity for livelihood diversity and welfare among small farm colonists in the Amazon. The Journal of Development Studies, 41, 1193-1220.

Peterseil, J., Wrbka, T., Plutzar, C., Schmitzberger, I., Kiss, A., Szerencsits, E., Reiter, K., Schneider, W., Suppan, F. & Beissmann, H. (2004). Evaluating the ecological sustainability of Austrian agricultural landscapes – the SINUS approach. *Land Use Policy,* 21, 307-320.

Rashid, H. R. (1991). Geography of Bangladesh. Dhaka, Bangladesh: University Press Ltd.

Rasul, G. & Thapa, G. B. (2004). Sustainability of ecological and conventional agricultural systems in Bangladesh: an assessment based on environmental, economic and social perspectives. *Agricultural Systems,* 79, 327-351.

Ruben, R. & Pender, J. (2004). Rural diversity and heterogeneity in less-favoured areas: the quest for policy targeting. *Food Policy,* 29, 303-320.

Saha, N. (1998). A studies on forest industries of Bangladesh. *The Bulletin of the Kochi University Forests,* 25, 1-107.

Saha, N. & Azam, M. A. (2004). The indigenous hill-farming system of Khasia tribes in Moulvibazar district of Bangladesh: status and impacts. Small-scale Forest Economics, *Management and Policy,* 3, 273-281.

Saha, N. & Azam, M. A. (2005). Betel leaf based forest farming by Khasia tribes: a sustainable system of forest management in Moulvibazar district, Bangladesh. *Forests, Trees and Livelihoods,* 15, 275-290.

Sunderlin, W. D., Angelsen, A., Belcher, B., Nasi, R., Santoso, L. & Wunder, S. (2005). Livelihoods, forests and conservation in developing countries: An Overview. *World Development,* 33, 1383-1402.

Virtanen, P. (2005). Community-based natural resource management in Mozambique: a critical review of the concepts of applicability at local level. *Sustainable Development,* 13, 1-12.

Walker, A. (2004). Seeing farmers for the trees: community forestry and the arborealisation of agriculture in northern Thailand. *Asia Pacific Viewpoint,* 45, 311-324.

Wu, B. & Pretty, J. (2004). Social connectedness in marginal rural China: The case of farmers innovation circles in Zhidan, north Shaanxi. *Agriculture and Human Values,* 21, 81-92.

Yin, R. K. (2003). Case Study Research Design and Method., Applied Social Research Methods Series, Vol. 5. *Third edition.* SAGE Publications.

Zhen, L., Routray, J. K., Zoebisch, M. A., Chen, G., Xie, G. & Cheng, S. (2005). Three dimensions of sustainability of farming practices in the North China Plain — a case study from Ningjin County of Shandong province, PR China. *Agriculture, Ecosystem and environment,* 105, 507-522.

In: World Poverty Issues
Editor: Marilyn M. Watkins, pp. 69-103

ISBN: 978-1-60456-057-2
© 2008 Nova Science Publishers, Inc.

Chapter 3

URBAN AGRICULTURE AS A MEANS OF REDUCING URBAN POVERTY

Nyumbaiza Tambwe

University of the Witwatersrand (Wits University), Johannesburg, South Africa

ABSTRACT

Social scientists are unanimous to acknowledge that urbanization in Africa is fast-growing. Unfortunately, the highest urbanization rate in the world is not accompanied by economic growth. Of greater importance is the fact that most of the researchers in the urban sector predict that by the year 2030 more people will live in cities and towns than in rural areas. A former Congolese Minister in charge of urbanism and habitat recently reiterated this view in his speech during the ceremony of handing-over to the Gizenga government. He declared that in the coming two decades more than a half of Congolese population (presently 60 million) will be living in towns and cities.

As a consequence, satisfying urban dwellers' basic needs in terms of health, food, education, housing, water and other needs could be challenging. Even though cities and towns benefit from most of the local and foreign investments, urban areas experience high rates of unemployment, food insecurity and poverty, which continue to exacerbate.

To alleviate some of these problems, a large number of urban residents in developing countries, particularly in Africa, resort to urban agriculture for food, income generation, and employment. City dwellers convert open spaces (backyards, parks, garbage deposits, power lines and railways, roads, and peri-urban zones) into gardens and farms as a means of reducing urban poverty.

Taking the city of Lubumbashi as a case study, this chapter explores push and pull factors, coupled with the presence of facilitating factors such as availability of land, market proximity, and support from municipal officials and non-governmental organizations (NGOs). This chapter would like to find out who is farming in the city of Lubumbashi, what is produced and for what benefit.

INTRODUCTION

The modernization of Lubumbashi (second largest city of the Democratic Republic of Congo (DRC) after Kinshasa (the capital city) with Gécamines[1] as the powerful capitalist instrument of industrialization and also the concentration of most investments give the impression that Lubumbashi dwellers get more and better goods and services than in the countryside. The presence of a number of public services, schools and the third institutions of education, shops, public and private hospitals and clinics, and even some companies provides jobs to Lubumbashi dwellers. But the existence of these infrastructures is not necessary sign of welfare. According to Makala-Lizumu and Mwana Elas (1979: 109), there exists an approach which conceives poverty in relative terms in urban areas and in absolute terms in the case of rural areas. This is to say that the presence of socio-economic infrastructures in towns and cities have the advantage to satisfy basic needs of urban residents in terms of health, education, housing, water, and so on. The same, the concentration of most investments in urban areas is said to generate employment and wealth. In measuring the importance of the socioeconomic infrastructures in the city, Makala-Lizumu and Mwana Elas advise to take into consideration not only the number of jobs provided, but also the level of salaries or wages allocated.

The collapse of Gécamines for example, in the 1990s forced this mining company to retrench more than 10,000 workers. The Gécamines' collapse resulted in the collapse and even disappearance of many other companies operating on its orbit. For example, workers at the national railway company (SNCC) remained unpaid for several years. The survey conducted by the University of Lubumbashi in 2003 showed that most of Lubumbashi residents have one meal per day and about 70 percent of their earnings are spent on food. They can hardly have access to health care services, education, and good housing. Only the high-income households representing 30 percent of the urban households can afford luxurious goods such as car, cell phone, etc. This reveals that the majority of urban households live under the poverty line of one dollar a day. But the common view is that Lubumbashi and Kinshasa benefit more than other cities and rural areas from the national health policy and expenditures.

This description clearly demonstrates that the living conditions in Lubumbashi city are not brilliant as they suppose to be. On the contrary, most people are poor like in the countryside. For their survival, Lubumbashi dwellers practice several economic activities. Urban agriculture seems to be the most practiced one. Therefore, this chapter firstly explores factors which have been at the origin of the emergence and expansion of agricultural activities within and around the city of Lubumbashi. Concretely, the section examines push and pull factors coupled with the facilitating ones. Secondly, the chapter demonstrates the importance of urban agriculture in Africa in terms of the number of urban dwellers involved, the quantity of foods produced and the superficies of urban land under cultivation. In the third section, the study describes main features of Lubumbashi farmers. This section answers question about who is farming in this city, what is cultivated or raised, and for what purpose. Semi-structured

---

[1] Gécamines (Générale de carrières et des mines) is the former Union-Minière du Haut-Katanga created in 1906. It is a mining company specialized in production and export of copper, cobalt and many other minerals. It was the most important company in DRC by the size of its contribution to the national budget (up to 60% until the 1990s).

interview was used as a principal method of data collection (from November 2004 up to March 2005). A conclusion is provided in which a summary of the study in given.

1. PUSH AND PULL FACTORS' THEORY

The livelihood perspective argues that households and individuals diversify assets, incomes, and activities in response to what Barred *et all* (cited in Awetori Yaro 2006) called "push and pull factors". By push and pull factors, I understand factors that force urban households or urban residents to resort to agricultural activities on one hand and those that attract them for nutritional, financial, and social reasons on the other hand. The first group of factors put pressure (negative) on urban population while the second group constitutes the type of response to the pressure. Both forces must be operating for urban agriculture to take place. In addition, facilitating factors must be present as well, such as availability of land, positive attitude of municipal officials towards urban agriculture, market proximity, and material support from outsiders.

According to the urban agriculture literature, push factors include: continuing rural-urban migration, economic recession, structural adjustment, rapid urbanization, ineffective agricultural policies, wage cuts, civil strife, war, and natural disasters (Mougeot 1994, Obudho and Foeken 1999, Pélissier 2000, De Lattre 1994). Among push factors, there is possibility to distinguish external factors (structural adjustment, the decline in world prices of the primary commodities, and dependency relationships between peripheral economies of the Third World and core economies of the First World) from internal factors (low wage and or salary, unemployment, rapid population growth, economic crisis, war, poverty, natural disasters, agricultural crisis in traditional sector) (Tambwe 2006: 201-02). Pull factors include: food security, income generation and employment (Freedman 1991, Mougeot 1995, Mbiba 1995). As it appears, these forces may be economic, political, social, or historical.

The United Nations Development Program considers the following as elements and components of urban agriculture: (i) location: urban and peri-urban areas; (ii) purpose: market oriented, local consumption and sale; (iii) products: food and non-food; (iv) roles: food, income, and employment; and (v) status: legal or illegal. Urban agriculture is the result of the interplay of various forces at upstream as well as at downstream of the process.

1.1. Push Factors

In this section, I distinguish external factors from the internal ones. Are considered external factors those that have their origins in the global economy, but having certain impact on the Congolese economy. Even though there are more internal factors than external at the basis of the emergence and expansion of urban agriculture, it is important to analyze some of the external factors. Nevertheless, more internal than external push factors will be analyzed.

1.1.1. External Push Factors

The Democratic Republic of Congo is part of the global economy with a specific role to play. Since the colonial epoch, the Congolese economy was and still be specialized in the supply of row materials such as copper, cobalt, zinc, diamond, etc. As long as the prices of row materials remain high, the Congolese economy is strong enough, meaning strong currency, stability of jobs and also creation of new jobs. In 1973 for example, one Zaire (Congolese currency during the Mobutu regime) was the equivalent of two American dollars. Zaire was one of the strongest currencies in the world. The contrary is also true. The decline of world prices of the primary commodities means the decline of Congolese economy having as a result, a weak currency, loss of jobs, an increasing number of unemployed people, and poverty. This happened in 1974 when the price of copper declined. The price of copper dropped from BF (Belgian Franc) 118,025 (approximately $US 3,370) per metric ton in April 1974 to BF 47,402 (approximately $US 1,350) in December 1974 to BF 45,482 (approximately $US 1,280) in December 1975 (Banque du Zaire cited in Kannyo 1979:63). As if it was not enough, oil price tripled at the same time. As a result, the rate of growth of the commercialized gross domestic product dropped from 7.6 percent in 1973 to 5.4 percent in 1974 (Banque du Zaire 1975).

With such a situation, the government often refers to IMF (International Monetary Fund) or World Bank to cope with the economic crisis. These institutions generally impose some conditions such as the devaluation of the local currency making imports more expensive, cut of social expenses, removing of interest rates to curb inflation and stop capital flight, and the abolition of price controls. The implementation of these policies is accompanied in most cases by the loss of jobs for many workers (public services particularly). At the same time there is rise in social service costs (hospital, school fees, transport, etc). The combination of the increasing costs of services, wages freeze, and the increasing unemployment rate engenders poverty. At the University of Lubumbashi in 1984 for example, transport service and restaurant were closed at the same time that student bursary was cut off. From that period, students started cultivating vegetables for food and income generation to meet their basic needs.

The relations of dependency which started since colonization are maintained between the Democratic Republic of Congo and some developed countries (such as France, United States, Belgium, and United Kingdom). This kind of relations is also taking place between DRC and South Africa as an African political and economic power. This means that the country is now exploited not only by the first world but also by the second world which is dominated in sub-Saharan Africa by the South African economy. Also, Chinese companies are currently exploiting and exporting copper and cobalt from Katanga province. Salaries earned by workers in the Chinese mining companies are so low that the new elected Governor (Moise Katumbi Chapwe) denounced the exploitation of Katanga population. The double exploitation far from helping the country is impoverishing Congolese population.

1.1.2. Internal Push Factors

The combination of external and internal factors puts pressure on urban population to practice urban agriculture among many other survival activities. The following factors are more specific to the city of Lubumbashi, even though some of them may be applicable to other Congolese cities.

1.1.2.1. The Gécamines' Collapse

The economy of Katanga province was dominated up to the early 1990s by the mining company of copper and cobalt. Gécamines was the main producer and exporter of those minerals. The mining sector provided about 80 percent of DRC's foreign exchange earnings in 1987; 65 percent came from copper (Economist Intelligence Unit 1989).

Created in 1906, the Union Minière du Haut-Katanga (UMHK), renamed Gecomin in 1967 and later on Gécamines (Générale des Carrières et des Mines in 1972) was a colonial mining company. It was specialized in the exploitation and export of copper, cobalt, zinc and many other minerals. UMHK started copper production in 1911 with an initial capital of 10 millions Franc-gold representing 100, 000 shareholders. As Katwala declares in *Export-Led Growth: The copper sector*, "UMHK had not only built a copper empire in Katanga that contributed to an autonomous development of the province but had also become the most powerful company operating in Congo, producing the largest single source of government revenue and three-quarters of its foreign exchange" (1979:123). With concessions of 34,000 square kilometres, the company was divided into three main groups:

- Group South-East concessions comprising Lubumbashi, Kipushi and Lukuni;
- Group Centre Concessions with Kambove, Kakontwe and Shinkolobwe; and
- Group West Concessions located in Kolwezi, Musonoi and Kamoto.

In 1913, Union Minière du Haut-Katanga produced 7,500 tons of copper. The production reached the level of 27,000 tons four years later. In 1929, 137,000 tons of copper were produced. Eight years before the independence (1952), UMHK could produce more than 200,000 tons. By producing 300,000 tons of copper in 1960, the company became the third producer of copper in the world. During the same year, 8,240 tons of cobalt was produced. Thus, Congo became the first producer of this mineral in the world (Joye and Lewin 1961:219). It can be said that Gécamines was the main instrument used by the colonialists to integrate DRC into the capitalist economy as a supplier of mineral and agricultural products.

Fearing the nationalization of the Union Minière du Haut-Katanga by the central government at the independence of the country (June 30, 1960), UMHK encouraged the secession of Katanga province. On July 11, 1960, Tshombe proclaimed the independence of Katanga and became himself the President. Nationalization of the copper company would have resulted in a massive departure of Belgians and in government interference in day-to-day management of the company (Katwala 1979:123). After the three years of secession, Joseph-Desiré Mobutu took power by coup d'état on November 24, 1965. In his search of economic independence, the Mobutu government took over UMHK's assets in 1967. Although the takeover, the company still controlled copper production and marketing in the country (Katalwa 1979: 124).

It was only in the mid-80s, under the Mobutu regime that the company reached the highest level of copper production: 476,000 tons and about 14,000 tons of cobalt, generating external revenue of about $US 1 billion a year. At that time the company had 24,378 employees. As a welfare mining company and example of success, Gécamines provided its employees with several benefits, which included monthly food distributions, free housing, water and electricity, free education and free health care for family members, free recreational facilities, cheap loans, a retirement package, free burials, etc (Frutchard 2004:12). It is important to mention that most of the companies in Katanga province economically depended on Gécamines. This was the case of the national railway (SNCC), which transported Gécamines minerals of copper and cobalt from Lubumbashi to Kalemie or from Lubumbashi to the Republic of Zambia. The company provided health care service to Lubumbashi population by taking over Sendwe hospital as the state was unable to manage it. In 2000, Gécamines paid as tax for its 24,378 employees an amount evaluated at FC 199,155,267,90 ($US 485,744) (Report of tax service 2003).

Table 1: Productions of copper (1986-2003)

Years	Quantity (in tons)
1986	486,000
1988	450,000
1990	150,000
1992	150,000
1994	40,000
1996	50,000
1998	40,000
2000	20,000
2002	10,000
2003	8,000

Source: Gécamines: Rapport 2003.

A combination of several factors precipitated the collapse of the giant capitalist company. The mine of Kamoto (one of Gécamines concessions) near Kolwezi collapsed in September 1990, bringing production levels down to 150,000 tons of copper. Since then, production of copper went every year down, reaching the lowest level of 8,000 tons in 2003. Also, mass lootings took place in almost all towns and cities of DRC in 1991 and 1993. Economic infrastructures were destroyed. Theft of Gécamines' production and predatory behaviour of government apparatus, political instability and mismanagement, international isolation of Kinshasa government because of the so-called "University of Lubumbashi massacre", and the expulsion of more than 300,000 Kasai populations from Katanga province in 1993 deepened the disintegration of the mining company.

Despite the collapse in copper production, the distribution of monthly food to employees continued as well as free health care and free school fees until 2003.

Because of the collapse, 10,364 Gécamines employees were retrenched. It must be said that this was presented as a voluntary departure program. The truth is that Gécamines workers did not have choice after many years without receiving their salaries. The main criterion was to have at least 25 years of employment with Gécamines. The package offered to the retrenched employees represented on average $US 2,903 for the workers, $US 11,901 for the managers, and $US 28,588 for the directors, (World Bank Report 2004). The amount of money each category of employees received was largely less than what the company should pay them after several years without salary.

Some consequences with financial and social costs were observed. In its fall for example, Gécamines took down a great deal of the economic and social infrastructures of the Katanga province in general and of Lubumbashi in particular. About hundreds of firms (SNCC, Swanepoel, etc) working in the orbit of Gécamines have gone bankrupt, increasing the unemployment rate in the province. By maintaining itself and its system (human capital, health, and education) despite the decline in production, Gécamines' debt reached $US 1, 6 billion in 2003. During that year, Lubumbashi city received only 2, 38 percent of the total values of the tax retro-cessions which were owed to it according to the law, and as a result had to function with an annual operating budget of $US 8,640 compared to the $US 485,744 in 2000, for a population of about 1, 2 million (Rapport de la Mairie de Lubumbashi 2004). The collapse of Gécamines has had a strong social impact. Roads have in some places disappeared, schools buildings are in a state of complete disrepair, lacking doors, windows, etc., hospital equipment lack repair parts. For example, the road linking Lubumbashi to Kolwezi (370 km of length) is no more practicable. People use airplane to travel. Also, best professionals in the education and health sectors have left (mainly for South Africa and Zambia). Recent figures on maternal death at birth however seem to indicate that there has been a considerable worsening of the situation: the rate of women dying at birth went from 20.4%o in 2000 to 88.1%o. According to the University of Lubumbashi survey (2004), 85 percent of retrenched Gécamines employees and 82 percent of the remaining only have one meal or less a day.

Gécamines health services represented an important part of the health infrastructure in Katanga province: 64 percent of all hospital beds in Lubumbashi, 42 percent in Likasi, and 47 percent in Kolwezi. The running of national hospital (Sendwe with 1,000 beds), 7 local hospitals, 3 clinics, 4 health centres, and 18 factory health centres cost $US 30 million to the company in 1990 as operating budget, which became zero in 2003. Sendwe hospital could any more play its essential role in the national medical system or served the medical needs of the whole Katanga. Gécamines local hospitals and health centres playing the essential role as the only medical facility available in areas like Kipushi, Mangombo, Kambove, Kakontwe, Kakanda, Kando, and Luena, ceased to function since 2002. As a consequence, people go to non-Gecamines health centers, but private clinics are expensive.

The DRC government decided the restructuring of Gécamines and of its welfare role vis-à-vis the communities in which it operates. Gécamines's restructuring plan included the voluntary departure of about half of the company's workforce (about 11,000 workers), a structural adjustment loan that marked the re-engagement of the Bank in DRC after ten years break, and the hiring of a new international management team at the head of Gécamines to help in the restart of production operation.

The restructuring of Gécamines obviously affected the education sector. One third of teachers have been retrenched and the remaining teachers have not been paid. Schools are in complete disrepair with missing doors, windows, etc. Educational level has been going down in the last ten years. Also, about 1,300 households living in formerly Gécamines-owned houses or apartments were vacated in 2004, as the houses and apartments they were living in were sold by the company to other company employees.

Agriculture in the contrary became the primary choice for the retrenched. Already during the many years without salary, 54 percent of Gécamines employees and the members of their family went into agriculture. But the lack of capital, bad roads, and the high cost of inputs constitute some of the constraints to success in this activity.

1.1.2.2. The Mobutu Regime

The Mobutu regime lasted 32 years (1965-97). Joseph-Desiré Mobutu took power by coup d'état on November 24, 1965. It is important to say that General Mobutu as a member of Lumumba's political party (Mouvement National Congolais) was appointed secretary of state in the first independence government. He was overthrown from power by Laurent-Desiré Kabila on May 17, 1997. The three decades of Mobutu regime were characterized by a relative stability and unity of the country, also by brutality, mismanagement, corruption, economic dependency on international economy, poverty, etc.

Collusion of interests between copper mining (Gécamines), the Belgian government, and some local political actors (Tshombe, Munongo, etc) was at the origin of Katanga secessionist movement (July 11, 1960), which was followed by the Kasai province. The actors' goal was to ensure control of mines in Katanga province in order to deprive the Lumumba government of the means of its politics. While Belgian government, banks and mining corporations feared that Lumumba nationalizes the Union Minière du Haut-Katanga, the United States viewed Lumumba as a communist leader. As a result, Patrice Emery Lumumba was assassinated in the Katanga Province.

One year after President Mobutu took power, some stability was restored in the country. To strengthen his power, Mobutu established a personal patrimonial regime in which high-level bureaucrats played a major role in policy making and implementation. According to Kannyo (1979:57), a technocratic elite of the politico-administrative class emerged as the immediate holder of political power and primary beneficiary of the Mobutu's economic policies. Clientage was the main feature of the political relationships of the Mobutu regime. In 1967, Mobutu created the Mouvement Populaire de la Revolution (MPR), a political party which, later on prohibited the existence of any other political party. It was decided by the *Bureau Politique* (one of the major structures of the party) that only the President of MPR, meaning Mobutu should become the President of the country.

In the search of political and economic independence, the Mobutu regime undertook a series of administrative and constitutional reforms. UMHK was nationalized and became Gecomin in 1967, and finally Gécamines in 1972. MIBA, the diamond mining-company was also concerned by the nationalization process in 1973. According to Nest (1979:127), the Mobutu government accepted International Monetary Fund (IMF) proposals and introduced in June 1967 a stabilization program to restore budgetary control and balance-of-payments equilibrium and to establish the profitability of the export sector. Radical measures including the devaluation of Congolese franc, the raise of taxation and abolition of the dual exchange rate were taken and implemented. Advised by IMF-IBRD experts, the government of Mobutu concluded that an increase in copper production and export would be the fastest and most reliable way of increasing foreign exchange earnings and of raising government revenues (Nest 1979). The high copper prices in the period 1965-70 on the London metal Exchange encouraged the Congolese government to give priority to copper production and export. Two-part Gécamines expansion program designed to increase production and export of copper and cobalt began in 1970. The first five-year expansion program (1970-74) provided for an increase in copper production of 100,000 metric tons to 460,000 metric tons. Investments for this first project were put at $US260 million and financed mostly from internationally generated funds and loans of about $US21 million from U.S and European banks. The second five-year expansion program (1975-79) was designed for the opening of two open-pit mines in the Kolwezi area and for the construction and expansion of treatment plants and infrastructure facilities. Copper and cobalt production was expected to increase by 120, 000 tons and 4, 000 tons, respectively, raising annual total capacity to 580, 000 tons of copper and 20, 000 tons of cobalt (Nest 1979: 132). It was always in the purpose of increasing copper and cobalt production that SODIMIZA (Société de Développement Minier du Zaire) in April 1969 and SMTF (Société Minière de Tenke Fungurume) in September 1970 were created.

For Kannyo (1979), the year 1974 can be regarded as the beginning of the political crisis of the Mobutu regime. He retained two factors: the zairianization measures and the decline of copper price on the international market. The truth is that the nationalization process of small and medium businesses started some months before the year 1974. On November 30, 1973, small and medium-sized wholesale and retail businesses, small factories, farms, and plantations were confiscated from Europeans, handing them over to cronies of the regime. Thirteen months later, zairianization measures were followed by radicalization measures designed to take over slightly larger businesses. And in 1975 stabilization committees were established to deal with the disruptive economic effects of the measures. In 1976 retrocession was decreed. Most former owners had taken their business back (Gould and Mwana-Elas cited in Kannyo 1979:98). As if it was not enough, the copper price dropped on the international market at the beginning of the year 1974. At the same time, oil price tripled.

Ignoring the economic crisis, Mobutu continued directing ever larger proportions of state revenue toward the presidency and maintenance of patrimonial systems of rule, and away from economic investment or public goods provision (Nest 2006:18-9). In this regard, President Mobutu used his position as many other dictators in the world to enrich himself leaving the rest of the population in extreme poverty.

For three decades, he put vast country, the second largest in sub-Saharan Africa at the disposal of the CIA and other Western agencies, which used it as staging base for their activities throughout the continent. In exchange, he enjoyed a free hand at home, diverting for his use billions of dollars from Zaire's mineral wealth while leaving most Zairians in poverty (Castells 2000: 99).

The economic crisis deepened in the 1990s when Gécamines' copper production dropped 90 percent, former Cold War patrons withdrew financial and diplomatic support, University of Lubumbashi students' massacre occurred, and when unpaid soldiers engaged in masse looting of private property.

What can be considered as the decisive factor in Mobutu's downfall was the first recent civil war started in late 1996 with Laurent-Desire Kabila as the head of the Alliance des Forces Démocratiques pour la Libération du Congo-Zaire (AFDL), which was military supported by the Rwandan and Ugandan governments. The government of Rwanda was engaged in the war to destroy the Interahamwe and Hutu power organizations located in DRC since the genocide in Rwanda, and the government of Uganda for getting rid of Mobutu. Seven months later, the AFDL took power when Mobutu fled the country, and Laurent-Desiré Kabila as the head of the movement became the President.

1.1.2.3. The Failure of Agriculture

It was previously demonstrated that the modern economic sector of DRC was and still dominated by the export of minerals. This sector comprises also agricultural exports. Palm oil, coffee, and rubber were the major export crops. An estimated 260, 000 people, meaning 30 percent of wage labour in DRC worked on large plantations in 1970 (Gran 1979:10). According to Gran, the modern sector was a disarticulated economy. The various sectors did not face each other as relative equals whose growths should be mutually stimulated, as happened in the internal economic growth of the United States of America or some of countries of Western Europe.

Two major periods characterize the history of agriculture in the Democratic Republic of Congo: the colonial and postcolonial periods. Agriculture during the colonial period was oriented into two directions: to supply towns and cities, especially the mining companies, and to export commercial crops to industrial countries for foreign currency. About 40 percent of the DRC's exports came principally from coffee, palm oil, cotton, etc. To achieve these objectives, several agricultural policies were implemented. Firstly, fertile rural lands were confiscated from local peasants and handed over to white farmers. Congolese peasants were either relocated in hostile land or recruited in the mining companies. As the mining companies should feed their workers (especially Gécamines), white farmers were the principal suppliers of agricultural products (maize, rice, cassava). In the meantime, peasants were discouraged to sell their produce to these companies. On the contrary, the majority of them were recruited as farm workers or mining companies' workers. Secondly, instead of encouraging them to practice subsistence crops, black peasants were forced to produce cotton, palm oil, coffee, etc for commercial reasons. According to Gran (1979:7), DRC was a net exporter of maize before independence. In 1959, the total imports of wheat, rice, and maize were 47,000 tons. Cotton production cycle for example took nine months before the harvest (December to July). This means that peasants submitted to this kind of agriculture did not have time to practice subsistence agriculture. Thirdly, rural populations were organized into peasantries to facilitate the control. In these farming organizations, they were obliged to grow cotton, palm oil, coffee, maize, and cassava. Priority was given to cash crops. As it appears, agriculture during the colonial period was practiced not to meet the needs of peasants, but to satisfy the needs of mining companies and the needs of the metropole. It must be added that during the same period, roads linking rural areas to towns and cities were practicable, facilitating the evacuation of agricultural products. About 10 percent of the main roads of the country were located in Katanga province and 24 percent of the secondary roads.

At the independence of the country (1960), populations enjoyed the freedom of movement. They could move from rural areas to urban ones without any restriction. The rural-urban migration deprived rural areas of their workforce. In his study, Michel Ngongo (2003) (cited in Mawazo 2005) retains five steps which were followed by the agricultural production in Katanga province since the independence of the country:

- 1960 to 70 is a step of relative extension;
- 1970 to 78 is characterized by a stagnation of agricultural production;
- 1980 to 89 is the beginning of decline of agricultural sector;
- Early 1990s is marked by the acceleration of the decline; and
- Beginning of the 2000s is featured by the dependence of the province on agricultural supplies.

According to Ngongo, stagnation, decline and regression of the agricultural sector in Katanga province (even in the rest of the country) resulted in the dependency of the province on the importation of 75 percent of peanut, 70 percent of fish and meat, and 100 percent of milk. To address the situation a series of policies were conceived and even implemented, but most of them failed. The first measure was the Mobutu Plan (1979-80), followed by the agricultural minimum program, which was followed by the agricultural revival program (1982-84). The last one was the five-year agricultural plan (1986-90).

Announced in the President's speech on November 25, 1977, The Mobutu Plan was really implemented in January 1980. The main goal was to boost the national economy by the revival of agriculture. To achieve this goal, the plan undertook the following actions (i) the rehabilitation of infrastructures of communication (roads) with the purpose to facilitate the evacuation of agricultural products from rural areas to towns or cities, (ii) the promotion of commercial agriculture to earn foreign currency, (iii) the promotion of subsistence agriculture to achieve the food security policy, and (iv) the improvement of living conditions of rural populations by the rehabilitation of sanitation, education infrastructures. The Mobutu Plan was too big to be implemented and relied too much for its implementation on foreign resources. So, the Mobutu Plan failed to reach its objectives. The failure of the Mobutu Plan pushed the authorities to conceive another one more realistic: the Minimum Agricultural Plan. Conceived to correct the first one, this plan should be financed by the government. Only the following three objectives were retained:

- intensification of subsistence agriculture;
- promotion of commercial agriculture; and
- production of row agricultural products for national agro-industries.

The Minimum Agricultural Plan was the strategy to improve the agricultural production in the country, which was decreasing each year.

Table 2. Agricultural production in tons

Products	Needs	Production	Deficit	Objective
Maize	700,000	509,500	190,500	1000,000
Rice	150,000	127,000	23,000	200,000
Cassava	4,000,000	2,284,000	1,706,000	5,000,000

Source: Conseil Exécutif, PAM 1980, p.6.

This table shows that the Minimum Agricultural Plan should deal with the deficit of each product in order to allow the country to become self-sufficient in maize, rice and cassava. Thus, the objectives of 1000,000 tons of maize, 200,000 tons of rice and 5,000,000 tons of cassava should be reached by the plan. But because of the short time (1 year: 1980) given to achieve these objectives, the Minimum Agricultural Plan also failed. From 1982, another agricultural program was conceived named Revival Agricultural Plan. Like the two previous, the revival plan should promote the subsistence agriculture, increase industrial agriculture, and promote production for commercial purpose. The major innovation introduced was the distribution of responsibilities between the government and the private sector. The government had the role of conceiving the agricultural policy, coordinating agricultural activities, and creating basic infrastructures while private sector had to produce and commercialize the agricultural products. The main objectives to be achieved were the improvement of subsistence agriculture and the rural development. Three cities were chosen as poles of development for the rest of the country: Kinshasa, Lubumbashi and Kisangani. As

many other plans or programs, the revival agricultural plan failed to reach its objectives. The
smallness of the budget affected to the promotion of agriculture can explain why agricultural
programs or plans failed. Since 1970 up to 1995, the amount of money affected to agriculture
was very insignificant: less than 2 percent of the national budget.

With an average of 1 percent of the national budget affected to agriculture, this sector
could not meet the needs of populations in food. As said by Mawazo (2005) in his thesis,
agriculture even though declared the priority of priorities was more a slogan than a reality.
Although the existence of the various plans or programs to promote agriculture, the state of
roads considerably deteriorated particularly those linking the centres of production (rural
areas) to the centres of consumption (towns and cities). About more than 50 percent of roads
in Katanga province are in bad conditions. The unique exception is the road linking Lwena to
Malemba, which is in good state. Because of the bad state of roads, many entrepreneurs
hesitate to send their vehicles in rural areas to gather agricultural products in order to supply
urban centres in food.

Table 3. Evolution of budget affected to agriculture in million of American dollars

Year	National Budget	Budget affected to agriculture	Percentage
1970	600	6	1
1975	1,240	13,1	1.05
1980	1,500	17	1.13
1985	1,120	13	1.16
1990	960	8.7	0.90
1995	1,111	9.14	0.82

Source: Ministère de Finances et Budget 1995.

Food production in Katanga as well as in Lubumbashi city accuses a deficit. This means
that the demand of food largely surpasses the offer. In other words, Lubumbashi must import
food to feed its population. Imported food (maize, rice for example) is not accessible to all
Lubumbashi residents. One bag of 50kg of maize flour costs 16 American dollars. This is
almost the salary earned by a teacher at primary school. The lowest salary in education is FC
10,000 ($US 20) while the highest is FC 18,000 ($US 30). Therefore, the majority of
population resorts to various means in order to feed themselves. The most used being urban
agriculture.

Table 4. food production compared to Lubumbashi populations' needs (2003)

City	Maize in tons			Cassava in tons			Rice in tons		
	Production	Needs	Deficit	Production	Needs	Deficit	Production	Needs	Deficit
Lubumbashi	13,214	274,340	261,126	28,706	174,152	145,446	-	59,003	59,003

Source: Rapport Annuel/Inspection Régionale de l'Agriculture/Katanga 2003.

The above table reveals that Lubumbashi residents produce many crops such as maize,
cassava, but not rice. Although they produce the first two products, the quantity produced in

not sufficient to cover the all needs of the city. This means that the city must either import or buy from rural areas of the province about 261,706 tons of maize, 145,446 tons of cassava and 59,003 tons of rice to meet the needs of its populations. But considering the shortage in maize (506,278 tons) and rice (252,809 tons) at the province level, the only option is to import. The needs of Lubumbashi residents in cassava flour are satisfied by the surplus of production from Haut-Katanga and Lualaba districts.

1.1.2.4. The Effects of Recent Civil Wars (1996-97 and 1998-2002)

After the collapse of Gécamines, the principal provider of foreign currency, there has been emergence and expansion of informal economy, involving primary commodities, trade, transport, urban agriculture, construction, etc. The informal sector enabled tens of millions of Congolese to survive despite crumbling state services and economic crisis.

The recent civil wars disrupted the informal social and economic networks that had enabled Congolese to survive. Many slid further into poverty. Speaking about the devastating effect of insecurity in Eastern DRC, Nest (2006) lists rape, murder, assault, and looting by Interahamwe, Mai Mai, and antigovernment forces as means used that made villagers afraid to travel to their fields, causing a sharp reduction in agricultural output and food scarcity that contributed to poor health and high mortality rates. If cruelty was most stigmatized in the eastern part of the country, the rest of DRC like Katanga province was not less concerned. Villages were destroyed, people killed, and women raped in the north Katanga. The only way out was to flee to towns or cities more secured or to the neighbouring countries like Zambia, Tanzania, Burundi, etc. To sustain and expand their military capacity, the Rassemblement Congolais pour la Démocratie (RDC), Mouvement de Libaration du Congo (MLC), and the Mai Mai undertook economic activities including extortion, looting, taxation, of commerce, and the illicit production and trade of commodities. The colombo-tantalum (called coltan) production and trade by the rebel movement characterized the Congo war. Key element in manufacture of cell phones, computer chips, and pagers, the rise in international prices for this mineral occurred in 2000. According to Nest (2006:37), there is evidence that of the four main processing firms-one each in China, the United States, Kazakhstan, and Germany-the latter two received supplies of coltan originating from the DRC, although the German firm has denied this.

The first civil war started in 1996 and ended up in May 1997 when Laurent-Desiré Kabila took power. The goal pursued was to overthrow the Mobutu regime. According to Nest (2006: 31), the principal actors (Rwanda, Uganda, Burundi, AFDL, Banyamulenge, etc) entered the first civil war for different motives. These were complex and evolving combination of regime security, concern at preventing ethnic-based harassment and killings, grievances related to access to land and citizenship rights, domestic political leaders' interest in obtaining a "seat at the table" of a new post-Mobutu regime, and the desire by neighbouring governments to maintain their political dominance within the region (Rwanda, Uganda, and Burundi). Economic agendas became a prominent part of the conflict later on. The second conflict began in August 2, 1998. Its specific origins can be traced to President Laurent-Desiré Kabila's desire to become more independent from his Rwandan and Ugandan sponsors, as well as domestic discontent with the extent and pace of the government's political and economic reforms. But economic interests became significant for many actors in the war when they were unable to achieve an early victory and had to finance ongoing military campaigns (Nest 2006:31). The taking over of power by Joseph Kabila Kabange in

January 2001 after the assassination of President Laurent-Desiré Kabila has frozen the hostilities. A power sharing government of transition including different factions and interest groups (MLC, RCD, Mai-Mai, civil society, and political parties) was inaugurated in 2003 as a result of the inter-Congolese dialogue which was held in South Africa. Three years later (2006), elections were held with a financial and political support of the international community. Joseph Kabila Kabange was elected the President of the third Republic, and his party, le Parti du Peuple pour la Reconstruction et la Démocratie (PPRD) won 111 seats out of 500 in the new parliament.

These two wars were economically, socially, and politically devastating, particularly the second one. More than 4 million Congolese died. Peasants' farms were destroyed. Rural population was constrained to abandon their fields and villages for security reasons. Cities and towns like Lubumbashi, Kalemie, Kolwezi, Kamina, Kipushi, and Likasi in Katanga province received a huge number of the so-called "déplacés de guerre" (internal displaced of war). The presence of internal displaced of war increased insecurity in the city. Also, trains linking rural areas (principal suppliers of food) to urban areas (consumers) were suppressed. Rural settlements such as Kongolo, Nyunzu, Kabalo, Malemba-Nkulu, Bukama, etc (where maize crops were produced) were isolated from the main centres of consumption. Some roads and even bridges disappeared. Those that still exist are impracticable. The only way to supply cities and towns in maize flour as the staple food for the majority of Katangese populations was to import maize flour from Zambia, South Africa, or Tanzania. Poor urban population could not afford imported maize flour. This means that although the availability of maize flour on the market, large number of Lubumbashi dwellers had not access. Also, the fact that neighbouring provinces like oriental and occidental Kasai depended on Katanga province for food supply, this resulted in the increase of maize flour price on Katangese market. To cope with food insecurity, urban dwellers mainly resorted to urban agriculture and many other strategies.

The following table shows that there were internal displaced of war settled in the peri-urban areas such as Kamakanga, Yandisha, Dilefwe, Bulanda, and Kimba). In addition to food they had been receiving, internal displaced of war were encouraged to grow maize crops and vegetables. Thus, agricultural inputs and tools (hoes, long knives) were distributed. Other displaced were living within the city (Kenya, Kamalondo, Katubal, KatubalI, Diana, and Elakat). Even though they were not explicitly encouraged to undertake agricultural activities, some of them grew vegetables by their own initiatives.

Since the end of the second civil war marked by the power sharing government of transition (2003), roads are not yet repaired. Urban dwellers still resort for their survival to several activities such as selling on streets, prostitution and corruption, exchange of foreign currencies, small business, urban agriculture, and so on. People turned to urban agriculture for example for food, employment and cash income. Thus, open spaces (park, backyard, railways lines, roads, power lines, etc) are used mainly to grow vegetables. Even though most farmers practice agriculture in the city for home consumption, part of the produce is sold.

Table 5. Displaced of war (in the city of Lubumbashi and its surroundings)

Sites	People Displaced
Kenya	1,542
Kamalondo	587
KatubaI	375
KatubaII	729
Diana	313
Elakat	460
Kamakanga	1,630
Yandisha	1,641
Dilefwe	1,969
Bulanda	1,597
Kimba	1,375
Total	21,218

Sources: Commissariat Général à la Reinsertion/Province du Katanga 2000.

1.2. Pull Factors

Urban agriculture is not only the consequence of a combination of several factors which pushed Lubumbashi inhabitants to resort to this kind of activity. It is also a solution to the urban unemployment, food insecurity, and urban poverty issues. The literature on this sector acknowledges its rich potential. Therefore, the practice of agriculture in the city is encouraged as a coping mechanism for poverty alleviation.

1.2.1. Urban Agriculture as Source of Employment

When speaking of Gécamines, it was demonstrated that since colonial period (1884-1960) up to the 1990s this mining company dominated not only the local, but also the national economy of DRC as the principal provider of foreign currency. Its collapse deprived the city of its resources and resulted in the closure of many companies in the province. As a result the number of unemployed people, which was already high, increased drastically. In his inaugural speech (December 2006), President Joseph Kabila acknowledged that only 20 per cent of active population constitutes the workforce in the country. To survive people undertake various socio-economic activities. The informal sector is very much in demand. It is currently the most important sector in DRC in terms of number of people involved in (more than 70 per cent). Among activities undertaken by urban dwellers there are small business, selling on street, urban agriculture, exchange of foreign currency, shops, public phones, etc. By considering the number of people involved in food production, the surface of urban land under cultivation, and the contribution to urban food demands, urban agriculture is the most practiced activity in the city of Lubumbashi.

According to the World Bank survey conducted in 2003, of more than 10,000 Gécamines workers retrenched, more than 54 per cent had agriculture as their substitute economic activity. The practice of urban agriculture started long before the retrenchment. During the long period of no salary, the majority of workers practiced agriculture in the city by growing vegetables and maize crop. Petit's (2003) survey confirms the fact when it reveals that one head of household out of six in Lubumbashi declares being involved in farming. Also, the number of agricultural associations supported by NGOs increases each year. World Vision DRC for example, distributed agricultural inputs including fertilizer and maize seed to 19 associations in 2003 and to 25 associations in 2004 and 2005. Each association comprising 25 households, this means that a total of 475 farming households (in 2003), 675 in 2004 and again 675 in 2005 received material support from this international NGO of relief and development. SADRI (Service d'Appui au Développement Integré) did the same in 2004 by distributing seeds and fertilizer to 26 agricultural associations representing 650 households.

1.2.2. Urban Agriculture as Source of Food and Income

The traditional agriculture has failed to satisfy urban food demands. This is due to a combination of several factors such as civil wars, economic crisis and lack of adequate agriculture policies, declining productivity and poor distribution systems. To meet the urban food needs, urban residents grow themselves various crops. During the interview it was noticed that three quarters of each yard in the largest ward of the city (Annexe) are occupied by gardens. On almost all vacant spaces (along roads, power lines, railways, etc) are grown crops. The common crops cultivated in the city of Lubumbashi are maize, beans, peanut, sweet potatoes, and vegetables. Maize production is not enough because of the smallness of plots' size. This is not the case for vegetables. The city of Lubumbashi has become self-sufficient in vegetables. This means that almost 100 per cent of vegetables consumed by Lubumbashi residents are produced within and around the city. According to the local Director of FAO, the quantity of vegetables produced is too abundant that it affects the price. Some cooperatives experience some difficulties to sell their produce because of the abundance and the low price practiced on the market. The abundance of vegetables can be explained by the fact that vegetables are alternatively cultivated all over the year.

Most of farmers in Lubumbashi are so poor that they practice urban agriculture for home-consumption. It is also true that part of their produce is sold to meet their basic needs. While low-income households produce primarily for own-consumption, middle- and high-income households produce for commercial reasons. The contribution of urban agriculture to urban food demands has been demonstrated by many social scientists in different African cities. In Bamako for example, the UNDP (1996) reports that 100 per cent of vegetables consumed are produced within and around the city. In other words, Bamako (Mali) is self-sufficient in vegetables. Concerning particularly vegetables, it can be said the same for Dakar and Kampala which are self-sufficient at 70 per cent while Accra is self-sufficient at 90 per cent and Guinea-Bissau self-sufficient at 90 per cent in poultry meat and eggs (Maxwell 1994, Moustier and Mbaye 1999). The case of the International Relations Professor at the University of Lubumbashi illustrates how urban agriculture can be a source of income. To pay an air-ticket in order to join his supervisor who was living in Kinshasa (more than 2000 km away from Lubumbashi), he grew ground nuts just beyond the faculty of social sciences. From the selling of his product he bought not only the air-ticket, but also a second-hand car he transformed into a taxi the following year.

1.3. Facilitating Factors

For push and pull factors to operate, there must be existence of what I call facilitating factors such as availability of land, positive attitude of municipal officials, market proximity, and support from NGOs. For this activity of rural areas to take place in the city, the attitude of municipal officials plays an important role. When the attitude is positive, urban agriculture is promoted and when it is not, UA encounters resistance. In general, Lubumbashi officials have positive attitude towards urban agriculture except in some areas of Ruashi ward. In Matoleo and Shindaika areas only vegetables are allowed to be grown. If an inhabitant grows maize crops, these are immediately destroyed. The reason is that maize crops attract mosquitoes which are at the origin of malaria. Most of the residents in these two areas grow only vegetables, sweet potatoes and beans.

Whatever the attitude of officials, the availability of land is the most important factor required for urban food production to take place. It must be said that land in the city is not for agricultural purpose. From November up to April, the city of Lubumbashi becomes a green belt zone. Everywhere in the city except the city centre, vegetables, maize, beans, sweet potatoes, peanut are grown. These crops are cultivated mostly in backyard, in the peri-urban zones and on any vacant space in the city. Urban agriculture is the dominant activity in Annexe ward and most parts of Katuba and Ruashi wards. The specificity of these wards is that they possess enough opened spaces. Almost each yard in Annexe ward has got a garden which occupies in most cases three quarters of the yard. The campus of the University of Lubumbashi for example, is surrounded by farms. Students like other categories of people practice urban agriculture. Along the railway separating Kamalondo ward from Kampemba ward, people grow maize crops, beans, peanut, vegetables and sweet potatoes. In Kamalondo police camp, a public road separating the camp from the rest of the ward serves as land on which vegetables are grown. Even though farmers still have land to cultivate, this is not enough to satisfy their demand of land. That is the reason why more and more urban farmers are moving either from backyard gardens to the peri-urban farms, or from the city to the surrounding villages.

Lubumbashi farmers benefit from a positive attitude of officials in general and have land on which to cultivate crops even though there is competitiveness with other urban activities like development and housing. The other facilitating factor is the existence of market in the neighbourhood. Contrary to rural populations who need to evacuate their produce from the centre of production (rural areas) to the centre of consumption (towns and cities), urban farmers have the advantage to have the market in their proximity. Distribution systems operate without any problem because the centre of production is at the same time the centre of consumption. In most cases farmers become vendors of their own produce. Sometimes vendors come to buy agricultural products at harvesting period.

The last factor and not the less that facilitates the emergence of urban agriculture in addition to push and pull factors is the support that farmers receive from NGOs and some development agencies. There are more than 40 NGOs in Lubumbashi, but only ten are involved in the promotion of agriculture in the city. Urban farmers receive tools, seeds, and fertilizers. Sometimes, NGOs organize training session to equip farmers with modern techniques in order to increase their productivity. Material support from NGOs like World Vision Congo, SADRI (Service d'Appui au Développpement Integré) and many small NGOs allow hundreds of farming households to increase their capacity of production. Some farmers who previously were farming just for own-consumption are now producing for cash purpose.

2. Importance of Urban Agriculture in Africa

The importance of UA is in relation with its contribution to urban food security. To measure its importance, researchers consider the following indexes: (1) the proportion of urban dwellers that produce food (Table 6 demonstrating the significance of urban food production), (2) the proportion of foods that come from production within and/or around the city (Table 7 focusing on the contribution of UA to urban food demand), and (3) the proportion of urban and peri-urban land under cultivation (Table 8 considering the dimension of urban land under cultivation). To constitute this section, I principally refered to Smith's (2002: 23, 24) chapter entitled *Overview of urban agriculture and food security in West African cities* in which are recorded data from several authors. This has the advantage of giving an overview of the phenomenon of urban agriculture in Africa. Also, I gathered data from other social scientists in order to highlight the dimension of lands under cultivation in some African cities. As it appears, urban agriculture is an economic activity in rapid expansion in Africa. This expansion is mostly due to the rapid population growth, which exercises a strong pressure on urban land.

The proportion of African people engaged in urban food production is high and still increasing. The highest proportion (table 6) reaches 80 per cent of the urban population. With 80 per cent in Zaria (Nigeria) and Harare (Zimbabwe), and 75 per cent in Kano (Cameroun), this means that urban farmers come from different categories of population, and not only from low-income households. According to the urban agriculture literature, most of these urban farmers are women. About 20 to 60 per cent of African people are involved in farming in the city (Anon 1996; Moustier 1998; Smith 2002).

Table 6. Significance of urban food production

City	Proportion of urban dwellers involved in urban agriculture (%)
Dar es Salaam (Tanzania)	44-70
Harare (Zimbabwe)	80
Kampala (Uganda)	25-57
Kano (Nigeria)	75
Kumasi (Ghana)	25
Lusaka (Zambia)	45-60
Nairobi (Kenya)	29 (Higher proportions found in smaller towns 57 in Kitui, 30 in Mombasa)
Ouagadougou (Burkinafaso)	36
Yaounde (Cameroun)	35
Zaria (Nigeria)	80

Source: Smith 2002:24.

Urban agriculture has rendered certain African cities such as Bamako (Mali), Guinea-Bissau (Guinea-Bissau), Accra (Ghana) and even Dakar (Senegal) self-sufficient in vegetables. As the above table (7) shows, urban farmers sell part of their produce even though they mostly produce for home consumption. It is argued that UA contributes to producers' well-being in different ways including cash-saving, income generation, nutrition, health, and employment

Table 7. Contribution to urban food demands by urban producers

City	Proportion of demands supplied
Dakar (Senegal)	70% of vegetables
Bamako (Mali)	100% of vegetables, 50% of poultry products
Accra (Ghana)	90% of vegetables
Guinea-Bissau (Guinea Bissau	90% of leafy vegetables
Kampala (Uganda)	70% of poultry meat and eggs
Singapore	80% of vegetables, 25% of poultry meat
Shangai	76% of vegetables

Source: Smith 2002:24.

Land in the city is not designed for agricultural purposes. But there is more and more urban lands used for agricultural activities. Table (8) below reveals that the largest dimension of urban land under cultivation reaches 50 to 66 per cent (Kampala and Zaria). For the whole African continent, about 20 to 60 per cent of urban lands are in agricultural use (UNDP 1996). Concerning particularly the city of Lubumbashi, about 21 to 25 per cent of its lands were under agricultural use in 1987 (Bruneau and Bukame 1987), today this might double as most of Annexe (the largest ward in Lubumbashi city) inhabitants are farmers

Table 8. Dimension of urban land under cultivation

City	Proportion of land under cultivation (%)	Source
Dar es Salaam (Tanzania)	23	DSM/ARDHI, 1992
Harare (Zimbabwe)	15-29	Mbiba, 1995
Kampala (Uganda)	50	Mougeot, 1994
Zaria (Nigeria)	66	UNDP, 1996
Lubumbashi (DRC)	21-25	Bruneau and Bukome, 1987

The importance of urban farming is also well estimated when evaluated in comparison with households' expenses on foodstuffs. Gathered data from authors such as Lee-Smith et al (1987); Diallo and Coulibally (1988); Khouri-Dagher (1987); Sawio (1993); and Pain (1985), helped Tiker (1994: 10-11) to illustrate that importance by giving some figures. For example, poor urban Kenyan households spent 40-50 % on food and cooking fuel alone in 1987. In 1983, surveyed households in Bamako spent 32-64% of their average income on food and cooking. In Egypt, food represents 60% of family budgets for more than 50% of all urban households. In Dar es Salaam, the percentage of income spent on food rocketed from 50% in

1940 to 85% in 1980. In Kinshasa, in 1982, food purchases were already absorbing an average 60% of total household spending. Quoting Young (1985: 2), Tinker showed that city dwellers of five developing countries surveyed paid 10-30% more for their food than rural dwellers.

3. LUBUMBASHI FARMERS

3.1. Demographic Characteristics

Variables such as sex and age of urban farmers are mostly referred to in the urban agriculture literature. The analysis of these variables is necessary for comparison reasons. Studies were carried out in different African cities such as Harare, Lusaka, Nairobi, Dar es Salaam, etc. In addition to sex and age of farmers, I have added the size of the household because of its implication on the weight of work to be carried out or the amount of money to be spent on food.

As figure 1 below reveals, women and men practice urban agriculture in the city of Lubumbashi. The majority of urban farmers are women (55%). That there are more women than men (45%) in UA confirms similar findings in other cities like Dar-es Salaam (Sawio 1994) and Nairobi (Freeman 1991). Social scientists such as Tripp (1990), Mvena *et al.* (1991), Sanyal (1984), Lee smith *et al.* (1987), and Mazwell and Zziwa 1992) cited in Sawio (1994: 30) noticed in their studies the predominance of women in urban food production. This may be explained by the fact that traditionally women are responsible for the household's food provision. For having a lower level of education, most of the women have more difficulties in finding other kind of employment (Obudho and Foeken 1999).

As age profile of the respondents who participated in the interviews, it can be pointed out that the largest proportions of respondents (more than 57%) were in the 35-54 age groups (table 9). Few farmers (23%) were in the higher age-groups (more than 55 years old).

With an average of six children per farming household, figure 2 below demonstrates that only 29% of households had less than 5 children, meaning that 63% had a higher number of children (varying between 5 and more than 8).The rest of the households (8%) were without children when the interviews were conducted.

respondents' sex

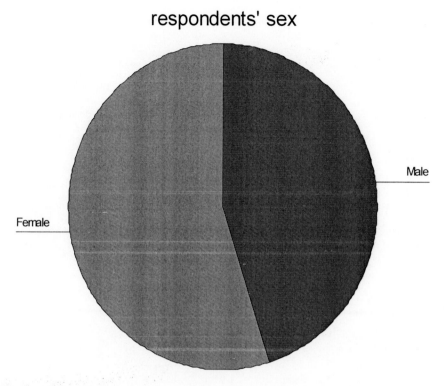

Figure 1. Distribution of farmers by sex.

Table 9. Distribution of Urban Farmers by Age

Group-age	Number
25-34	20
35-44	28
45-54	29
55-64	19
65 and more	4
Total	100

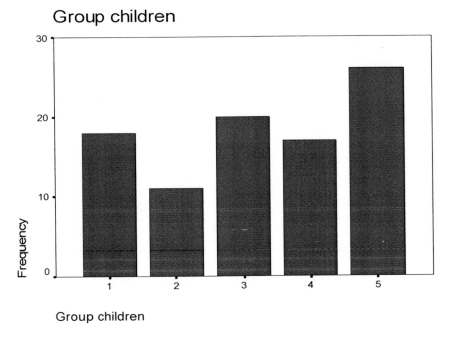

Figure 2. Respondents' number of children.

In his survey carried out in the city of Lubumbashi, Petit (2000) stated that a household of six members spent more than 60% of the income on food. This means that the more a household has children the more it has to spend on food. This was also pointed out by Sawio (1994:35) in his study on Dar es Salaam that the number of persons in household influences the amount of food consumed in the household and also the amount of labor the household can expend on UA.

3.2. Socio-economic Characteristics

Farmers were asked to describe their area of residence in order to fit it in between the unplanned, planned or residential. The unplanned area of residence (Annexe, parts of Ruashi and Katuba wards) is where the norm of urbanism is not applied. In that area there is generally lack of electricity, running water and other basic infrastructures. A high level of poverty is also observed. By contrast, the planned area (corresponding to the former indigenous cities occupied by black people: Kenya, Kamalondo, and Ruashi) possesses basic infrastructures even though most of them are now desegregated. People still have running water, electricity and housing. Finally, the residential area is what white people formerly occupied (Lubumbashi ward and Bel-air area). This area has the advantage of being cleaned and secured. It possesses the enviable infrastructures of the city like roads, hospitals, schools, etc.

According to table (10) below, the urban farmers are unequally distributed in the three areas (unplanned, planned and residential). Most of the farmers were living in unplanned areas (58%) corresponding to the Annexe and parts of Ruashi and Katuba wards. About 33%

of other farmers were living in planned areas of Ruashi, Kampemba, Kamalondo, and Kenya wards. And very few farmers (9%) were living in residential areas of Lubumbashi ward and part of Kampemba ward, particularly Bel-air. Contrary to Sawio's study (1994) in which it is pointed out that most of farmers in Dar es Salaam (Tanzania) were living in the planned area, the unplanned area was the most occupied by Lubumbashi farmers. The finding confirms the summary given by Okike (2002) about urban agriculture. According to this author, most of urban farmers produce food mostly for home consumption and most of them live in the peri-urban areas where land scarcity is not as acute as the city centers.

This table shows that there is a strong concentration of urban farmers of both sex in the unplanned areas representing Annexe, and parts of Katuba and Ruashi wards (32% of female farmers and 26% of males). The presence of farmers becomes less important in planned areas (22% of women and 11% of men), and much less important in residential areas (1% of women and 8% of men). As it appears, the number of farmers is decreasing from unplanned to residential areas through planned areas. This means that the more there are low-income groups in an area more likely the chance to find farmers increases.

Table 10. Distribution of farmers (%) by area of residence by sex

Typeof residence	Respondents' sex		Number
	Male	Female	
Residential	8	1	9
Planned	11	22	33
Unplanned	26	32	58
Total	45	55	100

3.2.1. Provenance of Farmers

In order to find out where farmers were living the last 10 years, the following question was asked: *where were you living the last ten years?* Table 11 below indicates that most farmers (94%) came from urban settlements. Only 6% declared coming from villages. This clearly shows that urban farmers are not necessarily the newcomers in the city. Some had been or are still working as miners (in Gécamines), public servants, teachers, etc before their involvement in farming.

Table 11. Previous residences of farmers 10 years ago

Previous residences	Number of farmers
Never change	11
From another commune	64
From another city	16
From another province	3
From village	6
Total	100

Table 11 indicates that 75% of farmers have been living in the city of Lubumbashi since the last decade, from which 11% were living in the same ward and 64 coming from other wards.

Only 16% of farmers declared coming from other cities of the province like Likasi, Kolwezi and Kipushi. Very few farmers (6%) acknowledged coming from surrounding villages (Kaponda, Kikanda, Katanga, etc).

3.2.2. Professional Background

People involved in urban agriculture were from different professional backgrounds. Thus, police officers of Kamalondo ward, primary and secondary school teachers, public servants from local administration, workers from different local companies, especially Gecamines and SNCC, street vendors, business persons, etc were involved in the practice of cultivation or raising livestock.

Figure 3 demonstrates that 27% of urban farmers are workers (most of them were from mining companies, and also public servants, police officers, teachers) while 23% were essentially farmers. The rest of the population interviewed was either practicing small business (20%) or doing something else in addition to growing food crops or raising livestock. As it appears, urban farmers in the city of Lubumbashi practice two or more activities in addition to their main economic activity.

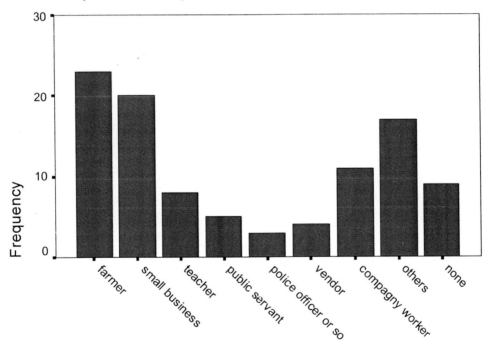

Figure 3. Professional background of farmers.

3.2.3. Level of Education of Urban Farmers

Table 12. Distribution of farmers by level of education

Level of education	Number
Primary	21
Secondary	67
Tertiary	12
Total	100

It can be concluded from this table that urban farmers were unequally distributed across the three education levels. 79% of the respondents were educated of whom 67% were of secondary school level and 12% of tertiary school. 21% of farmers did only the primary school. Among the 67% of the secondary school, 36% were women who most of them did only the first two years of the secondary school.

3.2.4. Income of Farmers

Table 13. Income of Urban Farmers per month ($US1= Fc 500)

Income earned	Number	Percent
D/K	24	24.0
0-5000 Fc	9	9.0
5001-10000 Fc	9	9.0
10001-15000 Fc	7	7.0
15001-20000 Fc	9	9.0
20001-25000 Fc	9	9.0
More than 25001 Fc	33	33.0
Total	100	100.0

This table shows at once glance that the majority of farmers (67%) earned a very small amount of money to survive (less than $US 51 per month). 24% of farmers were unable to remember how much they were spending per month as they were living on day-to-day basis. Only 33% of the farmers were earning more than $US 50 per month, reaching for some of them $US 2000 per month.

Considering the smallness of their earnings, Lubumbashi residents cultivate food crops or raise livestock either to supplement the meager wage or salary they earn or to supply their households with food and also to generate some income.

3.2.5. Members of Households Involved in Food Production

Interviewees were asked to describe other household members involved in the growing of food crops. Apart from wife and husband as the main actors, to some extent children at a certain age were included. Adult relatives such as aunts, uncles, nephews, nieces, cousins were employed in UA. Some high-income households used domestic workers, security guards, and mostly farm workers to cultivate crops and raise livestock. The last category of workers was especially used in big size farms.

As it appears, UA is an activity that includes all members of the household. But it is dominated by parents where both exist or by one parent when the second does not exist. Even in the case where husband and wife were both involved in farming, in many households women were the main producers (figure 1).

3.2.6. Experience of Farmers in Farming

Table 14. Time in farming-scale

Years in farming	Number of farmers	Percent
Less than 1year	14	14.0
1-5 years	48	48.0
6-10 years	28	28.0
11-15 years	6	6.0
16-20 years	4	4.0
More than 21 years	10	10.0
Total	100	100.0

As this table indicates, the majority of respondents (76%) had an experience varying between 1 and 10 years in farming. About 20% of farmers had more than 10 years of experience in farming. Almost 10 percent of the respondents acknowledged having been practicing UA since the 1980s. This period corresponds to the implementation of the structural adjustment measures that left many people without job. Many workers in public administration and public enterprises were dismissed. Student scholarships were cut off, transport facilities suppressed and canteens closed by the Mobutu government in 1984 as consequence of the implementation of the structural adjustment policies.

If most of the Lubumbashi residents started farming during the 1990s, this is due to a combination of many factors including economic crisis as consequence of the structural adjustment measures imposed to the Democratic Republic of Congo by the IFM and the World Bank (1984), the pillages that occurred in every Congolese city and town (1991 and 1993), the closure of many companies in Lubumbashi because of the collapse of Gécamines enterprise. At the regional level, there was a severe shortage in food production in Zimbabwe as well as in Zambia where maize flour was particularly imported. In addition, the 1990s were also characterized by two civil wars (1996-1997 and 1998-2001). Peasants were no more able to cultivate. For more than three years, trains stopped carrying agricultural produces from rural areas to cities and towns.

3.3. Production of Food and Livestock Raised

3.3.1. Main Food Crops Cultivated and Livestock Raised

Answering the question about the main food crops cultivated and livestock raised in the city of Lubumbashi, farmers listed the following: maize, sweet potatoes, beans, peanut and vegetables as crops; and sheep, goat, pig, and chickens as livestock. Lubumbashi farmers were cultivating several kinds of food crops mostly for home consumption and commercial reasons. Maize is the mostly cultivated followed by vegetables. The reason may be the fact that maize flour is the staple food for most Lubumbashi residents. Vegetables are more and more part of Lubumbashi residents' diet, and also generate some income.

In-depth question consisted in knowing the reason of the preference for those crops. Answers from this question gave more insight. Firstly, maize as the most cultivated crop is grown for different reasons depending on the socioeconomic status of farmers. Most farmers living in Annexe, large parts of Katuba and Ruashi wards were cultivating maize for home consumption. The quantity produced was generally insufficient to cover the household food needs. Therefore, they could not pretend to sell part of their produce. If this is true for low-income groups, it is not the case for those with high income. The latter was cultivating maize for commercial reasons while the middle-income groups were cultivating maize crop for home consumption and income generation. Secondly, the cultivation of sweet potatoes was justified by farmers of low-income category by the fact that it was giving them the possibility to link the previous and the coming harvesting seasons. Farmers declared that the period before the next harvest (November, December, January, February, March, April, even May) was characterized by food scarcity, high food prices, and therefore food insecurity in the city. Sweet potatoes were mostly consumed during this period. This crop might be sold for money, but it was considered by many farmers as a strategic reserve food for period of food insecurity. This was not the case for peanut, which was generally grown to generate income. Those of farmers involved in cultivating beans did so for home consumption and also for income generation when the quantity produced was sufficient. Thirdly, the growing of vegetables had two main purposes; home consumption and income generation.

In addition, few Lubumbashi farmers were raising livestock. For example, only 37% of farmers were raising chickens. About 55 per cent of Lubumbashi farmers acknowledged not raising livestock. Apart from chickens raised for commercial reasons, very few people were raising pig (particularly in Kenya ward), sheep, and goat in their houses.

During the visits of farming households, I constantly noticed the presence of fruit trees in many yards. Mango tree was the most cultivated followed by avocado tree.

It can be said that a household logic was beyond the growing of food crops in the city of Lubumbashi. There were crops grown for home consumption and commercial reasons (for example, maize, peanut, and beans). By contrast, crops like vegetables were particularly grown for home consumption. Sweet potatoes seemed the most strategic food crop cultivated by farmers as food reserve for the period of food insecurity. This denotes an evident rationality for farmers. In other words, crops were not grown by accident.

3.3.2. Spaces under Cultivation

A question was asked to farmers to indicate the area in which food crops were grown. As table 15 below reveals, 30% of farmers were growing food crops on open spaces (along roads, railways, under electric power lines), other 30% were cultivating in the peri-urban zones of the city, 23% of farming households were doing so in the surrounding villages, and 17% practiced only backyard gardens. Almost all farmers were growing vegetables in their yards. This is the reason why Bukome and Bruneau (1987), focused their study on backyard gardens. Here, it can be noticed that yard and periphery of the city (semi-urban areas) were the most common spaces where food crops were grown. In their search of much more available lands, some farmers were moving from the city to the surrounding villages (Kikanda, Kaponda, etc).

Of course, urban farmers might cultivate at two different places, for example on backyard and at the periphery of the city. It is important to point out that the periphery in question is part of the Annexe ward. This means that people growing food crops in the Annexe ward are not necessary from this ward even though most of them were residents. People from other wards were attracted by the availability of lands.

Table 15. Spaces under cultivation

Areas of cultivation	Number	Percent
Yard only	17	17.0
Around the city and yard	30	30.0
Surrounding villages and yard	23	23.0
Open spaces and yard	30	10.0
Total	100	100.0

3.3.3. Size of Maize Farms

Even though maize is the staple food and the most cultivated crop by Lubumbashi residents, its size was generally small and varied according to the (i) space where cultivation occurred (small or large spaces), (ii) the reasons for which it was cultivated (home consumption or income generation), and (iii) the category of farmers practicing it (low-, middle- or high-income groups). The size of maize farm was bigger (more than 150 square meters) when it was cultivated in abandoned farms or former farms surrounding the city or when maize was cultivated in the surrounding villages (Kapenda, Kafubu, Kikanda, etc). Most of farmers who were involved were from high-income groups. Their main reason was to make money. By contrast, the smallness size of farms can be explained by the fact that most farmers interviewed were poor and were cultivating it in their own yard and/or around it. The farm size increased from the moment there was a move from yard to the periphery of the city (along railways, around Luano Airport, under power lines). It became much important when crops were cultivated in rural areas (surrounding villages or in the abandoned farms). There, farmers found enough spaces to cultivate food crops. About 85% of farmers were cultivating maize on a small surface of less than 101 square meters. Only 15% of farmers did more.

Despite the meager harvest of maize crops, the majority of farming households were still growing this crop. Question was asked to find out the reason. One farmer from Kimbembe area in Annexe ward pointed out the social status this conferred to farmers: *even though maize farming does not give what is expected, it is better to cultivate maize if you want to be considered a farmer.* This answer reveals that maize as a staple food for Lubumbashi residents was cultivated not only for food and income, but also for its social status conferred to farmers.

Table 16. Dimension of maize farms

Size	Number	Percent
Less than 50 square meter	45	45.0
51-100 square meter	30	30.0
101-150 square meter	19	19.0
151-200 square meter	6	6.0
Total	100	100.0

3.3.4. Quantity of Maize Produced, Consumed and Sold

Table 17. Quantity of maize produced (2004)

Quantity of maize (bag sac of 50kg)	Number of households	Percentage
Less than 1 sac	23	23
1-10 sacs	48	48
11-20 sacs	10	10
21 and more	4	4
N/A	11	11
Missing	4	4

Table 18. Quantity of maize monthly consumed

Quantity of maize (bag sac of 50kg)	Number of households	Percentage
Less than 1 sac	44	44
1-5 sacs	31	31
6-10 sacs	6	6
11-15 sacs	3	3
N/A	11	11
Missing	4	4

Table 19. Quantity of maize sold

Quantity of maize (bag sac of 50kg)	Number of households	Percentage
Less than 1 sac	3	3
1-5 sacs	24	24
6-10 sacs	7	7
11-15 sacs	3	3
16 and more	3	3
N/A	11	11
Missing	44	44

Considering the importance of maize in the diet of Lubumbashi population and the status it confers, it was necessary to find out the quantity of maize produced, consumed and sold by the farming households.

Table (17) related to the quantity of maize produced the year before reveals that an insignificant quantity of maize was produced. In fact, 71% of the farming households produced less than 11 sacs of maize while 23% harvested less than one sac of maize a year. Only 4 households were able to produce more than 21 sacs, meaning less than 2 sacs of maize per month. As table 17 points out, 11 households started cultivating only during the year of interview. Therefore, they could not answer the question concerning the quantity of maize produced last year. The missing case is about households that cultivated other food crops than maize, for example vegetables.

Consequently, table (18) related to the quantity of maize monthly consumed reveals that 44% of households consumed less than one sac of maize flour per month regardless their size. Most of these households afford two or three meals a day only during the harvesting period, which lasts three or four months (from June to September).

Because priority was given to home consumption, only 13% (table 19) of households could sell 6 sacs of maize per year or more. The missing cases (44%) in table 19 concern households, which were cultivating just for their own consumption.

Despite the insignificance of their production, 77 per cent of households declared feeding their members through urban agriculture. But only 56% acknowledged improving their living conditions through urban agriculture. This reveals how crucial self-production is for the survival of this population. Even though farmers noticed a small improvement in their diet, this was in comparison with the 1990s, which was characterized by severe food insecurity. More than one farmer remained nostalgic of the prosperous period of Gécamines.

3.4. Benefits from Farming

Question was asked to respondents to identify the reasons why they have been cultivating. As indicates table 20 below, 60% of farmers were cultivating for food and money. 34% were doing so for food only. Very few people (6%) were practicing urban agriculture for money only.

Table 20. Households' benefits from farming

Benefits	Number
Food	33
Money	6
Food and Money	60
Others	1
Total	100

From the respondents' answers, three types of urban agriculture emerge in the city of Lubumbashi. The first one can be called "a survival urban agriculture." Low-income groups are the most involved in this kind of urban agriculture. It is practiced on small spaces (in yard or around the yard), meaning in the city. The survival urban agricultural is dominated by backyard gardens. The majority of farmers practicing this category of urban agriculture live in Annexe ward, large parts of Katuba and Ruashi wards, and also in almost all the suburbs of each Lubumbashi ward. Vegetables are the crops generally grown. The second category of urban agriculture is "semi-capitalist" in the sense that it is practiced not only for home consumption, but also to generate income. It is mostly practiced by the middle-income groups. Here, urban agriculture is mainly considered as source of income. This kind of agriculture is undertaken in the semi-urban areas, like around Luano airport, Kilobelobe concession of RTNC television, along Kipushi, Likasi, and Kasumbalesa roads. Some of the farmers in this category were benefiting some support from NGOs. Contrary to the first category, in the second category, farmers have enough lands to exploit for agricultural activities. And the last category can be called "capitalist urban agriculture". This category of urban agriculture is specifically dominated by the high-income groups of Lubumbashi residents. The main reasons being commercial, it is practiced on large surfaces, mostly in abandoned or former farms surrounding the city. Maize is the dominant crop grown. Few people are involved in this kind of urban agriculture because it requires hiring workers or the use of machine.

From the above table (20), it can be noted that most Lubumbashi farmers have been moing from simple home consumption as reason of cultivating to home consumption and income generation. Cultivating uniquely for money, very few farmers have reached this category.

3.4.1. Daily Expenditure on Food per Household

In the attempt to measure the importance of UA in the city of Lubumbashi, it was asked the question about the amount of money daily spent on food per household. The question gave insight on why many Lubumbashi residents engage in UA.

The table (21) below suggests that the highest amount of money that a farming household spent on food was more than 2 American dollars per day. But because most of them (61%) were poor, all they could spend on food was less than 2 American dollars in order to feed themselves and their household members.

Considering the average size of a household (eight members) and the high number of respondents with less than Fc 25,000 ($US 50) as income per month, urban agriculture becomes a real source of food and income.

One police officer declared: *"With Fc 5000 ($US 10) I earn as salary even though I don't pay rent it is impossible to feed my wife, my seven children and four grandchildren. Therefore I have to grow vegetables in front of the yard while my wife grows maize plants at Kilobelobe,"*

Table 21. Food expenditure per day ($US1= Fc 500)

Expenditure per day	Number of farmers	Percent
0-200 Fc	1	1.0
401-600 Fc	14	14.0
601-800 Fc	17	17.0
801-1000 Fc	29	29.0
1001-1200 Fc	5	5.0
More than 1201 Fc	34	34.0
Total	100	100.0

3.4.2. Diet of Urban Farmers

Table 22. Number of meals consumed in household per day

Number of meals per day	Number of farmers	Percent
1	56	56.0
2	39	39.0
3	5	5.0
Total	100	100.0

This table reveals that most of farmers (56%) had one meal a day. Only 5% of respondents were able to have three meals a day. The rest of farmers (39%) had two meals a day. With more than a half of urban farmers of the sample having only one meal a day, these data reveal the level of poverty that characterizes Lubumbashi farmers. This also reveals how important UA is for the survival of these categories of people.

The harvesting period (from June to September) was the period where most farmers could eat twice even three times a day. In Shindaika area located in Ruashi ward, one farmer stated: *"tunakuliaka muzuri mpaka wakati tukonavuna"* (we only eat well when we start reaping: from June to September). Crops plants corresponding to the harvesting period (between June and September) are maize, sweet potatoes, and peanut. On the contrary, local vegetables (matembele, lengalenga, ngaingai) are alternatively grown all over the year.

3.4.3. Daily Menu

Respondents were asked to answer the question about food frequently consumed in their household. 97 percent of respondents affirmed eating pap of maize flour (locally called bukali[2]). Rice is generally eaten during the festivity season (Christmas, for example).

Pap of maize flour is often consumed with bitoyo (local salted fish) or ndakala (local small fry). Vegetables grown within or around the yard are generally served with bitoyo or ndakala. In many poor households visited, pap of maize was sometimes consumed without bitoyo or ndakala, but served with only vegetables (ngaingai, lengalenga, matembele). This is to show that poverty has reached such a level that people are unable to buy even local fish. Emphasizing the importance of bukali (pap of maize flour) in Lubumbashi residents diet, one respondent from Kimbembe area (in Annexe ward) said: *"kama muntu yebado kulia bukali ata anakula kintu kyengine, ikosawahayakula bado"* (if somebody does not yet eat pap, even though (s)he has eaten something else, it is like (s)he does not yet eat).

From this emphasis, it must be understood that when farmers say they eat once a day, this means eating pap of maize flour. They may have eaten something like sweet potatoes, but they consider it not yet eating.

3.4.4. Self-sufficiency in Vegetables

The insignificance of maize production for most farmers cannot hide the fact that almost each farmer grows vegetables in Lubumbashi city (locally called lengalenga, matembele, bibwabwa, ngaingai, etc). The Director of FAO based in Lubumbashi acknowledged during

---

[2] The local food called Bukari is prepared by special processing of maize into flour, which is pour into boiling water and turn into a paste.

the interview that Lubumbashi residents were self-sufficient in vegetables. They could any more import vegetables from Zambia, except fresh tomatoes. According to this local FAO Director, vegetables were grown all over the year. This is one of the reasons why vegetables prices on the market are very low. During the rain season, farmers cultivate matembele, lengalenga, bibwabwa, ngaingai while during dry season they mostly cultivate cabbage for commercial reasons.

CONCLUSION

This chapter tried to show that the question of poverty in the city particularly in Africa must be taken seriously. Poverty is not necessarily relative in city because of the presence of infrastructure and investments and absolute in rural areas because of their absence. More critically, with more people to be living in African cities and towns in the two coming decades, poverty and food insecurity could exacerbate.

In the meantime, urban dwellers are not passive. They use different means as coping mechanisms for their survival. It is in this context that agricultural activities are taking place within and around many African cities. The proportion of urban residents engaged in food production, the quantity of foods produced and the surfaces of urban land under cultivation prove that urban agriculture is currently one of the most practiced informal activities in Africa.

Therefore it was indispensable to found out who is practicing this activity, what is produced or raised and for which purpose, taking the city of Lubumbashi in DRC as a case of illustration. It is worth noting that many studies have been carried out in East and West Africa. This study confirms findings from other African cities. There are more women than men involved in urban agriculture in the city of Lubumbashi. Although the female predominance, urban farmers come from all socio-economic categories (low-income, middle and high-income groups) for different reasons even though the majority is from the low-income groups. If for the low-income groups, home consumption is the main reason of their involvement, for the middle- and mostly the high-income groups, commercial reasons justify their engagement in food production. In the city of Lubumbashi, maize crop and vegetables are the most cultivated. Since then, Lubumbashi city has become self-sufficient in vegetables.

As land in the city is not designed for agricultural activities, conflicts often occur between farmers and developers. Most of Lubumbashi farmers have been now moving from backyard gardens to farms around the city for space reasons. There are those who have decided to cultivate in the surrounding villages (Kamakanga, Kikanda, Kaponda, etc). But food production within and around the city of Lubumbashi is still dependent on the use of hoe as the main means of production.

REFERENCES

ANON (1996) *Urban Agriculture: Food, Jobs and Sustainable Cities.* United Nations Development Program, New York.

Banque du Zaire (1975)

Bruneau, Jean-Claude et Bukome, Itongwe (1987) "La Répartition Spatiale des Petites et Moyennes Activities Economiques à Lubumbashi. Premier Inventaire et Essai d'analyse des Fréquences de Localisation." In: *Bulletin de la Societe Geographique de Liege.* No.22-23, pp. 79-97.

Castells, Manuel (2000) *End of Millennium.* Oxford: Brackwell.

de Lattre, A., (1994) Préface. In Snrech, S., De Lattre, A., Pour Préparer l'Avenir de l'Afrique de l'Ouest: *Une Vision à l'horizon 2000.* Paris: Editions Karthala.

Freeman, B. Donald (1991) *A City of Farmers. Informal urban agriculture.* Montreal: McGill-queens University Press.

Frutchard et *al* (2004) The Socioeconomic Situation of Gécamines. Unpublished Document assessing Gécamines' Reform.

Gran, Guy (Editor) (1979) Zaire. *The Political Economy of Underdevelopment.* New York. Praeger Publishers.

Joye, Pierre et Lewin, Rosine (1961) *Les Trusts au Congo.* Société Populaire d'Edition, Bruxelles.

Kannyo, Edward (1979) Postcolonial Politics. In: Guy Gran (ed.)., Zaire. *The Political Economy of Underdevelopment.* New York. Praeger Publishers.

Katwala, J. Ghifem (1979) Export-Led Growth: Copper Sector. In: Guy Gran (ed.) Zaire. *The Political Economy of Underdevelopment.* New York: Praeger Publishers.

Lizumu, Makala and ELAS MWANA (1979) Modernization and Urban Poverty. A Case Study of Kinshasa. In: Guy Gran (ed.)., Zaire. *The Political Economy of Underdevelopment.* New York. Praeger Publishers.

Mawazo, Kalunga (2005) *La Politique Agricole et le Sous-Développement de la République Démocratique du Congo.* Thèse de Doctorat en Sociologie, Université de Lubumbashi.

Maxwell, G. Daniel (1994) *The Household Logic of Urban Farming in Kampala. In: Cities Feeding People.* Ottawa: International Development Research Centre.

Mbiba, Beacon (1995) *Urban Agriculture in Zimbabwe: Implications for Urban Management and Poverty.* Harare: Avebury Ashgate Publishing Limited.

Mougeot, Luc J. A. (1994) African City farming from a World Perspective. In: *Cities Feeding People. An examination of Urban Agriculture in East Africa.* Ottawa: International Development Research Centre.

Moustier, Paule (1998) Définition et Contours de l'Agriculture Périurbaine en Afrique sub-Saharienne. In: *Agriculture sub-Saharienne. Actes de l'Atelier International du 20 au 24 Avril 1998.* Montpellier.

Moustier, Paule and Mbaye, Alain (1999) Introduction Générale. In: Moustier P. et al. (éd.), *Agriculture Périurbaine en Afrique sub-Saharienne.* Montpellier: Cirad, Colloques.

Nest, Michael et *al* (2006) The Democratic Republic of Congo. Economic Dimensions of War. London: Lynne Rienner Publishers.

Okike, I., (2002) Socioeconomic Implications of Emerging Urban Food Producton Systems. In: *Advances in Crop-Livetock Integration in West African Cities.* Ottawa: International Development Research Centre.

Obudho, Robert and Faeken, Dick (1999) *Urban Agriculture in Africa: Bibliographical survey.* Leiden: African Studies.

Pelissier, Paul (2000) Allocution d'Ouverture. In: *Les Interactions Rural-Urbaines.* Dakar: University Cheik Antadiop Press.

Petit, Pierre (2003) Lubumbashi: La Situation des Menages dans une Economie de Precarite. *Rapport des recherches Effectuees Durant la Premiere session des Travaux de l'Observatoire;* Juin-Octobre 2000.

Provincial Tax Service Report (2003)

Rapport de la Mairie de la Ville de Lubumbashi (2004)

Sawio, J. Camillius (1994) Who are the farmers of Dar es Salaam? In: *Cities Feeding People: An Examination of Urban Agriculture in East Africa.* Ottawa: International Development Research Centre.

Smith, B. Olanrewaju (2002) Overview of Urban Agriculture and Food Security in West African Cities. In: *Advances in Crop-livestock Integration in West African Cities.* Otawa: International Development Research Centre.

Tambwe, Nyumbaiza (2006) "Urban Agriculture as a Global Economic Activity with Special Reference to the City of Lubumbashi in the Democratic Republic of Congo (DRC)." In: *African and Asian Studies,* Volume 5, No 2. Leiden: Brill Academic Publishers

Tinker, Irene (1994) Urban Agriculture is Already Feeding Cities. In: *Cities Feeding People: An Examination of Urban Agriculture in East Africa.* Ottawa: International Development Research Centre.

UNDP (1996) *Urban Agriculture. Food, Jobs and Sustainable Cities.* United Nations Development Program. Publication series for Habitat II, volume one. New York: UNDP.

World Bank Report on Gécamines (2004).

Yaro, A. Joseph (2006) "Is Deagrarianisation Real? A Study of Livelihood Activities in Rural Northern Ghana." In: *The Journal of Modern African Studies,* Volume 44, No 1. Cambridge University Press.

In: World Poverty Issues
Editor: Marilyn M. Watkins, pp. 105-121

ISBN: 978-1-60456-057-2
© 2008 Nova Science Publishers, Inc.

Chapter 4

IS THERE A WAY TO ALLEVIATE POVERTY?

Michael H. Kottow
School of Public Health, University of Chile

ABSTRACT

Poverty should no longer be understood solely as scarcity of material resources, but reather as the lack of capabilities to gain the social and political empowerment required for a life fully integrated in society. Economic, teological and political views on poverty have been one-sided and uninspiring, suggesting that a fresh approach from the vantage point of ethics is necessary, notwithstanding that ethics has traditionally been devoted to interpersonal relationships and neighbourly assistance.

Poverty is marginal and distant. Does distance elicit ethical concern? The contrary has been the case up till now, for global processes have proved detrimental to the poor, without offering any compensatory policies. According to Pogge, reducing poverty is mandatory because it is a man-made evil that requires a "global resources dividend", to be levied in favour of the destitute.

Since justice is a theoretical principle that has failed to inspire political or social policies, it can hardly be expected that poverty might be reduced by resorting to a just distribution of goods and resources. Instead, it is here proposed to replace the quest for justice with an ethics of protection, where all dealings between individuals, communities and societies would include mandatory clauses demanding the powerfull to benefit the less advantaged in order not only to secure fair dealings and eliminating exploitation and coercion, but also to progressively improve the lot of the destitute.

INTRODUCTION

Possibly no social condition has been historically so prevalent as poverty. Although generally deplored, poverty hardly qualifies as an urgent problem, for it is characteristic of problems to press for solutions, whereas human misery receives no more than lip-service indignation. Rather, poverty is an issue that has gained much academic attention, but little in the way of effective proposals to reduce it. A wide range of suggestions have been brought forth, including support for the idea that the best way to combat poverty is to ignore it. International aid, it is argued, would only perpetuate the condition and increase the number of poor people, whereas sufficient assistance to improve their lot is bound to unacceptably threaten the living standard of the affluent [Ryberg 1997].

BEING POOR

International agencies tend to measure poverty in terms of buying power, stating that almost half of the world population lives under the extreme constraint of having a buying power of less than $1 USD a day. Access to less the 1 liter of water per day is also a way of illustrating dire living conditions. Further quantitative refinements are hardly necessary to grasp the enormous magnitude of human plight involved. Numbers can be easily manipulated by stating that those living with $3 USD are "no more" than 25% of the world population. Moving the poverty line has political clout, but doesn't say much about the living conditions of the deprived. Poverty is insufficiently defined by economic parameters which, in any event, are no more than rough estimates because the poor constitute marginal, and for the most part, invisible populations. A. Sen [1995] has very perceptively shown that poverty is not only material scarcity but, much more important, includes lack of capabilities to make use of personal liberty in order to give meaning to a person's life.

Destitution goes beyond material scarcity, for it involves exclusion from civil rights and social relief programs, and marginality from other forms of aid, which do not exist or lack effectiveness, otherwise people would cease being poor. The situation of utter deprivation has been characterized as the *homo sacer* condition, which denotes the naked human being, devoid of any attribute beyond his physical existence. Recalling Aristoteles, *homo sacer* is the human being whose residual life has lost the *bios* characteristic of humanity –of existence in the Sartrian sense or the *Dasein* as described by Heidegger-, and whose *Lebenswelt* –life world- is void of any possible development, least of all of flourishing. What remains is the *zoe* or strictly animal life, struggling to survive in the lost battle that condemns the poor to a precarious existence under harsh conditions of undernourishment, disease and disability, with a life expectancy that is often under 50 years.

FACING POVERTY

The theoretical approach to poverty and possible ways of reducing it have been suggested from the economic, political, social, theological and ethical vantage points, which shall be briefly reviewed and found wanting, suggesting the need for a fresh approach through the perspectives of an ethics of protection. All these approaches need to confront the issue of justice which, it could be said, is trascendental to the problem of poverty, for referring to justice is a necessary prerequisite to broaching the subject of poverty.

In spite of the pivotal position of justice in many discourses, influential voices have been raised that are proposing justice in inequality, arguing that equality is not an ethical dimension at all, and that it has a somewhat dubious origin, being nurtured less by some higher quest for fairness than by comparisons of what people in different wakes of life have or lack [Krebs 2000]. Fortunately, this thorny question, although not easely dismissed, is of little concern to the debate on poverty, because philosophers agree that inequaliy may be reasonably postulated only after all have achieved a fair coverage of their basic needs. A society may indulge in unequal schemes of goods or privileges once it has fulfilled its responsibility of eliminating dire need and equally empowering all its members with the necessary capabilities to take charge of their lives, pursue their interests and fulfill their desires in personal life plans. In another approach, social arrangements should allow people to flourish, but such more egregious goals presuppose a "decent society" that has provided all its members with the capabilities to survive in a respectable way. Rather than being concerned with flourishing, the indigent must gain the required empowerment to become integrated and productive citizens, so that justice in inequity is not their primary concern.

For similar reasons, talk about the Pareto proviso or Rawls idea of the difference principle, appear as well-meant efforts to avoid increasing economic disparities, but these schemes do not address the essential ethical requirement –more often than not politically neglected-, that societies must first eradicate poverty, and only after having done so can fairness, justice in inequality, meritocracy or any other social order be suggested to support private initiative, laboriousness or even luck. Meritocracy can legitimately be postulated once basic equality regarding essential goods and fundamental capabilities have been obtained.

THE ECONOMIC APPROACH

Anchored in the traditional idea that the mark of poverty is lack of material resources to cover basic needs, economists have suggested that this may be due to an absolute scarcity of goods or, alternatively, to situations where resources are on the whole sufficient but distributed in a perversely skewed fashion. A diversity of parameters and indexes tend to support this second view. For example, the amount of nutrition being produced world-wide amounts to approximately 3500 calories per human being, but it is distributed in such a way that the severely undernourished population is as prevalent as the obese and the overfed. The 19th century economist Gini developed an index that compares the highest income with the lowest. The greater the distance, the worse is the income distribution, so that, whereas European countries have a Gini index of 0.3, the poorer countries of the Third World show values of 0.6. Obviously, the distribution of resources and the availability of means to obtain them are skewed to the detriment of the poorest.

Economic parameters show a dramatic but not very vivid picture of poverty, for data is provided by statistics, hardly showing the everyday plight of the deprived. Also, as the German sociologist Luhmann will have it, social sub-systems are responsive to a single codex, which in the case of economics extends between the extremes of solvency and insolvency, but has no receptivity for ethical considerations regarding the distribution of wealth, thus failing to provide any reason for the affluent to part with their wealth in an effort to assist the destitute.

THEOLOGICAL ATTITUDE

Medieval thought offers scholastic distinctions between pity, compassion, benevolence and mercy, all of which have slightly different connotations. Mercy was often associated to leniency in matters of justice or morality, showing also common roots with terms like mercenary, merchandise. Mercy is associated with power, being shown from the heights of well-being towards the weak, the guilty, the injured and the poor. An equally emotional reaction is pity, which tends to include a feeling of superiority in regard to the sufferers, and has therefore been rejected by such militant groups as the disabled. Benevolence is equated with goodness, and is an expression preferably employed in the context of kind concern for others. Although now rarely used, benevolence is the forerunner of beneficence, which has become one of the major principles of applied ethics, especially bioethics. Beneficence is a bulwark of ethical thought, strongly advocated by consequentialist schools of thought, but lacking specificity since it does not necessarily refer to the needy, for anyone who is better off than before will have benefited.

Compassion is an empathic feeling towards the suffering, with a tendency to offer assistance. As a feeling, it addresses the individual and can hardly apply to an abstract appreciation of poverty. Compassion reenters contemporary thought through the writings of Nussbaum [1996], who rescues its ethical value, at the same acknowledging that compassion needs to be buttressed by justice in order to transcend the personal realm.

Nietzsche's rantings against compassion come to mind, especially in a predominantly secular world that observes the paradox of compassion having become a callous, because passive, way of confronting human misery. In the so-called social encyclicals, frequent mention is made of the need to treat the poor graciously, but no thoughts are lost on the deeper issue of eradicating poverty since, after all, it is a social arrangement sanctioned by God, as was explicitly sated in the social encyclicals of the Leonine period (1878-1958).

POLITICAL ASPECTS

There surely is some arbitrariness in separately handling economic, political and social attitudes towards poverty, for they are firmly intertwined. Nevertheless, their realm of action differ in important ways. Possibly the most purely political program to ever be raised, was the one inspiring the French Revolution. Equality, fraternity and liberty were proclaimed without securing social and economic support, and understandably had an ephemeral existence. Whereas economics is an observational form of studying financial flows and arrangements, politics is concerned with power, its shifts, concentrations, the feuds and alliances it induces. Those in power are rarely willing to share or relinquish it, whereas those who lack power are unlikely to gain it by peaceful means. Promises of sharing power with destitute majorities have failed to obtain, and some of the harshest dictatorships have been exercised in the name of the people and against them.

The political issue is of special importance in discussions on poverty, ever since A. Sen [2000] insisted that being poor meant first and above all, to lack the capabilities of exercising one's liberty in the pursuance of the basic goods and a flourishing life. To be poor is to be disempowered, and the only reasonable way of reducing poverty is to empower the poor both politically and socially. Unless people acquire the political power to co-decide the way they want to be governed, they remain chained to destitution and lack of freedom. In other words, politics is not about preferring one or another form of government, but on exercising the freedom to chose both the form of government and the amount of power it should wield. Empowerment can only be distributed through social institutions capable of removing those factors that make people destitute, by developing programs like health-care, education, housing, acquisition of specific skills.

SOCIAL ASPECTS

Political and social issues blend into each other, but they should be analyzed separately, for designing political programs will have little effect unless society is willing and able to restructure itself accordingly. Gender and ethnic discrimination are typical anomalies that continue to plague societies even after political forces have established equal rights for all. Poverty is another example where human rights seem to guarantee basic social goods to all citizens, and yet the richest country in the world has a poor population that unwieldingly comprises 12-15% of all its citizens and, according to one observer, up to 40% of the total population will spend one in every ten years of their lives being poor. Obviously, the social structure needed to make the poor healthier, better educated and more securely sheltered, in order to boost them definitely above the poverty line, are absent or insufficient. To be effective, political intentions must blend into social institutions and thus become enmeshed in society's fabric.

ETHICAL PROPOSALS

Scholastic philosophy elevated misericordia, understood as compassion imbued by reason, as the second highest virtue after the love of God. The decline of theology led to the obsolescence of this term, and nowadays hardly anyone speaks of misericordia. Pity has a double connotation, positive in that it leads to assist the suffering, but negative because pity implies the inferior quality of the one being pitied.

The most neutral term, therefore, is compassion, but its moral value needs to be explored. Opinions differ, but a minimal consensus has been reached that it is a feeling of sympathy which, by its mere expression, should alleviate at least temporarily the sufferers distress or, at the very least, being surrounded by compassionate people should provide solace and reduce the isolation of pain. But, it may be argued, showing compassion is an effortless way of moral empathy which may preclude more effective support. In fact, pity seems to have characteristics that disqualify it to evaluate poverty: it "takes up the onlooker's view" and is related to her "conception of human flourishing"; pity is especially sensitive to misfortunes that might also befall the pitier, thus creating a community between pitier and the pitied [Nussbaum 1996]. When ruminating about pity and compassion, philosophers have seen the trees but not the forest. Pity and compassion are elicited by viewing the suffering of others. They are, above all, feelings that are triggered by the unhappy other, requiring the proximity of those involved.

None of this obtains in relation to dire coditions, which are distant, unrelated to the casual observer, and more concerned with covering basic needs than with flourishing. In spite of these shortcomings, it is argued thatcompassion nurtured by the humanities that increase our sensitivity towards the lives and sufferings of others, should predispose us favourably towards a more just society. The link is weak, if at all existent, for compassion has been always with us, but so has injustice.

Ethics is about concern for others. Since human beings cannot live in isolation, they will relate to other humans and necessarily share expcriences, goals, hopes. Consequently, ethics is at the basis of interpersonal relations or, as Apel will have it, human beings are transcendentally ethical: they cannot but develop their thoughts and actions from a common ethical stance. Levinas has written some seductive passages on the encounter of I and the other, which sparks an ethical concern triggered by the other's plea for care. Philosophy offers many suggestions on how human encounters are basically steeped in ethics, thus giving reason of the biblical commandment "Love thy neighbor". The problem encountered is the persistently unsuccessful effort to extend personal values to social ethics, that is, how to generalize the strong bond between neighbors and make it determine social relations.

Nothing in our occidental upbringing shows us the way to develop an ethics for the distant or the absent. One needs to distinguish at least the categories of beings who may, or may not, be recipients of ethical attitudes. First are the absent, which are those who were here, perhaps should be here, but have lost contact with us. Absence does not cancel the claim to moral treatment, as is shown by the most definite absence of all, death. Dead people have not forfeited, for example, their expressed desire to donate organs, to have their will appropriately carried out, their intention honoured to secure continuing support for a person or an institution. Basically, posthumous actions fall under the broad category of promise keeping. A second category of non present candidates to moral treatment, are future generations, an issue forcefully developed by Hans Jonas and later taken up by much of the literature on bioethics. Whereas it is obvious that the world should remain hospitable to human beings not yet born, it is less convincing that they should receive special moral attention. Whatever is needed to secure human life in the future, is also necessary now, and whichever rights and claims actual people are entitled to, will also be valid in the future. If societies behave morally and take care of the environment, they will be benefiting humanity at large, both actual and future.

This leaves us with the third category, the geographically distant, and the question whether being far away and in need has sufficient moral pull to develop an ethics of assistance, a question most germane to the subject of this text, for the poor are always far away, either at the margins of society or in distant countries. After having cultivated interpersonal ethics for two and half centuries, it does not come easy to bring into the moral arena individuals or communities one is not familiar with. Recently, A. Sen raised the question why people were more than willing to help out in a catastrophe like the 2004 tsunami in Asia, but have become oblivious to the chronic suffering of those who live in absolute destitution, and his answer was, that tsunamis and earthquakes receive strong exposure through the media, whereas hunger rarely makes the news and therefore remains distant. More coverage might bring poverty into the light and, perhaps, motivate action to reduce it. Rendering human misery visible should move people to not only experience the emotions of pity and compassion, but towards taking additional steps to "transform human values into meaningful and effective programs that will serve precisely those who need our empathy and solidarity most." [Farmer 2005: 152]

Bringing the poor closer by way of media exposure will probably be of little impact in terms of kindling a proactive ethical attitude. Image reproduction is a weak substitute for experience, and viewing pain through the veil of a TV screen will hardly mobilize much more than a fleeting sensation of compassion, for the media may well achieve the unwanted effect of stressing how far these depicted worlds are from our own sheltered existence. S. Sontag [2003] has something to say on this matter, being critical of watching others suffer if nothing more than the "unstable emotions" of compassion or pity ensue. To her mind, picturing human misery is justified if it leads to a double awareness: that it poignantly remind us that suffering continues to plague a substantial part of humanity and, perhaps more important, that "our privileges are located on the same map as their suffering" [Ibid. 102-103]. The more fortunate are in no way innocent of the plight of poverty caused and entrenched by such global practices as colonialism, exploitation, avid consumerism.

Farmer believes that viewing misery and hunger will drive compassion and pity to an ethical response based on the recognition of rights entitlements, not only of the universal and negative kind of rights, but more importantly of the positive ones represented by social and political rights. Such a view is of more theoretical than practical plausibility, for the world has been talking about human rights for at least sixty years without achieving major inroads in their implementation.

The specifics of this thorny problem are preceded by the impression that a new process in social ethics has been developing throughout the second half of the 20th century along four strands [Lichtenberg 2004]: 1) Increased affluence of the already well-to-do. 2) Awareness of the misery in distant parts of the world, mediated by communications and the media. 3) Productivity has increased and would, in principle, allow more efficient aid to the destitute, and 4) The need for egalitarianism has become more evident. Nevertheless, world affairs have not developed accordingly, for these 4 factors can easily be contrasted with their opposites: 1)Poverty has been on the rise, 2) Making misery more visible can be seen as an anæsthetic that does not stimulate action, 3) Whereas it is true that productivity has risen, so has consumerism, so that most of the goods being produced cater to the solvent and the well to do. As a corollary, the overweight and obese are as numerous as the undernourished human beings; 4) Socioeconomic inequality is on the rise; whereas big corporations increase their earnings, salaries have remained stagnant for decades, an the Gini coefficient has deteriorated in many parts of the world.

Humanitarian Aid

International assistance programs have been forcefully promoted as efficient forms of material aid to areas beset by catastrophic need due to war, epidemics, acute food shortage, natural disasters. Humanitarian aid developed in the 19th century, based on fourfold roots: power strife between church and secular rulers, the Christian notion of human nature as equal before God, social interdependence, and humanism which foster beneficence and fraternity. Initiatives were at that time related to war and the care of wounded soldiers, as exemplified by Florence Nightingale, the foundation of the Red Cross by Dunant in 1863, and the Geneva Convention of 1864. During the 20th century, more emphasis was placed on the plight of civilians, investing humanitarian aid programs with a number of distinct features. First, in order to reach critical scenarios, humanitarians must enter political alliances, often with local dictators; second, their aid must be specifically atuned to local needs, leading to a neglect of justice or other principles; thirdly, conflict is easily kindled between non-governmental aid agencies and such entities as transnational banks, peace forces, rival international task forces. In spite of magnificent work done by such organizations as Médecines sans Frontiers or Partners In Health, humanitarian groups have been criticized for devoting more time and resources to promotion and to organizatorial planning, than to actual helping the needy so that, in the final analysis, their main asset is to aid in emergencies rather than securing a more sustained improvement of poverty and allied conditions.

Ethics and Distance

Distance being unbridgeable, it has become necessary to deliberate whether an ethics for the distant can be posited and justified. One of the first to raise this question was P. Singer in a polemic article where the obligation to aid the distant was emphatically asserted. This position, called impartialism, recognizes that we are bound to assist our nearest of kin, but that this support should not be unlimited. Once the basic needs of our family and neighbours have been met, any surplus income should be made available to the most needy, wherever they may be, thus complying with a principle of beneficence which states that if one can prevent some significant bad from occurring, without sacrificing anything of comparable moral importance, one ought morally to do so. [Singer 1973, 2004]. Such an apparently judicious position is somewhat of a trap, for any benefit one might desire after having covered one's basic needs, will necessarily be of less weight than the dire needs of the distant and the marginal. The principle being advocated is social consequentialism, for the amount of good reaching a maximum of people will be better served by aiding the many in distress than concentrating on the good life of the few at hand. Curiously, Singer insist on the correctness of his principle, at the same time recognizing its impracticability [Singer 2004], raising the question whether implausible ethics are really ethical at all.

Nevertheless, the issue is on the table, posing a question which is germane to the discussion of ethics and poverty: Is distance a relevant feature to determine ethical responsibility? Singer's contribution to this issue is less than could be hoped for, since he uses analogies taken from proximity and extrapolates for distance. The fact that a drowning child ought to be assisted by anyone passing by, does not automatically extend the obligation to assuage the distress of non identified children in faraway countries. In fact, a number of scholars have represented the opposite idea, that it is morally correct to indulge in privileging family, neighbors and local community.

Whether distance is a morally relevant factor has been positively answered by R. Miller [2004] when stating that responsibility for one's dependents and, ultimately, to onself, determines that aid should first be given to proxies. In fact, it is justified to privilege those with whom we share interests, because this commonality entails responsibilities both to keep our partners' well-being, and to secure that our common interests will be best served, but the need of the distant must also be considered.

Much talk about foreign aid and humanitarian actions is based on the irrelevancy of distance. Kamm discusses this point with Igneski, who suggests that it is not distance, but moral determinateness that matters [2004] . A situation is morally determined when it entails a specific agent, requires a specific act aimed at a specific person in order to free her from an immediate peril. The description seems to better fit a situation of rescue than of aid, and the way it presents is more likely to be an obligation than a moral act.

The philosophical discussion on the matter of what distance does to ethics has not, and probably will not, come to port because aiding the unnamed poor does not depend on purely consequentialist arguments that mandate distributing justly around the globe, nor on any moral duty to assist, which as yet has to be justified. The argument of shared moral responsibilities within a bound society, like a community or a nation, is plausible if all members share a common culture and abide by the same moral rules, including respect for human rights. This will justify tax arrangements that distribute available wealth in such a way that poverty and material destitution are eradicated. Beyond national boundaries, nevertheless, the common bond no longer exists, and additional thoughts need to be developed in order to gain support for international aid. In other words, the anæsthetizing effect of distance must be countered with ethically relevant arguments.

Responsibility and Poverty

What are the possible claims of the poor against the affluent? It suffices not to make poverty visible in order to elicit compassion for, unless compassion is welded to an additional ethical dimension, like justice, it will not become a motivating power to inspire assistance. Nor can the poor effectively appeal to human rights, for the recognition of basic rights does not entail the responsibility of assistance. Not even to witness the violation of these rights is *per se* an unfaltering call for remedial intervention, unless one feels, in some way, co-responsible of these misdeeds.

Having denied that any consequentialist argument will reasonably lead to distribute to the poor at the cost of oneself or by neglecting one's proxies, it will be necessary to explore the crevices of deontology in search for a binding motive that might turn mere awareness of misery into proactive assistance.

Philosopher T.W. Pogge [2005] has devoted his academic career to tracing and denouncing world poverty, the widespread violation of human rights, and the global order under which conditions have become more precarious. World affairs would ideally be regulated by a form of moral universalism, with moral principles being valid for all human subjects and securing equal moral benefits and burdens for all, to the exclusion of privileges or discriminations. So general a proposition will find no opposition, but it also is far from applicable in the real world. Moral tenets that are contingently inapplicable need support, but those that essentially cannot be realized are devoid of the necessary moral fiber.

Pogge suggests two ways to become morally relevant. First, the problem of world poverty is so vast, chronic, pervasive and neglected, that action is mandatory. Indigence and massive misery are usually not, by themselves, classified as unjust, as little as a tsunami killing thousands is to be morally blamed. For a situation or condition to be unjust, it must have been caused by human action, and that is exactly what Pogge believes has happened. Global economic orders, exploitation, unbridled consumerism all tend to funnel goods towards the already affluent, unjustly deteriorating the chronically deprived.

If world poverty is the consequence of abusive practices, it becomes mandatory to actively change global conditions in favor of the poor, and specific policies are suggested to this purpose. Additional moral support is given by pointing out that we all share common values, must stand up to historical injustices committed in the past, and will be wise to eradicate poverty in order to avert a future of angry social revindications, uprisals and war. This can best be achieved through a scheme called "global resources dividend" [GRD] which evolves from the basic idea that natural resources are owned by the world at large, so that when rich nations exploit their own resources, they should share a small part of the revenues with poor countries: "This payment they must make is called a dividend because it is based on the idea that the global poor own an inalienable stake in all limited natural resources." [Ibid. p.196]. This sounds like another name for taxes levied on resources extraction.

The main problem with Pogge's scheme is his belief that the distribution of money by way of a GRD will eradicate poverty promptly and create fair market conditions that will remain immune to unhealthy social inequities. Not even Locke was so optimistic when he suggested an initial social contract where each one got an equal share of natural goods, for he accepted that fair market transactions might eventually create disparities in wealth which would be legitimate if acquired through morally and legally unimpeachable means.

SOLIDARITY

The 19th century social movements aimed at improving the working conditions of labor forces, were expected to be more effective if a compact front of demands was presented. Solidarity (= *solidum*) was invoked for a diversity of political, social and religious purposes, having in common the concept that "the essence of solidarity is a symmetric, mutual and reciprocal relationship. Solidarity means cooperation." [Jaeggi 2001:291]. Papal Encyclicals often refer to solidarity as an attitude requiring the rich to take care of the poor [Juan Pablo II 1981:40. Pablo VI [1967:47]. In the 20th century, solidarity has taken a more bureaucratic connotation, having been adopted by insurance companies to develop schemes where the costs of high risk individuals are absorbed by the community of all insured. In fact, solidarity and insurance have been suggested as the basis of the social contract, where all contribute equally and receive services according to their needs.

"In general, the idea of solidarity is associated with mutual respect, personal support and commitment to a common cause." [ter Meuelen, Arts & Muffels 2001]. "[I]nasmuch as we share a common life, solidarity should be understood not only as a commitment to the others, but also as the preservation of a common form of life." [Jaeggi 2001:295].

There is an obvious convergence of perspectives, seeing solidarity as a relationship between equals, aimed at preserving a common interest but remaining, in the final analysis, as a very difuse and uncommitted social proposition, showing no propensity to become a useful strategy to confront poverty. Solidarity, it has been noted, tends to lull into conformity in the wake of chronic and unchanging misery, but becomes very much alive, albeit for a limited period of time, when tragic emergencies occur. In the view of Rorty [1999], solidarity require a more specific bond than shared humanity because there is always some sort of distinction that separates "us" from "them". Moral progress does not consist in developing an unlikely "human solidarity", but in being more inclusive about who qualifies as "we" so as to reduce the population of "they".

The Frail Concept of Justice

A. Sen´s characterization of poverty as not only lack of basic material goods, but more importantly as reduced capability of applying one´s liberty to forge a meaningful existence, shifts the emphasis of being poor from material destitution to lack of empowerment.

"What the capability perspective does in poverty analysis is to enhance the understanding of the nature and causes of poverty and deprivation by shifting primary attention away from *means* (and the one particular mean that is usually given exclusive attention, viz., income) to *ends* that people have reason to pursue, and, correspondingly, to the *freedoms* to be able to satisfy these ends." [Sen 2000 p. 90].

Important thinkers are rejecting the idea that equality is an ethical dimension, and they see no reason to decry differences in interests, desires, merits, material wealth, since people are intrinsically diverse to begin with. Such a form of justice in inequality presupposes, nevertheless, that basic needs have been taken care of by a fair social order or, as Margalit [1996] puts it, a "decent society".

Even if it seems counterintuitive to accept justice in inequality, there does remain a strong suspicion that, for all that it has been hailed, justice remains elusive and has never become a reality in any social arrangement. No one would be willing to disbar justice from the ethical discourse, but it seems unhealthy and unethical to insist on a principle that is unattainable. The main reason why justice does not transcend the theoretical realm is arguably that just social orders are based on redistribution of material goods, an unsavory proposition to all who believe, even unknowingly, in Locke´s above mentioned proviso that advantages gained in the wake of legal and morally correct transactions are legitimate and need not to be further accounted for. In consequence, redistribution of what has been fairly earned is unjustified.

"Indeed, the overuse of the concept of justice reduces the force of the idea when applied to the terrible deprivations and inequities that characterize the world in which we live. Justice is like a cannon, and it needs not be fired (as an old Bengali proverb puts it) to kill a mosquito." [Sen 2000, p.254]

Of course, its more than a mosquito that needs killing, but the idea remains that justice is a theoretical proposition that does not purchase much social change. Perceptively, Sen goes the extra mile needed to bring his ideas closer to a policy proposition:

"*Protective security* is needed to provide a social safety net for preventing the affected population from being reduced to abject misery, and in some cases even starvation and death. The domain of protective security includes *fixed* institutional arrangements such as unemployment benefits and statutory income supplements to the indigent as well as ad hoc arrangements such as famine relief or emergency employment to generate income for destitutes." [Ibid. p. 40]

Seeing that theories of justice do not lead to practical approaches, and that schemes of redistribution are unpalatable enough to remain unfulfilled, different approached need to be explored. The idea of protection as the fundamental function of the state has been with us for over 300 years, and more recently, philosophy has recognized that highly vulnerable human beings, both actual and potential, –the newborn, future generations- need a protective mantle to survive and strive.

In pursuing an ethics of protection, emphasis is shifted from distributive justice to the recognition that the destitute are powerless, and that the basic function of protection is to provide the *tectum*, the shelter until the helpless gain sufficient empowerment to take care of their lives in terms of acquiring the capabilities necessary to unfold a meaningful existence.

Writers like O'Neill, Sen, McIntyre believe that society is to be organized in such a way as to render the necessary services that will meet the basic needs of the population. Furthermore, protection must transcend the private, the social and the national realm, hoping to offer a global answer to human misery, in a similar vein as justice, solidarity or human rights aspire to universal reach. Such universality can only be suggested from the vantage point of ethics.

ETHICS OF PROTECTION

When the idea of sovereign nations became reality, political philosophers devoted much time to developing the notion of state, political power, and social contract. Thomas Hobbes was convinced that man was his own worst enemy –*homo homini lupus*-, the only way of avoiding the disastrous condition of permanent war being that individuals relinquish their arms to the State in exchange of being guaranteed personal and patrimonial protection. The idea of a strong and protective Leviathan was so forceful, that it remained the key notion of the liberal understanding of the State. In the 20th century, R. Nozick , anxious to reduce the influence of the State upon its citizens, acknowledged that the minimal State could be dispensed of all central functions except the protection of its subjects [1974].

This individual protection was eventually extended to collective safeguards, to include public health in the wake of epidemic disease; the State was also called upon to protect individuals and communities that were victims of natural catastrophes they could not cope with. In spite of the debilitating effect of globalization, the State remains under the obligation to protect and defend its population, thus explaining that nations of all political shading have an army, a police force and public health policies, in compliance with the protective functions that remain the quintessential *raison d'etre* of the State.

Human beings are all equal, we are told, even though this tenet is contradicted by everyday experience. Consequently, equality requires fair treatment, and ethics is supposed to be universalizable in that it applies indiscriminately to all, regardless of gender, age, color or any other distinctive features. The tradition of ethics stresses its egalitarian nature and yet, human beings are so different that fairness is breached in the face of different needs, interests and desires. Concerning poverty, invocation of justice, egalitarian distribution, and fair ethical treatment have not gone beyond theoretical pronunciation, leaving actual circumstances unchanged. So it may be time to think about ethics less in terms of justice, but rather from the vantage point of asymmetry.

Contemporary philosophers have essayed some thoughts along these lines. When Hans Jonas developed his principle of responsibility, he based it on two examples of protection.

The newborn shows a helplessness that calls for protection without the need for any ethical justification and, in the same vein, not yet existent future generations must be protected from the deleterious effects of ecological pollution and scarcity. Levinas believed that a primary ethical moment is kindled whenever two human beings meet, presenting in the form of a plea for protection that is detected in the face of the other. The care element of ethics is built on this initial need for protection, much as handshaking is a form of assuring that no concealed weapons are being introduced, so that the parties concerned may feel safe.

Canadian philosopher R. Brandt [1995] ascribes to a utilitarian form of ethics sustained by a form of sympathetic altruism that will secure conviviality. Nevertheless, he also believes that a basic sort of security must prevail, based on a social order that assures protection.

An initial and most formidable hurdle to be taken is given by the paradox that fighting poverty is forcefully presented as an imperative, whereas ethical approaches are by nature watered down to bland suggestions, recognizing the lack of a universal mandate to erradicate poverty. But there are strong arguments in favor of a widespread protection of citizens *qua* members of societies that choose public governance by a democratically constituted State. And there are equally convincing arguments that human beings live in communities where the weak are taken care of by the strong, as excercised in paternalism, medical care, education. In fact, in many wakes of life protection becomes an obligation, parents by law being required to look after their chidlren, just as the State is constitutionally mandated to protect its subjects.

A number of dearly held convictions tend to oppose any scheme of universal ethics, be it in terms of distributive justice or of protection. In taking a second look at these objections, they may be less convincing than they seem at the first blush. Common sense upholds the idea that identifiable subjects are more readily and justifiably assisted than statistical populations, in the sense that actual people prevail over numbers. Similarly, "common sense morality permits, and often requires, preferential treatment of family and friends." [Temkin 1995, p. 89]. Thirdly, philosophers like Rawls distinguish between natural misfortune and perpetrated injustice, so that the unfortunate may be voluntarily assisted whereas it is society's duty to compensate the unjustly treated.

Being just or, as here proposed, exercising protection towards others depends less on their degree of anonimity than whether we have dealings and share interests with them or not. If someone buys diamonds from distant Congo or imports elephant tusks, he becomes morally responsible to oversee that mining and hunting be carried out under conditions of fairness and care, just as the buyer of a piece of art makes sure that it is not stolen good. If giving preferential treatment to proxies implies regaling them will ill-gotten goods, than ethics is being severly insulted.

As for the much cherished difference between natural and man-induced disadvantages, two considerations obtain. First, many apparently natural misfortunes are the product of human misconduct. Poverty, for example, is more often than not the results of colonialism, exploitation and neglect. Second, genuine natural deprivations become all the more severe if they lead to social disempowerment. The disabled are much worse off in poor societies than in affluent ones where compensation, rehabilitation and other forms of social support are available, so that what is a natural handicap becomes a major social disadvantage if not adequately cared for.

An ethics of protection will go beyond these duties and call upon those in power to take care of the disempowered. Power should not be curtailed, provided it has been legitimately obtained, but it should be required to share its advantages to some extent. To be effective, the extent and the realm of power-sharing ought to be specified. How much power is to be devoted to protecting the weak depends less on the authority wielded than on the needs of the powerless. In a father-son relationship, a cascade exists from power to authority to paternalism, and paternalistic attitudes can be defined as those that take vicarious decisions for the weak because, supposedly, they are not autonomous. Therefore, protecting a child will not depend on the amount of power the parent wields, but on the lack of autonomy of the child. As the child matures and gains autonomy, the need for protection diminishes and the parent in power is expected to relent his paternalistic attitudes.

As for the realms where power can be expected to exercise protection, it can be schematically segmented into concentric circles, somewhat in the spirit of Walzer's partition of justice into spheres [1983]. There is an undisputed inner circle where people take care and protect their next of kin, meaning those with whom they share existential interests that are emotional and vocational rather than contractual. Next, one can draw an intermediate circle of care including all those with whom we share a limited but important aspect of our lives: neighborhood, professional affiliation, working place and groupings of diverse kind. More often than not, we will be willing to take care of those members of our group that have been hit by misfortune and require support, and the ethical call for protection is present because we share significant portions of our lives.

As the circles widen, protection becomes harder to pinpoint because relationships turn more diffuse and less binding. At the national level, protection must become State policy which, up to a limited point, it already is. States have armies for protection against external threats, they have police forces to protect citizens from being harmed, and they have a public health policy to protect their subjects from epidemics, toxic damages, preventable diseases. These protective mandates are political rather than ethical, but the way the State implements them requires ethical deliberation. Is the protective coverage related to need or is it equally available to all citizens? Are all inhabitants of the nation included, or only its citizens? Does marginality mean exclusion? These are ethical issues concerning the protective function of the State, which does not mean proposing a specific political agenda, but only confirming that under any form of government, the State must protect the needy and those at risk, and empower the weak. According to A. Sen, social and political empowerment for all is best achieved in democracy, for the aim is not to have a paternalistic State, but one that is true to its basic funcions. If the national circle of protection is expected to take remedial care of the poor, it will be ineluctable to commission the State to create and support social institutions that will protect and empower the needy to the point of erradicating poverty in the national realm [O'Neill 1998].

Poverty being a universal scourge, can only be reached by protective ethics in a wider, transnational circle which, on the other hand, is impervious to ethical considerations. International aid is suggested, promised, agreed upon, but remains invariably short of expectations and insufficient to even palliate worldwide indigence. Repeatedly proclaiming universal human rights has not fared better, and poverty remains a vast and increasing problem. Experience teaches that loudly proclaiming protection or any other form of international ethics, will be of little import and finally remain beset by the inmorality of prescribing the unreachable, much like a physician who excels in diagnostic proedures but has no effective therapy to offer.

History has shown that international relationships have always been commanded by interests and enforced to the benefit of the powerful. To a great extent, poverty is the product of colonial and oppresive policies, exploitation and injustice. It has been suggested that these are sufficient reasons for powerful nations to recognize the need for retribution and embark on major schemes of compensation, but such appeals have created a benevolent yet expectant attitude: if someone starts, we'll follow.

Dealings between nations of unequal power continue to be marred by authoritarian self-interests. When international Conferences plea for equity, environmental sustainability or preferential clauses for the disadvantaged, they get little more than lip-service agreements at best, occasionally explicit rebuttals. Therefore, in order to safeguard poor nations in their dealings with the affluent, explicit protection provisos needs to be incroporated into any agreement that entails commercial, research, educational or other kind of interactions between nations of unequal power. To exemplify what is being meant, a brief look upon international scientific research may be in order.

The Non Protectiveness of Biomedical Research

Biomedical research has been subject to a double migration: from universities and traditional centers of knowledge to commercial research enterprises. More to the point, developed countries have moved their research endeavors to the Third World at increasing speed. The Nuffield Council [2002] reports that between 1990 and 2000, the amount of research protocols placed in less developed countries has had a 16-fold increase. Two developments make this scientific migration ethically suspicious. First, the scientific world has identified the 90/10 inequity, caused by devoting 90% of the worldwide available resources for biomedical research, to the study of 10% of diseases that affect the richer countries, thus creating huge pockets of so-called neglected diseases that are endemic and ferocious killers in poor areas, of which malaria is a prime example. Second, most of the pharmaceutical research done is devoted to "me too drugs", that is, therapeutic agents that will redundantly duplicate without improving on what is available, being aimed at gaining a place in the lucrative pharmaceutical market [Angell 2004].

If biomedical research being siphoned into poor countries has objectives that are of no interest to these hosts, it becomes downright unacceptable once the underlying research ethics is revealed. Again, only two aspects need to be stressed, although many more are being discussed in the pertinent literature. First, researchers have proposes to distinguish between "aspirational" ethics of research, marked by excellency and to be applied in affluent couuntries, in contrast to "pragmatic" research ethics which adapt to local context and are less stringent. Host countries have resented this big stick doctrine, and insist that ethics cannot conform to what has been called a "double standard." [Macklin 2004]. In the second place, although the Declaration of Helsinki has insisted that research subjects are entitled, both during and beyond the research period, to the benefits that the trial might unveil, investigators and other stakeholders have diluted such demands to the point of honoring them in the breach.

Biomedical research tactics are a prime and current example of asymmetric interactions between rich and poor countries, which often disregard elementary ethical tenets to the point of increasing the vulnerance and unprotectedness of the weak An ethics of protection, in addition to the punctillious fullfilment of research ethics, would require investigators to safeguard their subjects and eventually the community where they place their study, in all those aspects that are touched upon by the research protocol, so that, at the end, the host parties, by accepting to be research subjects, will have made some lasting gains in their quest for empowerment.

If affluent nations, and transnational enteprises, continue to be interested in the resources of poor countries, or to create scenarios for research purposes, they should enter ethical agreements that go beyond the minimum of avoiding maleficence and managing risks, to include the commitment of protecting their hosts. Researchers tend to select so-called "vulnerable" research subjects because they are more pliable, less demanding and easier to recruit. In reality, these people are not vulnerable in the sense of being fragile, they are vulnerated or harmed by diseases, malnutrition, marginality, lack of empowerment. These handicaps increases their willingess to be recruited for research purposes, but should also move researchers to take therapeutic care of subjects who willingly participate in investigations that entail risks and often have neither benefits nor relevance for them. Collaborative efforts imply equality, which in turn requires empowerment of the weak by means of protective policies developed by the stronger participants.

CONCLUSION

The track record of suggestions and policies to reduce world-wide poverty has been far from impressive, for poverty has both increased and deepened. Most proposals have been based on compassionate attitudes and presented schemes of distributive justice. Channeling resources and material goods towards the needy has been met with indifference and frank opposition till, finally, the idea of justice itself has come under the suspicion of not representing an ethical goal, at least not a workable one.

In recent decades the idea has been launched that poverty is not only a matter of material destitution, it is also, and to a great extent, a matter of lacking the capacity to acquire the social and political abilities required to take one's place in society. Only by being productive can individuals obtain the resources necessary to cover their needs and desires, and productivity will require opportunity and access to developing capabilities. In order to achieve these capabilities, the destitute must receive the necessary protection to ameliorate the lack of empowerment they suffer. An ethics of protection should support the suggestion that power wielded should share benefits and make the weak less disempowered as they enter joint ventures between the rich and the poor.

REFERENCES

Angell M. How the big drug companies deceive us. *The New York Review* 2004. 51: 52-58.

Brandt RB. Foundationalism for moral theory. In Couture J & Nielsen K. (ed.): *On the relevance of metaethics*. Calgary, University of CValgary 1995.

Farmer P. Never Again? Reflections on Human Values and Human Rights 2005 /www. tannerlectures.utah.edu/efgh.htm (Downloaded July 7, 2007)

Jaeggi R. Solidarity and indifference. En: ter Meulen R, Arts W & Muffels R (eds.): *Solidarity in Health and Social Care in Europe*. Dordrecht, Kluwer Academic Publishers, 2001:287-308.

Kamm FM. The new problem of distance in morality. In Chatterjee DK (ed.): *The ethics of assistance*. Cambridge, Cambridge University Press 2004: 59-74.

Krebs A. (Ed.). *Gleicheit oder Gerechtigkeit*. Frankfurt aM., Suhrkamp 2000.

Lichtenberg J. Absence and the unfond heart: why people are less giving than they might be. In Chatterjee DK (ed.): *The ethics of assistance*. Cambridge, Cambridge University Press 2004: 75-100.

Macklin R. *Double standards in medical research in developing countries*. Cambridge, Cambridge Univ. Press 2004.

Margalit A. *The decent society*. Cambridge, Mass. Harvard University Press 1996.

Miller RW. Moral closeness and world community. In Chatterjee DK (ed.): *The ethics of assistance. Cambridge,* Cambridge University Press 2004:101-122.

Nozick R. *Anarchy, State, and utopia*. Oxford, B. Blackwell 1974.

Nuffield Council on Bioethics. The ethics of research related to healthcare in developing countries.. London, Nuffield Council on Bioethics 2002.

Nussbaum M. Compassion: The basic social emotion. *Social Philosophy and Policy* 1996; 13: 27-58.0.

O´Neill O. *Towards justice and virtue*. Cambridge, Cambridge University Press 1998.

Pogge T. *World poverty and human rights*. Maldon, Polity Press 2005.

Pope Juan Pablo II: *Laborem excercens*, 1981.

Pope Pablo VI: *Populorum progressio*, 1967.

Rorty R. (1999) *Contingency, irony, and solidarity*. Cambridge, Cambridge University Press

Ryberg J. Population and Third World assistance. *Journal of Applied Philosophy* 1997; 14: 207-219.

Sen A. *Inequality reexamined*. Cambridge, Hardvard University Press 1995.

Sen A. *Development as freedom*. New York, A.A. Knopf 2000.

Sen A. (2005) Ethics, development, and disaster. . Digital Library of the Inter-American Initiative on Social Capital, Ethics and Development of the Inter-American Development Bank (IDB) – www.iadb.org/ethics.

Singer P. Famine, Affluence, and morality. *Philosophy and Public Affairs* 1972: 1: 229-243. Singer P. Outsiders: our obligation to those beyond our borders. In Chatterjee DK (ed.): *The ethics of assistance*. Cambridge, Cambridge University Press 2004: 11-32.

Sontag S. *Regarding the pain of other*. New York, Picador 2003.

Temkin LS. Justice an equality: Some questions about scope. *Social Philosophy & Policy*. 1995; 12: 72-104.

ter Meulen R., Arts W & Muffels R. Solidarity, health and social care in Europe. En: ter Meulen R, Arts W & Muffels R (eds.): *Solidarity in Health and Social Care in Europe*. Dordrecht, Kluwer Academic Publishers, 2001:1-11.

Walzer M. *Spheres of justice*. Basic Books 1983.

In: World Poverty Issues
Editor: Marilyn M. Watkins, pp. 123-138

ISBN: 978-1-60456-057-2
© 2008 Nova Science Publishers, Inc.

Chapter 5

INCOME MOBILITY IN LATIN AMERICA: A PSEUDO-PANEL APPROACH

José Cuesta, Hugo Ñopo and Georgina Pizzolitto[*]
Inter-American Development Bank, World Bank

ABSTRACT

This paper presents a comparative overview of income mobility patterns in Latin America. We construct a pseudo-panel for 14 Latin American countries between 1992 and 2003, unprecedented in the Region for its length and breadth. Estimates of time-dependence unconditional income mobility show that this is rather limited, as previously found in the scarce existing literature. However, after introducing personal, socioeconomic, demographic and geographical controls, conditional income mobility rises substantively for the Region. Also, unconditional and conditional income mobility show large variations across countries.

Keywords: Income Mobility, Poverty, Pseudo-Panels, Latin America

1. INTRODUCTION

Latin America is the most unequal region in the world. The discussion behind this salient feature has agreed on some of its causes: pervasive levels of macro-economic vulnerability, inequality in political voice and problems of social exclusion that are rooted in history (Vos et al. (2006), World Bank (2003) and IADB (1998) among others). The role of mobility on the analysis of inequality has been emphasized only recently, however (see Fields (2005), Galiani (2006) for recent reviews). The static measures of inequality are not enough to picture the

[*] Cuesta and Ñopo: Inter-American Development Bank; Pizzolitto: World Bank. The results and conclusions expressed in this research document are those of the authors and do not compromise the views of neither Bank nor their Boards of Directors.

well being of individuals in a society, and so they need to be complemented by the dynamics of mobility. For example, societies with prevailing exclusion (that is, individuals or groups neglected of access to services, consumption goods and assets) should expectedly have low upward mobility. Instead, societies that have actively combated exclusion should reflect high upward mobility (as reported for Chile by Scott 2000). In societies vulnerable to macro-economic shocks and ineffective social protection mechanisms, individuals may face high levels of downward income mobility (as reported for Argentina by Corbacho et al 2003).

This study is a contribution to the limited literature on income mobility in Latin America.[1] The lack of analysis has been the result of data requirements that the Region has been unable to provide fully yet, that is, panel data. By constructing, alternatively, a pseudo-panel for 14 countries between 1992 and 2003, this regional study applies the new methodological developments on the analysis of mobility in an unprecedented number of countries and years. There are several reasons for choosing a regional focus, but the most important one, from a policy-making stance, is that it allows for country-specific effects to be compared with sub-regional and region-wide effects. Of course, the analysis of regional mobility has shortcomings on its own, such as the need to exclude countries and periods from the analysis due to data limitations —as explained below. After this introduction, Section 2 defines mobility along the lines of the categorization in Fields (2005) and discusses the methodology used to estimate *unconditional* income mobility and *conditional* mobility (after controlling for personal, socioeconomic demographic and geographical features). Section 3 describes the construction of the pseudo-panel used in this study and explores mobility trends for the Region. Section 4 discusses the main results of the analysis: one, unconditional mobility is very low but rises significantly when controls are introduced; two, country-specific income mobility varies largely. Section 5 provides concluding remarks.

2. THE ESTIMATION OF MOBILITY

The measurement of income mobility started with Lillard and Willis (1978). It basically involves the establishment of a relationship between past and present income:

$$y_{i,t} = \beta y_{i,t-1} + \mu_{i,t} \tag{1}$$

Where $y_{i,t}$ is the total labor income for household i at time t, μ_{it} is a disturbance term and the parameter β, the coefficient of the slope in a regression of the income over its lagged value, is the measure of mobility. Fields (2005) refers to it as *time-dependence* mobility and it will be the focus of our paper. A value of β equal to 1 represents a situation with no income convergence; a value of β below 1 corresponds to a situation in which there is convergence, while zero represents an extreme case in which mobility would be total (as there would be no

---

[1] However, this literature is recently growing with the use of several methods to analyze mobility from transition matrices to econometric techniques or by estimating measures of permanent incomes. These techniques may refer to panel data, pseudo-panel or longitudinal data. The unit of observation can also vary, from individuals to workers, districts within a city or cities and regions in a country. For a detailed description see Fields et al (2006).

relationship between past and present incomes). Although there are no ex-ante restrictions about the range of values that β should take, they are regularly within the [0,1] interval. Additionally, the mobility estimator obtained from (1) is called *unconditional* in the sense that it does not take into account the presence of covariates (other than past income) that may explain present income. When the estimation is performed with additional controls, we have the time-dependence conditional estimation of mobility:

$$y_{i,t} = \beta y_{i,t-1} + \delta X_{i,t} + \mu_{i,t} \qquad (2)$$

Provided that an analysis of mobility of this sort implies to follow individuals (or households) over time, the quintessential data tool has been panel data. Unfortunately the development of this kind of tool has been only recent in Latin America and the few panels of data available as of today cover only short periods.[2] This has constituted an important barrier to the analysis of mobility in the Region. The development of pseudo-panel techniques that was initiated by Deaton (1985) has been an interesting alternative to overcome this data limitation. A pseudo-panel is formed creating synthetic observations obtained from averaging real observations with similar characteristics (regularly, birth year) in a sequence of repeated cross sectional data sets. In this way, the synthetic units of observations can be thought as being "followed" over time. The model then requires an appropriate modification:

$$\overline{y}_{c(t),t} = \beta_c \overline{y}_{c(t-1),t-1} + \delta_c \overline{X}_{c(t),t} + \mu_{c(t),t} \qquad (3)$$

Where the individual index, i, has been replaced by a cohort index, $c_{(t)}$, that is time-dependent. Analogously to Equation (1), the slope β_c is the parameter of interest. The literature has then focused on exploring the conditions under which such parameter can be consistently estimated in a context of repeated cross-section (instead of real panel data). The works of Browning et al. (1985), Moffit (1993), Collado (1997), Mckenzie (2004), Verbeek and Vella (2005) and Antman and Mckenzie (2005), among others, have provided set of conditions that the interested reader can explore.

Not surprisingly, there are pros and cons about the use of pseudo-panels for the analysis of mobility. Among arguments in favor of it we can cite at least three. The first is that they suffer less from problems related to sample attrition (because the samples are renewed at every period). Other is that, being constructed averaging groups of individual observations, they also suffer less from problems related to measurement error (at least the individual-level one). A third argument in favor, more practical, is that because of the wide availability of cross-sectional data it is possible to construct pseudo-panels that are appropriately representative covering long periods back in time, substantially more than what can be covered by real panels. The main argument against its use has to do with the fact that the decision about the clustering of observations in cohorts depends on a trade off (number of

---

[2] This is the case of a two-period Chilean panel available in the CASEN survey of 1996-1998 or a two-period panel in El Salvador, for rural areas. A panel can also be constructed for Mexico, using the Encuesta Nacional de Empleo Urbano (ENEU), that have a rotating panel, with household followed for five consecutive quarters. Also in Argentina (1988 to date), Brazil (1980 to date), Peru (1991-1997), and Venezuela (1994-1999) have household survey with the same design. See Fields et al (2006) for more details.

cohorts vs. number of observations in each cohort) for which the literature has not been conclusive yet. The larger the number of cohorts, the smaller is the number of individuals per cohort. One the one hand, one would like to have a large number of cohort observations such that the regressions performed with the resulting pseudo panels suffer less from small sample problems. However, on the other hand, if the number of observations per cohort were not large enough, the average characteristics per cohort would fail to be good estimates for the population cohort means (McKenzie 2004). In addition, Antman and McKenzie (2005) note two caveats from the use of pseudo-panels. They may introduce biases if the average cohort household fails to account for changing trends in household dissolution and creation (such as migration, for instance). Also, intra-cohort mobility is utterly ignored.

The pseudo-panel approach has been recently undertaken in the region to estimate mobility as defined above, at least by Navarro (2006) for Argentina, Antman and Mckenzie (2005) for Mexico and by Calónico (2006) for a set of 8 countries (Argentina, Brazil, Chile, Colombia, Costa Rica, Mexico, Uruguay and Venezuela). The latter found low patterns of mobility for all these countries during the 1992-2002 period. When trying to compare the results from both papers for Argentina we still found some differences. First, they use different time spans. Navarro computed mobility for the period (1985-2004), while Calónico did it for (1992-2003). Second, the studies differ in the concept of income that is used. While Calónico uses monthly labor incomes, Navarro based her analysis in hourly wages received by individual in their main occupation. Third, Navarro narrows her estimations to the conglomerate of Gran Buenos Aires in Argentina in order to construct a much larger pseudo panel. All in all, Navarro (2006) presents a higher degree of income mobility than Calónico (2006), a result supported by Albornoz and Menendez (2004) and Fields and Sanchez-Puerta (2005) using panel data for Argentina. Likewise, Antman and McKenzie (2005) report for specific age-education cohorts in Mexico between 1987 and 2001 little mobility between the earnings of rich and poor households but rapid convergence in the average household's earnings, suggesting higher levels of conditional mobility.

Our study complements the previous three both in scale and scope as it explores 14 countries during the period 1992 to 2003. On top of obtaining the cohort-mobility estimators - (both unconditional and conditional β and β_c in Equations (2) and (3), respectively), we also explore the role of the initial level of income on the change magnitude observed in the incomes of the pseudo-individuals as well as other controls. This new estimator will tell the impact that the changes, rather levels, of initial income has on the variation of that income to be expected in the next period.

$$\Delta \overline{y}_{c(t),t} = \beta_c \overline{y}_{c(t-1),t-1} + \delta_c \Delta \overline{X}_{c(t),t} + \mu_{c(t),t} \tag{4}$$

3. DATA

The raw data for this study comes from national household surveys of 14 Latin American countries in the region. These surveys have been harmonized to ensure a comparable definition of household incomes across countries. Countries included in the pseudo-panel share the same sources of labor incomes: labor –approximately 75% of the Region's average household incomes– and non-labor incomes –accounting for the remaining 25%. Countries that fail to report non-labor incomes in their household surveys were excluded of the pseudo-panel. That was the case of Dominican Republic, Guatemala, Nicaragua and Ecuador. Due to problems in the income variables, we also excluded from the analysis data from Brazil and Mexico for the year 1992.[3] All incomes were deflated using the Consumer Price Index of each country and year. We also adjusted the incomes using the Purchasing Power Parity – reported in the World Development Indicators – to make them comparable across countries.

We construct the pseudo-panel with data from these 14 countries using surveys between 1992 and 2003 and focusing on household heads aged 21 to 65. Birth cohorts include household heads born in seven-year spans, starting with those born between 1927 and 1933 and ending with those born between 1976 and 1982. Cohorts are constructed based on year of birth, country of residence and gender. Our pseudo-panel averages observations pertaining to the same cohort that appear in subsequent household surveys (each observation is appropriately weighted by the sample expansion factors). As a result, the constructed pseudo-panel follows eight birth cohorts over six periods. This comprises a total of 139,132 individual observations collapsed into 1,024 synthetic observations representing household heads. That number of observations is the result of collapsing the dataset by country (14 countries), gender (1 for men and 0 for women) and the eight birth cohorts (from 1927-33 to 1976-82), for the six periods of analysis. That would imply a total of 14x2x8x6=1,344 synthetic observations. However, some countries had missing household surveys for some years (especially the earlier ones subject to analysis) and some others were not usable due to the lack of a possibility to harmonize variables, as mentioned in the previous paragraph. As a result the number of synthetic observations was reduced to 1,024. Table 1 below reports cohorts' sizes (and annex 1 reports the information sources used to construct the cohorts in each country).

Table 1. Cohorts' sizes

Year	Period						Total
Birth Cohort	T1	T2	T3	T4	T5	T6	1993-2002
	1992-3	1994-5	1996-7	1998-9	2000-1	2002-3	
1927-33	2,055	1,284	851	303	…	…	4,493
1934-40	2,554	2,513	2,296	2,339	1,639	1,468	12,809
1941-47	3,084	3,098	2,845	2,879	2,768	3,121	17,795
1948-54	4,030	4,035	3,727	3,867	3,701	4,190	23,550
1955-61	4,516	4,585	4,171	4,519	4,570	5,166	27,527
1962-68	3,901	4,281	3,949	4,434	4,856	5,565	26,986
1969-75	9,34	2,319	2,411	3,182	3,968	4,858	17,672
1976-82	…	…	1,837	1,544	2,144	2,775	8,300
Total	21,074	22,115	22,087	23,067	23,646	27,143	139,132

Source: Own calculations based on IDB Research Department Harmonized Household Surveys.

---

[3] We observed that even after adjusting for consumer price index, incomes presented dramatic fluctuations. The high inflation rates (and currency changes in Brazil) explain these inconsistencies in the evolution of incomes variables.

Table 2. Data Descriptive Statistics

Variable	Number of observations (in pseudo panel)	Mean	Standard Deviation
Log Per Capita Household Incomes	1,024	5.36	0.68
% Female-headed households	1,024	0.50	0.50
Age	1,024	43.22	13.84
Years of Education	1,010	7.15	2.26
No Education	1,024	0.10	0.11
Primary incomplete	1,024	0.23	0.13
Primary complete	1,024	0.21	0.09
Secondary incomplete	1,024	0.19	0.10
Secondary complete	1,024	0.13	0.07
Tertiary complete	1,024	0.07	0.07
Tertiary incomplete	1,024	0.07	0.05
Number of Children aged 0 to 16 years	1,024	1.84	0.69
Number of other relatives living in the household	1,024	0.60	0.40
Dwelling Index	864	…	…
Southern Cone	1,024	0.38	0.49
Andean Region	1,024	0.38	0.46
Mexico and Central America	1,024	0.33	0.47

Source: Own calculations based on IDB Research Department Harmonized Household Surveys.

This pseudo-panel exceeds both the depth and breath other pseudo-panels for the Latin American region. Also, this pseudo-panel strikes a balance between a relevant number of cohorts and a meaningful size of the cohort. An insufficiently large number of cohorts cause pseudo-panel estimations to suffer from small sample problems. An insufficiently large cohort size causes its averages not to be good estimates for the population cohort characteristics.

Table 2 provides the basic descriptive statistics of the pseudo-panel: personal, socioeconomic, demographic and geographical characteristics of synthetic household heads of the constructed cohorts. The average household head in the pseudo-panel earns about US$ 456 dollars per month with a standard deviation of US$ 419 in PPP-adjusted real terms. The average household head is 43 years old and has seven years of education. Regarding attainment, 10% of the household heads have no education; 44% have primary education – either incomplete or complete–, while 33% have started or completed secondary education. The remaining 14% have college education. The average household has two children. We also construct an index of the dwelling characteristics to reflect the assets of the household. The index varies from zero to two and reflects the quality and availability of services in the dwelling.[4] The mean of the dwelling index is 1.27. Table 2 also reports the distribution of observations by sub-regions.[5]

Figure 1 below depicts regional and sub-regional trends of per capita monthly household incomes for selected birth cohorts (results do not change for the rest of cohorts). These trends confirm previous evidence based on individual labor incomes pointing to limited mobility in the region (see Calónico 2006). Even when trends differ among sub-regions, cohorts of young adults, prime-age and retirees follow similar patterns within each sub-region.[6]

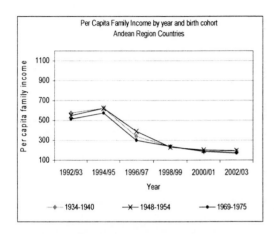

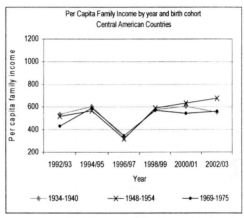

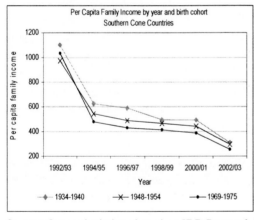

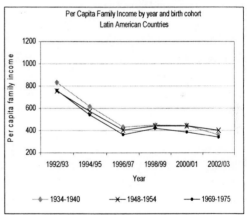

Source: Own calculations based on IDB Research Department Harmonized Household Surveys.

Figure 1. Income Trends by Sub-Region.

---

[4] The index takes into account the quality of the materials used for the walls, the number of rooms, if the household has a restroom with a toilet connected to a sewerage system or to a septic tank, the access to a source of safe water, and the possession of a phone, refrigerator and stove. The index is constructed taking the average of the selected dwelling characteristics.

[5] Southern Cone includes: Argentina, Brazil, Chile, Uruguay and Paraguay. Andean Region includes: Bolivia, Colombia, Perú and Venezuela. Central América includes: Costa Rica, El Salvador, Honduras, México and Panamá.

[6] Interestingly, these trends differ from nominal per capita household incomes and even PPP-adjusted national per capita GDP. It is worth noting that the former refers to the nominal purchasing power of each national currency in its respective country, while the latter to the international purchasing power of local currency based on estimated incomes from national accounts. The PPP-adjusted real trends that we report refer to the real purchasing power of local currencies in the international economy or, more specifically, how, for instance, the purchasing power of a Chilean peso or a Venezuelan Bolivar would fare in the US over time.

Table 3. Poverty Mobility

Period	Mobility around the US$1/day threshold (% of synthetic households)		Mobility around the US$2/day threshold (% of synthetic households)	
t+1	Poor	Non Poor	Poor	Non Poor
t				
Poor	11.72%	4.86%	36.74%	8.09%
Non Poor	4.61%	78.8%	7.60%	47.57%
	Incidence with respect to US$1/day threshold (distribution of synthetic households in each category)		Incidence with respect to US$2/day threshold (distribution of synthetic household in each category)	
N	178	846	536	488
%	17.38%	82.62%	52.34%	47.66%

Source: Own calculations based on IDB Research Department Harmonized Household Surveys.

When we analyze mobility with respect to poverty lines (using the international thresholds of US$1/day and US$2/day/person for extreme and total poverty, respectively), we also conclude that mobility is limited. Before discussing these results, it is worth noting that the US$1 /day and US$2/day per person are widely used international poverty lines accepted to estimate global poverty. World Bank (1990) introduced its use. The construction of the US$1/day line is based on an average of six country specific extreme poverty lines (Bangladesh, Indonesia, Kenya, Morocco, Nepal and Tanzania) that are subsequently expressed in national 1985 PPP$ terms –and updated in 2000 to US$1.08 to reflect 1993 PPP$. Criticisms1 accuse this methodology of either consistently underestimating the number of the poor (Reddy and Pogge, 2003) or of having grossly overestimated them (Sala-i-Martin 2006). Others consider that these income or consumption-based lines overlook other dimensions of poverty (UNDP 2006), and recommend the inclusion of early death, adult illiteracy, child's malnutrition and population access to safe water in the calculation of poverty (which has, in effect, resulted in the construction of the Human Poverty Index). Notwithstanding the relevance of such criticisms, they are not the focus of the paper. We follow the vast tradition of considering the US$2/day international poverty line as an appropriate threshold for international comparisons across the typically middle-income economies in Latin America (and further compare them with estimates accruing from a US$1/day line)

Table 3 below reports that about 15% of the households (represented by their household heads) crossed the US$2/day/person threshold and less than 10% did so with respect to the US$ 1/day/person line. Interestingly, the numbers of households slipping into and moving out these thresholds are almost identical: 51% of these mobile households moved out of the threshold line; the remaining 49% slipped into poverty.

Further analysis reveals that households moving in and out of extreme poverty (threshold of US$1/day/person) share more characteristics than those moving around the US$2/day/person poverty line. Table 4 shows that households pertaining to the two cohorts defined between 1955 and 1968 represent two thirds of the 'mobile' households around the extreme poverty line. In contrast, those cohorts only explain 37% and 25% of the mobility out and into the US$2/day/person line, respectively. Households whose heads are aged 18 to 34 represent some 57% of those slipping into poverty but only 28% of those able to escape from poverty.

Table 5 confirms the existence of disparities between mobility around the US$1 and US$2/day/person lines. There are not statistically significant differences between households moving in and out of the US$1/day/person line in terms of gender and education of the household head, household size and dwelling characteristics. Only age plays a role, with poor households able to move out of extreme poverty being older, on average, than other 'mobile' households. In contrast, younger and more educated household heads in smaller households are more likely to slip into poverty than are such households to move out of poverty. This may simply reflect the different initial conditions of non-poor households before slipping into poverty rather than conditions that cause a household's slipping into poverty at any given time.

Table 4. Cohorts Mobility

Birth Cohort	Poor to Non Poor	Non Poor to Poor
US$1/day/person		
1927-1933	0.00	0.03
1934-1940	4.08	2.49
1941-1947	4.35	2.09
1948-1954	3.42	7.02
1955-1961	18.97	31.01
1962-1968	46.09	34.96
1969-1975	15.90	5.53
1976-1980	7.20	16.88
Total	100.0	100.0
US$2/day/ person		
1927-1933	1.80	0.55
1934-1940	7.43	5.56
1941-1947	10.01	2.74
1948-1954	15.19	9.92
1955-1961	23.91	9.98
1962-1968	13.50	14.31
1969-1975	26.05	36.61
1976-1980	2.10	20.33
Total	100.0	100.0

Source: Own calculations based on IDB Research Department Harmonized Household Surveys.

Table 5. Differences in Characteristics among Households

Characteristics	Poor to Non Poor	Non Poor to Poor	Remains Poor	Never Poor
US$1/day/ person				
Age	44.86	38.84	41.25	38.91
		[6.02]**	[3.61]	[5.95]***
Gender	0.23	0.25	0.41	0.48
		[-0.03]	[-0.18]**	[-0.25]***
Years of education	6.79	7.29	7.52	7.20
		[-0.50]	[-0.73]**	[-0.40]
Number of Children	2.01	2.10	2.42	1.83
		[-0.09]	[-0.40]***	[0.18]
Number of Other relatives	0.77	0.67	0.73	0.38
		[0.10]	[0.05]	[0.39]***
Dwelling Characteristics	1.18	1.13	1.22	1.35
		[0.05]	[-0.04]	[-0.17]***
US$2/day/ person				
Age	42.79	34.11	39.13	39.55
		[8.68]***	[3.66]**	[3.24]*
Gender	0.50	0.41	0.36	0.52
		[0.09]	[0.14]**	[-0.02]
Years of education	7.18	8.25	7.25	7.01
		[-1.08]***	[-0.07]	[0.17]
Number of Children	1.86	1.85	2.11	1.77
		[0.01]	[-0.24]***	[0.09]
Number of Other relatives	0.57	0.44	0.58	0.32
		[0.13]**	[0.00]	[0.25]***
Dwelling Characteristics	1.31	1.22	1.20	1.42
		[0.09]*	[0.11]***	[-0.11]***

Source: Own calculations based on IDB Research Department Harmonized Household Surveys.
*** statistical significance at 1%; (**) at 5%; (*) at 10%. T-statistics are presented in brackets.

4. ESTIMATION RESULTS

In this section we provide estimates of income mobility. Table 6 below reports estimates of time-dependence income mobility for Latin America as a region. Mobility is first reported as the elasticity of current incomes with respect to past incomes. As indicated in the Section 2, the inclusion of personal, socioeconomic, demographic and geographical controls determines several specifications of conditional mobility. In addition to specification I, the unconditional mobility model, specifications II to IX are constructed by introducing progressively such controls. The lower part of Table 6 reports the controls included in each specification. The sequential introduction of such controls allows us to better understand the marginal impact of socioeconomic and demographic factors versus geographical location. A second time-dependence mobility indicator is also reported as the elasticity of future income changes with respect to initial incomes. This indicator differs from the former most traditional measure of time-dependence mobility in that captures how the magnitude of changes rather than levels of incomes affect the expected income mobility of that pseudo-individual.

Results confirm a very low degree of income mobility for Latin America as a region, as previously found in literature. The estimate of the unconditional mobility indicator, β, is as high as 0.996 (see specification I in the upper panel in Table 6). This changes substantially after controls are introduced. Specifications II to IV gradually introduce personal and socioeconomic controls such as age, gender, education, number of children and housing conditions (that is, the dwelling index acting as a proxy for satisfaction of basic needs). The estimated mobility indicator falls from 0.99 to 0.70. Furthermore, specifications V to VIII introduce regional controls. A meager additional 0.5% of inter-temporal income variation is captured when these regional controls are added to previous specifications. When country dummies are introduced instead of regional dummies (specification IX), they capture an additional 10% of the inter-temporal income variation. This evidence suggests that a misleading attribution of demographic and socioeconomic impacts to past incomes may well generate a false sense of limited time-dependence income mobility.

Table 6. Estimates of Unconditional and Conditional Time-Dependence Income Mobility in Latin America[7]

	I	II	III	IV	V	VI	VII	VIII	IX
Estimated Income Mobility - Equation (3) $\overline{y}_{c(t),t} = \beta_c \overline{y}_{c(t-1),t-1} + \delta_c \overline{X}_{c(t),t} + \mu_{c(t),t}$									
B	0.966	0.744	0.707	0.704	0.949	0.723	0.69	0.693	0.588
	(645.45)**	(64.85)**	(55.59)**	(50.24)**	(199.03)**	(62.07)**	(55.40)**	(50.50)**	(46.91)**
R^2	0.998	0.997	0.998	0.999	0.999	0.997	0.999	0.999	0.999
N. observations	800	800	800	672	800	800	800	672	672
Estimated Income Mobility - Equation (4) $\Delta \overline{y}_{c(t),t} = \beta_c \overline{y}_{c(t-1),t-1} + \delta_c \Delta \overline{X}_{c(t),t} + \mu_{c(t),t}$									
B	-0.034	-0.196	-0.184	-0.182	-0.051	-0.203	-0.196	-0.196	-0.202
	(22.41)**	(16.25)**	(15.75)**	(13.64)**	(10.65)**	(17.94)**	(18.16)**	(15.85)**	(16.76)**
R^2	0.390	0.520	0.550	0.560	0.550	0.590	0.620	0.630	0.720
N. observations	800	800	800	672	800	800	800	672	672
Controlling By									
Age	No	Yes	Yes	Yes	No	Yes	Yes	Yes	Yes
Age²	No	Yes	Yes	Yes	No	Yes	Yes	Yes	Yes
Gender	No	Yes	Yes	Yes	No	Yes	Yes	Yes	Yes
Years of Education	No	Yes	No	No	No	Yes	No	No	No
Number of Children	No	Yes	Yes	Yes	No	Yes	Yes	Yes	Yes
Number of Other relatives	No	Yes	Yes	Yes	No	Yes	Yes	Yes	Yes
Educational Dummies	No	No	Yes	Yes	No	No	Yes	Yes	Yes
Dwelling Characteristics	No	No	No	Yes	No	No	No	Yes	Yes
Regional Dummies	No	No	No	No	No	Yes	No	Yes	No
Country Dummies	No	No	No	No	Yes	No	Yes	No	Yes

Source: Own calculations based on IDB Research Department Harmonized Household Surveys.

---

[7] For presentation reasons, complete estimates for all specifications in this table and Table 7 are not reported in this paper. They are available upon request to the authors.

Table 7. Country-specific Estimates of Unconditional and Conditional Time-Dependence Income Mobility in Latin America

Country	Estimated Income Mobility Equation (3) $\bar{y}_{c(t),t} = \beta_c \bar{y}_{c(t-1),t-1} + \delta_c \bar{X}_{c(t),t} + \mu_{c(t),t}$		Estimated Income Mobility Equation (4) $\Delta\bar{y}_{c(t),t} = \beta_c \bar{y}_{c(t-1),t-1} + \delta_c \overline{\Delta X}_{c(t),t} + \mu_{c(t),t}$		
	Specification I (*)	Specification IV(*)	Specification IV		N
	β	β_c	β_c	R2	
Argentina	0.975	0.74	0.035	0.37	70
	192.20**	2.70**	0.44		
Bolivia	0.973	0.37	-0.026	0.47	40
	125.66**	5.24**	0.35		
Brazil	0.982	0.85	-0.051	0.95	56
	840.59**	20.14**	3.87**		
Chile	0.995	0.68	-0.068	0.89	56
	333.34**	7.60**	2.70*		
Colombia	0.964	0.81	-0.136	0.96	70
	204.16**	20.66**	7.80**		
Costa Rica	0.973	0.53	-0.472	0.85	28
	238.98**	2.59*	2.31*		
Honduras	0.96	0.09	-0.118	0.9	44
	123.32**	1.71*	2.27*		
Mexico	0.945	0.42	-0.32	0.9	56
	133.95**	12.54**	7.44**		
Panama	0.999	---	---		
	281.24**	---	---		
Peru	0.945	0.15	-0.056	0.87	44
	133.95**	17.1*	1.45		
Paraguay	0.996	0.88	-0.069	0.95	42
	175.12**	10.00**	2.69*		
El Salvador	0.955	0.47	0.017	0.53	28
	257.19**	2.86*	0.17		
Uruguay	1.005	0.3	-0.465	0.87	70
	306.65**	8.68**	10.11**		
Venezuela	0.896	0.4	-0.342	0.98	54
	151.62**	16.27**	15.08**		

* R^2 for specification I in all countries revolves around 0.95 and for specification IV exceeds 0.99.
Source: Own calculations based on IDB Research Department Harmonized Household Surveys.

The impact of previous incomes on today's incomes is additionally explored by looking at how initial levels of income affect changes observed in the following period. See the middle panel in Table 6. This alternative set of specifications confirms that the level of previous incomes plays a significant role in explaining today's incomes. The higher is the starting level of income, the lower its variation should be expected in a subsequent period. Its magnitude, however, varies according to the selected specification. Unsurprisingly, those with higher incomes are more capable of sustaining them, either because they possess larger stocks of human capital or have better access to insurance against shocks. When controls are introduced (specifications II to IX), this result becomes stronger, turning sizeable variations even less likely.

If initial levels of income play a significant role in explaining mobility, a country-specific analysis of mobility should reveal the heterogeneity of existing income levels across the Region. Table 7 reports country-specific estimates of mobility for the specification IV, which includes all personal, socioeconomic and demographic controls.

The estimates of income mobility in Table 7 are expressed as elasticities, which allows for a meaningful comparison across countries with different starting income levels. Estimated elasticities vary widely across country, as predicted. High levels of time-dependence income immobility (β exceeding 0.8) are only found in Brazil, Colombia and Paraguay, while the rest of the Region shows much higher levels of mobility (lower β). Countries such as Chile or Argentina show a moderate immobility (β between 0.66 and 0.79) compared with other 'mobile' countries (β below 0.66). These results confirm that a higher mobility is found across countries when countries are considered separately than when countries are being pooled regionally (as it was the case with results for Argentina using Navarro (2006) and Calónico (2006). Also, our results are consistent with Contreras et al (2004)'s conclusion of restrained mobility in Chile. Even when this limited evidence does not allow for generalizations, it may be that region-pooled estimates average out different country-specific patterns of income mobility.

The above conclusion holds when country specific estimates of mobility are obtained using changes in income (equation 4) instead of levels of income (equation 3). The right hand side columns in Table 7 show that the level of past incomes may exert either a positive or negative impact in future incomes. Higher levels of past incomes are associated with larger increases in current incomes in Argentina, Chile and El Salvador, although it is only Chile (which managed to sustain growth during the last 20 years) where such an impact is statistically significant. In the remaining countries, higher levels of previous incomes are associated with lower variations of future incomes. Poorer countries exhibit larger time-dependence income mobility.

5. Conclusions

Difficulties in the construction of panel-data have prevented a comprehensive analysis of mobility in Latin America and elsewhere in the developing world. This paper sheds more light on the implications of mobility in the Region by constructing, alternatively, a pseudo-panel for 14 countries over 11 years and 8 birth cohorts. Our analysis focuses on the standard notion of income mobility and, in addition, explores a notion of mobility around poverty lines. We show that the Region as a whole is highly immobile in income terms. However, a sizeable part of this immobility results from failing to account from the effects that personal and socioeconomic controls have on mobility (over 30% of the unconditional time-dependence mobility). Country-specific differences are also substantive and tend to cancel out when grouped into traditional sub-regions (Andes, Southern Cone, Central America). Current levels of incomes not explained by past levels of incomes vary widely across countries, well exceeding in some cases 50% of estimated changes.

Household mobility around poverty lines was found symmetrical in size: as many as those households moving into poverty, moved out of poverty. The analysis of the characteristics of 'mobile' households shows interesting features, such that younger households being twice as likely to slip into poverty as to move out of it. Despite the limitations of the analysis (an econometric analysis of the effects of such controls on poverty mobility is also needed), we reject as simplistic and misleading the widely accepted notion of a dominating socioeconomic immobility throughout the Region. This is a first step towards uncovering the underlying dynamics of poverty mobility in a Region that for long has implemented one-size-fits-all economic reforms and poverty strategies.

ANNEX 1.

Table A.1. Household Surveys – and periods considered to construct the pseudo panels

Country	Survey	Period					
		T1	T2	T3	T4	T5	T6
		1992-1993	1994-1995	1996-1997	1998-1999	2000-2001	2002-2003
Argentina	Encuesta Permanente de Hogares (EPH)	x	x	x	x	x	x
Brasil	Pesquisa Nacional por Amostra de Domicilios (PNAD)		x	x	x	x	x
Bolivia	Encuesta de Hogares	x	x	x	x	x	x
Chile	Encuesta de Caracterización Socioeconómica Nacional (CASEN)	x	x	x	x	x	x
Colombia	Encuesta Continua de Hogares	x	x	x	x	x	
Costa Rica	Encuesta de Hogares de Propósitos Múltiples (EHPM)	x	x	x	x	x	x
Honduras	Encuesta Permanente de Hogares de Propósitos Múltiples			x	x	x	x
México	Encuesta Nacional de Ingreso y Gastos de los Hogares (ENIGH)		x	x	x	x	x
Panamá	Encuesta de Hogares		x	x	x	x	x
Paraguay	Encuesta Permanente de Hogares			x	x	x	x

Table A.1. Continued

Country	Survey	Period					
		T1	T2	T3	T4	T5	T6
		1992-1993	1994-1995	1996-1997	1998-1999	2000-2001	2002-2003
Perú	Encuesta Nacional de Hogares sobre Medición de Niveles de Vida			x	x	x	x
El Salvador	Encuesta de Hogares de Propósitos Múltiples (EHPM)				x	x	x
Uruguay	Encuesta Continua de Hogares	x	x	x	x	x	x
Venezuela	Encuesta de Hogares por Muestreo		x	x	x	x	x

Source: Own calculations based on IDB Research Department Harmonized Household Surveys.

REFERENCES

Albornoz, F. y Menéndez, M. (2004). *"Income dynamics in Argentina during the 1990s: 'Mobiles' did change over time"*. World Bank, forthcoming.

Antman, F. and Mckenzie, D. (2005). *"Earnings Mobility and Measurement Error: A Pseudo-Panel Approach"*, World Bank Policy Research Working Paper # 3745.

Bourguinon F. and Goh C. (2004). *"Estimating individual vulnerability to poverty with pseudo-panel data"*. The World Bank, Washington DC.

Browning, M., Deaton, A. y Irish M. (1985). "A profitable approach to labor supply and commodity demand over the life-cycle". *Econometrica* 53, (3): 503-544.

Calónico S. (2006). *"Pseudo-Panel analysis of Earnings Dynamics and Mobility in Latin America"*. Research Department, Inter-American Development Bank, Washington DC.

Collado, M.D. (1997). "Estimating dynamic models from time series of independent crosssections". *Journal of Econometrics* 82: 37–62.

Contreras, D., Cooper, R., Herman, J. and Neilson, C. (2004). *"Dinámica de la pobreza y movilidad social en Chile"*.Universidad de Chile. Mimeo.

Corbacho, A., M. Garcia-Escribano, M. and G. Inchauste (2003) *"Argentina: Macroeconomic Crisis and Household Vulnerability"*, IMF Working Paper.

Deaton, A. (1985). "Panel data from times series of cross-sections". *Journal of Econometrics* (30): 109–126.

Fields, G.F and Sánchez Puerta, M. (2005). "Earnings mobility in urban Argentina". *Background Paper Prepared for the World Bank.* World Bank, Washington DC.

Fields G., Duval R., Freije S. and Sánchez Puerta M. (2006). "Inter-generational income mobility in Latin America". Economia, forthcoming.

Galiani, Sebastián (2006). "Notes on Social Mobility." Mimeo. Universidad de San Andrés.

Inter-American Development Bank, IADB (1998).*Economic and Social Progress Report 1998/9*. IADB, Washington DC.

Lillard, L. y Willis, R. (1978). "Dynamics aspects of earnings mobility". *Econometrica 46* (5): 985-1012.

Mckenzie, D. (2004). "Asymptotic theory for heterogeneous dynamic pseudopanels". *Journal of Econometrics*. 120(2), 235-262.

Milanovic, B. (2006). "Global income inequality: What it is and Why it Matters?". World Bank Policy Research Working Paper 3865. World Bank, Washington DC.

Moffit, R. (1993). "Identification and estimation of dynamic models with a time series of repeated cross-sections". *Journal of Econometrics* 59: 99–124.

Navarro A. I. (2006). "Estimating income mobility in Argentina with pseudo-panel data". Department of Economics, Universidad de San Andres. Mimeo

Reddy, S. and Pogge T. (2003). "How not to count the poor". Available at www. socialanalysis.org

Sala-I-Martin, X. (2006)."The world distribution of incomes: falling poverty and convergence, period". *Quarterly Journal of Economics,* May 2006, 121 (2): 351-97.

Scott, C. (2000) "Mixed Fortunes: A Study of Poverty Mobility among Small Farm Household in Chile, 1968-86," *Journal of Development Studies*, 36, 155-180.

United Nations Development Programme, UNDP, 2006. *Human Development Report.* New York: Oxford University Press.

Verbeek, M. y Vella, F. (2002). *"Estimating dynamic models from repeated cross-sections". Mimeo,* K.U. Leuven Center for Economic Studies.

World Bank (2003) *Inequality in Latin America and the Caribbean. Breaking with History?* World Bank, Washington DC.

World Bank (1990). *World Development Report 1990*. World Bank, Washington DC.

In: World Poverty Issues
Editor: Marilyn M. Watkins, pp. 139-153

ISBN: 978-1-60456-057-2
© 2008 Nova Science Publishers, Inc.

Chapter 6

ALLEVIATION OF RISKS AND VULNERABILITY FACING ISOLATED COMMUNITIES THROUGH CONSERVATION AND MANAGEMENT OF BIO-DIVERSITY: THE LOWER KUISEB RIVER BASIN, NAMIBIA

Josephine Phillip Msangi
University of Namibia, Namibia

ABSTRACT

Aridity characterizes an expansive area of Southern Africa and almost the whole of Namibia. Although known to be hot and dry, Namibia is characterized by a wide range of microclimates and varying habitats that include some sizable wetlands rich in biodiversity that supports a wide range of plant and animal life. The Namib, the oldest desert in the world, straddles the extremely arid coast of Namibia along its border with the Atlantic Ocean. The Kuiseb River Valley forms one of seven linear oases traversing the Namib Desert. The Kuiseb River Valley and other linear oases traversing the Namib are dotted with numerous small settlements whose inhabitants, depending on the bio-resources, until recently, had successfully adjusted to the conditions created by varying hydrological and climatic elements. Indigenous groups settled here include the Topnaar of the lower Kuiseb valley who had over the last few centuries sustainably exploited the biological resources for food, medicine and fodder for their livestock. Their survival techniques were greatly determined and shaped by the biological resources as determined by climatic variability characterizing their narrow relatively moist habitat along the lower Kuiseb valley. However, recent new developments and interventions in the upper and lower reaches of the valley tipped the scales against the Topnaar. The paper discusses the interactions between biological resources, habitat modifications and society in the lower Kuiseb valley through time and by analyzing recent developments and interventions in the Kuiseb River basin management strategies, highlights undermining of old-age coping mechanisms and increasing vulnerability to risks facing the Topnaar. The strong community spirit and community based activities have been thrown into disarray; the very existence of the Topnaar settlements hangs in balance. Conservation and management of biodiversity based on people centered planning should be adopted where social, economic and environmental consequences of an undertaking are given deserving emphasis. Conservation strategies ought to be multi-disciplinary in nature and consider the entire river basin. Social-economic as well as environmental impacts should be considered alongside the often over-emphasized profit maximization. Stable policies that form part of broader national development strategies need to be formulated and/or revised so as to enhance resilience to dwindling biological resources dictated by recent interventions leading to biodiversity changes affecting the indigenous community inhabiting the lower Kuiseb River Valley. Strong partnerships and indigenous knowledge considerations are necessary to ensure that all aspects of the biological resources on which the inhabitants depend on are included in such studies.

INTRODUCTION

Namibia, a large country (823,680 km²) with a coastline 1,440 km long, is located on the west coast of the Southern Africa sub-continent (Figure 1). Namibia is a dry country with very limited water resources; its climate is the second in aridity to that of the Sahara (Bethune, 1996; Mendelsohn et al, 2002). The rainfall is variable, unpredictable and unreliable; it varies between 20mm along the west coast to 850mm in the extreme northeast. The rainfall occurs mainly during summer months for most parts of the country, the southwestern part receiving winter rainfall. Evaporation rates are extremely high throughout the country; the average evaporation rate being 2500mm in the northwest and 3700mm in the southeast (Bethune, 1996, Christellis & Struckmeir 2001).

Namibia's climate is highly variable and difficult to understand. It is a direct interplay of various factors including its relative location on the southwestern part of the Africa continent, spanning a zone between 17° and 29° south of the equator. Thus Namibia is exposed to air movements driven by three major climatic systems. The Intertropical Convergence Zone (ITCZ) feeds in moisture-laden air from the north while the Sub-tropical High Pressure System positioned across the country pushes the moist air back with dry cold air. The effect of this system is more pronounced than that of the ITCZ so that Namibia is characterized by dry hot weather for most of the year. The Temperate System to the south of the country with predominantly moisture laden westerly winds which carry a succession of low pressure systems and cold fronts from west to east feeding bursts of cold air from the Antarctic, sweep across southern Africa during southern hemisphere winter, bringing some moisture to the south-western part of Namibia. These three systems move south and northwards in response to the overhead sun (Mendelsohn et al 2002). (Figure 1).

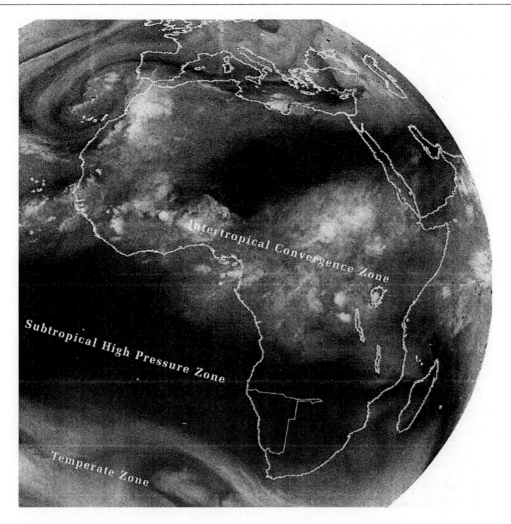

Figure 1. Major Climatic Systems Affecting Namibia (Mendelsohn, et al 2002).

Other factors influencing the climate in Namibia include the cold Benguela current flowing from South Atlantic Ocean and the Drakensberg range mountains that span the eastern coast of the continent. The cold current cools the easterly flowing air stream from below occasioning fog formation along the coast extending to about 100 km inland. No clouds form and therefore most years pass without rain in this part of the country. The mountain range along the eastern coast of Southern Africa force moist airstreams to rise, condense and drop most of the moisture on its eastern side descending as dry air on the mountains' western side reaching Namibia as dry airstreams; thus the presence of the Kalahari desert on the eastern part of Namibia.

Although known to be hot and dry for most of the year, Namibia's climate is highly variable. Temperatures and rainfall vary greatly over space and time, variability being compounded by the shifts in the relative position of the three major climatic systems. Temperatures are usually very high for most part of the year (in the mid and upper 30°C reaching 40°- 44°C in the northern and southern part of the country as well as over the Namib Desert only cooling off during the short winter period. Winds blow strongly for most part of the year being strongest along the coast where dry hot sand-laden winds fill up hand dug wells and compounding difficulties and risks facing communities dependent on natural resources exploitation for their livelihood.

KUISEB RIVER VALLEY

In Namibia, there are only four perennial rivers that are confined to the southern and northern borders of the country. They are shared with neighbouring countries of Angola, Zambia, Botswana and South Africa (Msangi, 2005). Due to vast distances, the high costs of water abstraction and transfer as well as high evaporation rates, these rivers are not extensively utilized. Namibia largely depends on groundwater and twelve westward flowing ephemeral rivers that have been dammed severally (Table 1). The ephemeral rivers with catchments in more relatively wet parts of the country (250-600mm), flow westwards to disappear into the Namib sands and gravels before emerging as springs and discharges at the ocean margin or discharge directly out to sea as groundwater base flow. A few of them traverse the desert forming oases across the Namib offering habitats to both people and animals inhabiting the desert.

The Kuiseb river valley forms one of the oases traversing the central Namib Desert. The Kuiseb river catchment is the third largest of the ephemeral rivers with an area of approximately 15, 500 km (Jacobson et al, 1995). Its source lies at 1,500m above sea level on the Khomas Hochland mountain plateau near Windhoek (Map 1). After crossing the Namib it empties into the Atlantic Ocean through a 30 kms wide delta. Variable rainfall is received over the catchment area; an amount of 400mm is received in the upper catchment (Botelle & Kowalski, 1995) and 21 mm in the lower catchment (average for 32 years -1962-1992) (Henschel et al, 2004). Like the rest of the country, rainfall varies considerably not just over space but over time as well. Temperatures are extremely high in the lower catchment area during the day particularly during summer months dropping to below freezing during winter; evaporation rates are astronomical made worse by the strong desiccating winds characterizing the lower reaches of the valley.

Table 1. Water availability in Namibia: (dependent on precipitation and aquifer size)

Source	Quantity	Remarks
Groundwater	300Mm³ per year**	Long-term sustainability
Ephemeral Surface Water	200Mm³ per year	95% assurance of supply
Perennial Surface Water	150Mm³ per year	Installed abstraction capacity 2001
Unconventional	10Mm³ per year	Reclamation, re-use and recycling

** Some of the groundwater reserve exists as fossil water in aquifers found below the earlier larger lake that covered areas in northern Namibia and southern Angola. This water accumulated tens of thousands of years ago when the climate in Southern Africa region was much wetter than now.
Source: Christelis, G and Struckmeir (eds.) (2001): Groundwater in Namibia.

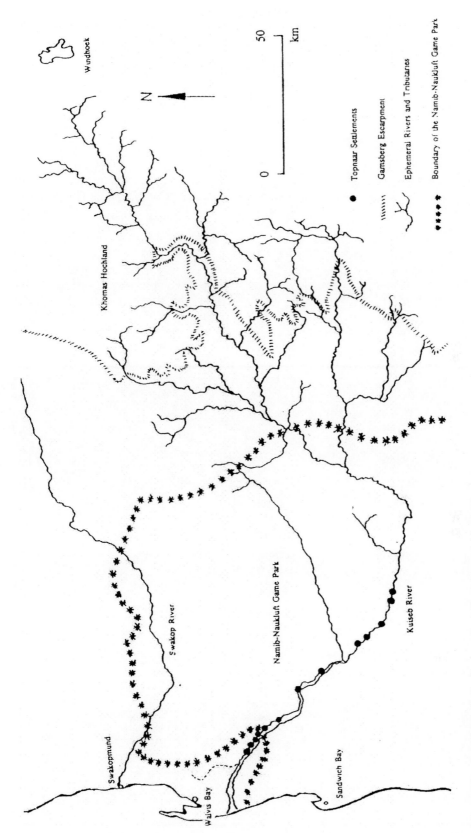

Map 1. The Kuiseb River Catchment (Botelle & Kowalski, 1995).

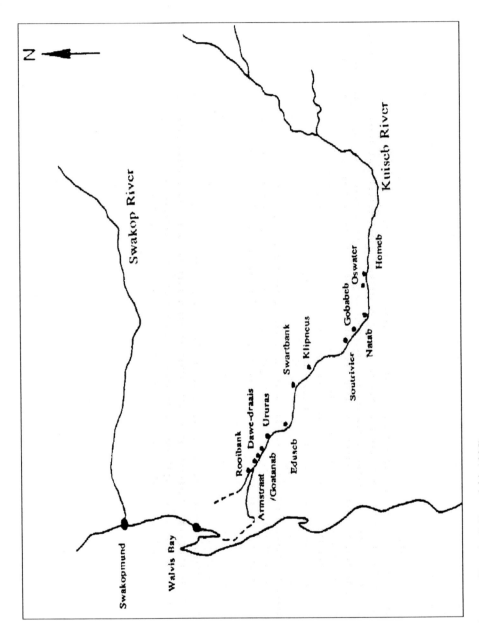

Map 2. Topnaar Settlements (Bottele & Kowalski, 1995).

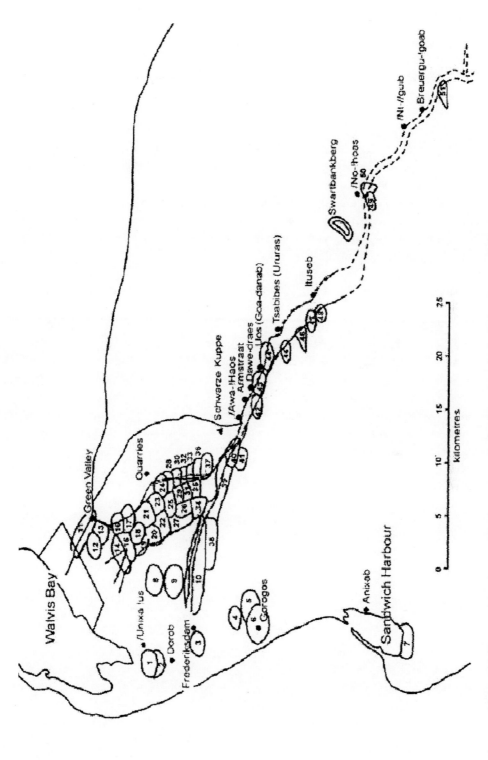

Map 3. Nara Fields and Villages of the Topnaar in the Lower Kuiseb Valley and Delta (Henschel et al, 2004).

While the 20mm received at the lower catchment is augmented by fog varying between 30mm-180mm per year (Botelle & Kowalski, 1995), it is important to note that all life forms for the lower catchment is concentrated along the riverbed and therefore interventions in the upper catchment directly affects the life at the lower catchment of the Kuiseb. An array of life forms including plants and animals depends on the fog for their water needs.

The upper catchment comprising 63% of the Kuiseb catchment supports 109 private farms and a large number of livestock and wildlife (Jackobson, et al 1995). These private farms depend on 407 farm dams and 591 subsurface water sources of which 90% are boreholes. These interventions dating only back to the mid 1970s have reduced the runoff from the Khomas mountains and the escarpment by 21% thus drastically reducing runoff reaching the lower catchment area of the Kuiseb where the Topnaar community is found (Botelle & Kowalski, 1995). The lower catchment life forms rely heavily on the flow from the upper catchment (either periodic floods or subsurface flow) that has been heavily reduced by the interventions in the upper catchment. High floods reaching the delta have only been recorded in 1990/1991, 2000 and 2006.

During earlier times, the floods brought down not only much needed water to the lower Kuiseb but also nutrients for the woodland vegetation and home gardens as well as logs for fuel wood and for protecting wells and fencing off the gardens. Recent years have seen a decline in the frequency as well as magnitude of the floods. Recent years have also witnessed much fluctuation in the structure and density of the riverine vegetation. The fluctuations in the woodland structure being a direct outcome of the reduced flood frequency that determines water and nutrient availability in an otherwise barren desert sand dunes and gravel environment. The riverine vegetation and abundance of other resources have fluctuated with the flooding regime of the river. According to recent surveys carried out on the woodland resources of the lower Kuiseb, there are many climatic and hydrological cycles (seasonal, yearly, wetter periods and drier periods), each superimposed one on top of the other (Botelle & Kowalski, 1995). As a result the lower river system is very fragile and dependent on the erratic rainfall and abstractions further up-river. Thus hydrological changes taking place upstream directly affects life forms downstream.

TOPNAAR COMMUNITY

The Topnaar are a community of about 300 inhabitants of hunters and gatherers living in the lower Kuiseb valley in the Namib Desert (Map 2). One of the oldest indigenous people of Namibia belonging to the Khoekhoen who have lived in the Namib Desert for many centuries, traditionally depended on small stock farming, vegetable gardening and !nara harvesting and processing for their livelihood. The Topnaar were identified through their association with the !nara plant, a cucurbit adapted to the Namib. A leafless thorny melon-bearing bush, the !nara is an important component of the dune ecosystem providing shelter and food to many different animals. It survives the harsh environment by tapping water from deep underground (down to 40-60m deep) through its deep tap root. In the past individual Topnaar families claimed ownership to individual !nara plants. This ownership was recognized and respected by other families in the community (Map 3).

The Topnaar community had evolved a self-sufficient system where the whole family served as a productive unit around which multiple activities like food and clothing production were organized. They had learnt to live and interact with their ever changing environment determined by the inherent climatic variables which shaped the way they utilized what was available in their natural physical environment (Henschel et al, 2004; Botelle & Kowaliski, 1995). The Topnaar had adjusted to their environment and sustainably exploited natural resources to obtain food, shelter and later since mid nineteenth century traded with outsiders to obtain consumer goods not available in their immediate environment.

The Kuiseb River was and still is the lifeblood of the central Namib Desert, the home to the Topnaar community. However fast changing policies and subsequent interventions are negating earlier interactions and adopted strategies. Studies conducted during mid 1990s and early 2000s, have revealed that in the past the Topnaar moved up and down over a vast area (about 200 kms along the valley) in search of food and building materials. They also moved freely along the narrow seaboard along the Atlantic Ocean fishing and scavenging local marine resources. They evolved a land tenure system, utilizing a wide range of resources determined by the climatic variability of their otherwise harsh desert environment. They moved their livestock to the upper reaches of the valley during low rainfall periods and back to their homeland in the lower Kuiseb during wetter periods. During lean times when the land did not have much to offer they relied on the sea to augment whatever their gardens and livestock offered them (Botelle & Kowaliski, 1995; Henschel et al, 2004).

Although the Namib has always been the driest and barren part of the country, the Kuiseb river regime enabled the Topnaar to live and sustainably use the bio-resources therein for thousands of years. However, what is emerging today is a people unable to cope with their arid environment and unable to make a living from the land in the same way as they did in the past. The field studies conducted during the last 10 years, have demonstrated that although droughts and floods always occurred interchangeably in the lower Kuiseb, in the past, the people had devised sustainable coping strategies through manipulating the available bio-resources and adjusting to these environmental vagaries. However, currently, their social organization and their economy are in a state of flux; the Topnaar have a much smaller area in which to maneuver. They live in more or less sedentary settlements dependent more on inputs from outside their environment due to various interventions which have not only confined them to a smaller area but have also changed the river regime and the nutrients brought down by the floods to support the rich vegetation and home gardens.

INTERVENTIONS

Detailed analyses of the various interventions through time have been presented in various documents. However, according to the book by Henschel and others, the first event that reversed the trend and way of living for the Topnaar occurred as a consequence of political developments affecting Namibia as a country. In 1884 Namibia, then a British colony was transferred to German rule and in 1920 the country was entrusted to South Africa by the League of Nations. A direct consequence of these shifts in colonial powers was the development of fishing and harbour industries in Walvis Bay at the delta of the Kuiseb River. Many coastal Topnaar moved further inland while others were absorbed into the industrial workforce. Further developments at Swakopmund necessitated the construction of water extraction schemes along the lower Kuiseb Valley at Rooibank (1927) and near Swartbank (1960's), both main Topnaar settlements. In 1962 a high flood barrier was constructed in the Kuiseb delta to protect Walvis Bay from flooding whenever the river flooded. This blocked the river surface flow thus reducing groundwater recharge in the northern delta area. This killed some of the !nara fields and lowered productivity from 1970 onwards. This further led to the abandonment of long established tending practices such as family ownership of the !nara plants to communal ownership due to the fact that some families lost their plants in the northern delta area. Communal ownership of the fields ruined the caring practices of the plants as it led to over harvesting and general mismanagement of the fields (Henschel et al, 2004).

It is further stated that while all this was taking place in the lower catchment area, developments in the upper reaches of the valley occasioned the construction of private farm dams with the resultant effect of lowering the water table in the lower reaches of the Kuiseb thus negatively affecting the riverine vegetation and the water source of the Topnaar who depended on hand dug wells for their domestic water needs and that for their animals and home gardens.

The second event that tipped the scales against the Topnaar is documented to be the proclamation of the Namib Game Reserve by the German colonialists in 1907 and the establishment of the Namib-Naukluft Park by the South Africa Government in 1975. The formulated park regulations were in direct conflict with traditional land use practices of the Topnaar such as periodic hunting of wild game for meat and the trapping of predators that killed their domesticated animals. Also prohibited by these regulations is the burning of the !nara bushes to improve productivity (Henschel et al, 2004). In the same publication, it is documented that the park boundaries limits the freedom of movement of the Topnaar in response to the variable climatic conditions within the Kuiseb valley. Park rules are reported to have influenced and eroded gender roles that once supported traditional systems of land tenure. Key land use activities that once satisfied the needs of entire households are reported to require supplementation with new sources of income, food and shelter.

Furthermore, the third event that led to changes in the situation facing the Topnaar is documented to be the sinking of deep boreholes (down to 10-30m deep) fitted with a windmill or a diesel pump engine to supply all settlements with domestic water and for their home gardens. The outcome of this undertaking is reported to have caused further lowering of the water table and hence the final death to hand dug wells for the Topnaar. Further negative impact of this intervention is the fact that the windmills pump water continuously and subjecting it to evaporation (wastage of a scarce and valuable resource) while the diesel pumps require diesel, which is not easy to get in these remote settlements. In the absence of wind, it is reported that people go without water for long periods. The situation becomes worse when once consideration is given to the fact that the people are not trained to maintain these engines and where an engineer attached to the settlements is not always available; the spare parts are difficult to come by due to either the unaffordable high costs of the parts or unavailability. Another observation on the disadvantage of the boreholes as permanent water sources is that the Topnaar have become more or less permanently settled. Permanent water source encourage growth in livestock numbers and subsequently over utilization of water, grazing and the deterioration of land and other resources. The Topnaar no longer move their animals up and down the valley because of prohibitive park regulations.

Additionally, another event that affected the Topnaar and their bio-resources management practices was the independence of Namibia in 1990. Article 95 of the country's constitution states that "The state shall actively promote and maintain the welfare of the people by adopting, *inter alia*, policies aimed at improving the following: maintenance of ecosystems, essential ecological processes and biological diversity of Namibia and utilization of living natural resources on a sustainable basis for the benefit of all users to make a living from the land..." However, to date, the issue of actions to be taken by independent Namibia Government to reverse actions taken during colonial times that have negatively affected the indigenous residents of lower Kuiseb Valley remains unresolved. According to available literature, there is uncertainty as to how to satisfy the different needs of all resource users living in the entire Kuiseb catchment.

Furthermore, it is reported that the establishment of the Walvis Lagoon Park in 1990 introduced additional restrictions on the area available to the Topnaar to occupy and practice their traditional land use and bio-resources management practices particularly those surrounding the harvesting and processing of the !nara. As stated in paragraphs above, the earlier interventions in the upper catchment lead to the reduction of silt load reaching the lower valley and its delta. This has in turn led to a chain of related impacts including a receding shoreline by wave action, salinization of some of the coastal dunes where rich !nara fields were located and substantial loss of productivity of the fields which has further robed the Topnaar an avenue of practicing their annual migration to the delta to harvest and process the !nara, previously an important source of food and income.

Other documented interventions that have affected the Topnaar of the lower Kuiseb include the urban developments along the coast in the vicinity of their traditional land area. The towns of Walvis Bay and Swakopmund have acted as a pull factor to the process of rural-urban migration for the Topnaar. This has influenced the way of life in the various settlements whose considerable numbers of working-age men and the youth have migrated to the towns to seek employment. Some send back cash, consumer goods and clothing to their family members back in the settlements while some have abandoned their villages altogether and settled in the poor sections of the two towns. Western way of life has penetrated some parts of the Topnaar settlements introducing inequalities not inherent before. Like in the case of all urban poor neighbourhoods where the unskilled and uneducated Topnaar migrants find themselves living in, alcoholism and petty crime is affecting the entire extended families both in the rural areas and in the urban segments. The quality of life for some part of the community is reported to be deteriorating fast.

It is reported that in the past, entire families carried out important activities together and family members complemented each other by dividing their labour along gender lines. For example extended families moved *en masse* to the Kuiseb delta to harvest the !nara during summer months (December-March). Women stayed near the camp to process the !nara and carry out domestic chores while the men and older boys were away collecting !nara fruit and selling the !nara pips. While the division of labour is still evident, currently, gender roles are less clearly defined. Social and economic activities are carried out by both men and women who make decisions independently as individuals rather than as a family unit. Unheard of in the past, women, like men, exchange stock for consumer goods and collect second hand building materials from the neighbouring towns to construct their make shift homes and to fence gardens.

The Topnaar are highly dependent on the riverine vegetation. Various tree species which provided building materials, fuel, stockades, medicine and fodder no longer satisfy their needs due to lowered water table and subsequent dying off of some of the vegetation. The Topnaar's reliance on the river and its ability to support plant life has left them vulnerable to the highly variable river regime especially during droughts when upstream users let through little or no water at all for the down stream users or during years with excessive rain when the upstream users let through excess water from their dams resulting in floods and destruction of property and !nara fields downstream (for example during 2006 rain season). In the past the Topnaar overcame the Kuiseb's climate and hydrological variability by adopting a variety of strategies such as moving their stock along the river and balancing their reliance on riverine vegetation with other resources in the delta and from the sea. Currently this is not possible due to the park rules, the fishing regulations and restrictions as well as Walvis Bay municipality regulations.

The rural-urban migration as well as schooling is said to have deprived the rural area of labour reserves. The better off Topnaar see formal education as the way out of their deteriorating quality of life. Families struggle to send their children to school in the hope that they will do well and secure good jobs that will generate a source of livelihood for them back at the settlements. This in turn has deprived the rural areas of much needed labour to look after livestock and harvest the !nara. Schooling has altered household division of labour and the way natural resources are utilized. The poorer families loose out to wealthier and well connected ones. The rural population find themselves more and more alienated from each other as their struggle has become that of survival of the fittest, giving less and less consideration for each other. Whoever reaches the !nara fields first harvests everything including unripe fruits which deprives others and at the same time lower the quality of the pips and therefore fetches less income. A new trend is reported to have emerged in recent years where the people are less and less dependent on each other and their own initiative; rather they look to the Government and outside NGOs for solutions to their problems. Solutions that are not readily available!

IMPLICATIONS OF INTERVENTIONS

The above interventions have produced many negative implications for the lower Kuiseb valley Topnaar. The changed river regime has jeopardized Kuiseb's inherently fragile environment. With permanent water sources, the Government discourages the movement of stock.. Fewer and fewer Topnaar travel to the delta to harvest and process !nara melon and no Topnaar exploit marine resources as they did in the past. They are only dependent on dwindling riverine forest resources thus remaining very vulnerable to the dying off vegetation resources. The anaboom tree on which livestock depended on has completely collapsed (Botelle & Kowalski, 1995) leaving the livestock to feed from less palatable species which has adversely affected the milk and meet quality. Other species such as palm trees are also said to be dwindling and those that remain such as fig trees do not bear fruit. To compound this vulnerability is the unsustainable exploitation of the groundwater resources.

Similarly, wildlife that formed an important part of the Topnaar diet is reported to have ceased frequenting the valley with the dying of important tree species. Animals such as elephants, rhino, leopard, lion and giraffe no longer visit the valley while springbok, gemsbok, ostriches and wild dogs and cats, and hares, are much fewer in number and less frequent due to building of farm dams and fences upstream which obstruct migration routes. All that is left are the destructive predators such as jackals and hyena, which kill livestock in the absence of wildlife. In the past there was a period set aside for hunting wildlife, a period outside mating and calving season. The Topnaar only hunted for food and skins, never contravening established traditional regulations. Currently, it has been observed that individuals hunt excessively whenever it is possible because otherwise they are hunting against park regulations.

The Topnaar continue to live in their traditional land and remain relatively isolated. Poorer than they were in the past, they continue to adjust to changing situations and have devised new coping mechanisms of utilizing their traditional land despite its reduced size and deteriorating environmental health. Most families are reported to still keep livestock (mostly small stock and no cattle) and harvest and process !nara or keep home gardens albeit smaller than before the interventions. The Topnaar acknowledge that some land uses such as livestock farming exert great pressure on their much-reduced land yet without viable alternatives, they are forced to overuse an already stressed environment (Botelle & Kowalski, 1995). The earlier key land use activities that once satisfied the needs of entire households have to be supplemented with new sources of income, food and shelter. Subsistence activities are less secure and thus emigration is on the increase. Many are emigrating to seek employment opportunities elsewhere yet without skill and education, the immigrants are very vulnerable and are subjected to great risks in their new habitats.

CONCLUSION AND RECOMMENDATIONS

Recent studies have demonstrated that since time immemorial, the Topnaar community of the lower Kuiseb had established a thriving livelihood based on bio-resources exploitation. Currently the Topnaar live in a marginalized socio-economic situation; their livelihoods based on livestock rearing and !nara harvesting and processing with some pension and remittance from town-employed members of their extended family. They no longer have access to marine resources that used to be a mainstay of their livelihoods. Future of the socio-economy based on bio-resource management looks bleak for the Kuiseb Topnaar. It is recommended that what could get the Topnaar out of this depressing situation is not abrupt abandonment of traditional life style; rather concerted efforts to promote wise-use of the bio-resources that would encourage gradual social change through value addition to products manufactured locally. Building indigenous small enterprises that neither depends on external guidance nor on alien processes and products will lead to increased opportunities for training and recruitment from within the community thus enabling the community to improve its livelihood. What the community requires is assistance and cooperation of interested parties to enable it realize these goals (Henschel, et al 2004).

The study conducted in 2000 and published in 2004 involving a cross-section of the Topnaar community members, primary and secondary wholesalers and retails as well as relevant Government institutions and NGOs, concluded that with training and better resource management, the quality of livelihoods could be substantially improved. It is observed that the potential for developing sustainable bio-resources management exists so long as cooperative management techniques are resorted to. It is therefore recommended that development of any available local potential should be encouraged so as to reduce importation of foreign products and processes because importation tends to alienate people from their local environment, resources, traditions and skills. Reliance on livestock under the constraints of limited resources in the Kuiseb Valley demonstrated no future; on the other hand improved !nara management could lessen this dependence and conserve the constrained and degraded riverine bio-resources. The study further recommends using traditional knowledge and principles of community-based natural resources management to increase sustainability. Recommended also is improved marketing of !nara seeds and other products that could be generated from !nara fruit. Efforts ought to be made to increase incentives to those involved in harvesting and processing of the fruit so that they have direct access to the seed markets. The aim is to maximize profits for the !nara harvesters/processors and eliminating the middlemen so as to cut down on distribution and handling costs.

Furthermore, it is observed that while it is not possible for the Topnaar to completely divorce all newly acquired features in their way of life, it is important that they be assisted to adopt profitable and modern aspects of communal farming and aspects of rural entrepreneurship. This could include for example diversified micro-enterprises that would produce consumer products required by the rural community as well as others such as handcrafts, which could be marketed in the nearby crafts outlets in the neighbouring towns. The documentation observes that the community requires encouragement to work together again as family units forming units of a cooperative society so that there should be equal access to the resources, markets and profits accruing from whatever processed products from !nara and other local resources. Urgent support and assistance in promoting eco-tourism and appropriate product-packaging to improve their marketability is necessary. Observed also is the fact that tourism could serve as an outlet for the handcrafts and other locally produced products.

Other conclusions of the study include the fact that it is important for the Topnaar to diversify the products from their local resources particularly the !nara plant. The study identified several products that could be produced from !nara. These include staple food for the community, dried or roasted seeds, various baked products, oil/body lotion, dried fruit flesh, jam, juice, liqueur, medicinal products from root or stem extracts and a range of souvenirs. Equally as important is the need to legally protect the prospective !nara products through registration and acquisition of a trademark (Henschel et al, 2004). Future success in this area lies in further research on potential products from !nara and identification of possible marketing outlets. Cooperation between the Topnaar and research organizations and supporting institutions (both Governmental and Non-governmental organizations) is appreciated as essential in securing a future for the products and stimulating community development.

The Government and the Walvis Bay Municipality need to review the policies that are negatively affecting bio-resource usage and conservation at the lower Kuiseb Valley. Policies on land use and land conservation ought to take into consideration the needs of the entire Kuiseb River Basin bearing in mind the fact that the lower catchment is being adversely affected by the activities being undertaken in the upper and middle sections of the basin. While earlier reactions of the Government were to relocate the Topnaar to another part of the country, this was done without proper consultations with the community (Henschel et al,

2004). If indeed relocation is unavoidable due to earlier decisions already implemented such as the establishment of the Naukluft Park and vital commercial farms, there is need to conduct proper consultations, education and training involving sociologists, social workers and land use planners as well as the entire community. Proper assessment of properties that would be left behind need to be undertaken, compensation worked out and receiving area well prepared in advance of relocation exercise. Successful translocation of the community should bear in mind the fact that giving ones home, culture and all that it holds for him requires much more than minimal parallel compensation. Deliberate extra attractions ought to be included in the package, attractions such as employment opportunities, consumer goods outlets as well as educational, health and entertainment facilities.

REFERENCES

Bethune, S. 1996. Namibia's Challenge: Sustainable Water Use. In Tarr, P. (ed.) *1996. Namibia Environment,* Vol. 1, Windhoek, Namibia.

Botelle, A. & Kowalski, K. 1995. *Changing Resource Use in Namibia's Lower Kuiseb River Valley: Perceptions from the Topnaar Community.* Institute of Southern African Studies, Roma, Lesotho.

Braune, E. 1991. Hydrology of the Lower Kuiseb River, In Slabbert, A. (ed.) *Water Development for Walvis Bay.* Department of Water Affairs and Forestry, Windhoek, Namibia.

Christelis, G and Struckmeier, W (eds.) 2001. *Groundwater in Namibia: An Explanation to the Hydrogeological Map.* Windhoek, Namibia.

Dausab, F. Francis, G., Johr, G. Kambatuku, J.R., Molapo, M., Shanyengana, E.S. & Swartz, S. 1994. *Water Usage Patterns in the Kuiseb Catchment Area (with emphasis on sustainable use).* Desert Research Foundation of Namibia Occasional Paper No 1. Windhoek, Namibia.

Henschel, J., Dausab, R., Moser, P. & Pallet, J. (eds.) 2004. *!NARA. Fruit for development of the !Kuiseb Topnaar.* Namibia Scientific Society, Windhoek, Namibia.

Jacobson, P.J., Jacobson, K.M. & Seely, M.K. 1995. *Ephemeral Rivers and their Catchments.* Desert Research Foundation of Namibia, Windhoek, Namibia.

Mendelhson, J; Jarvis, A; Roberts, C & Robertson, T 2002. Atlas of Namibia: A Portrait of the Land and its People. The Ministry of Environment and Tourism of Namibia. David Philip, Tien Wah Press Singapore

Msangi, JP. 2005. *Water Resources and Management Practices along the Namibia's Coast.* TWOWS International Conference Proceedings, Bangalore, India.

INDEX

D

E

H

I

M

S

T

U

V